THE FUTURE AND WHY WE SHOULD AVOID IT

THE FUTURE
AND WHY WE SHOULD
AVOID IT
KILLER ROBOTS, THE APOCALYPSE
AND OTHER TOPICS OF MILD CONCERN

SCOTT FESCHUK

Douglas & McIntyre

Douglas and McIntyre (2013) Ltd.
P.O. Box 219, Madeira Park, BC, VON 2H0
www.douglas-mcintyre.com

Edited by Cheryl Cohen
Cover art and design by Dave Murray
Interior illustrations by Dave Murray
Text design by Carleton Wilson
Printed and bound in Canada

Canada Council   Conseil des Arts
for the Arts   du Canada

BRITISH COLUMBIA
ARTS COUNCIL
An agency of the Province of British Columbia

Douglas and McIntyre (2013) Ltd. acknowledges financial support from the Government of Canada through the Canada Book Fund and the Canada Council for the Arts, and from the Province of British Columbia through the BC Arts Council and the Book Publishing Tax Credit.

Cataloguing information available from Library and Archives Canada
ISBN 978-1-77162-033-8 (paper)
ISBN 978-1-77162-034-5 (ebook)

To our future overlords, be they robots, monkeys or Clintons

CONTENTS

INTRODUCTION

The future!

It sounds so great and exciting until you give it some thought. That's when you realize that the present—the time we're living in right now—once *was* the future. Look at the calendar: politicians and futurists once forecast that this very day would exist as a utopia in which poverty would be eradicated, the races would live as equals and Nicolas Cage would no longer make terrible movies. The children of the children who were *our* future would be busy being *their* future. Or something. Point is: by now, life should be awesome and leisurely and you should be wearing a spacesuit and high-fiving your wisecracking robot sidekick. Except instead your dishwasher is broken, your goddamn iTunes won't sync up and right now you're reading this book on a toilet in your bathroom instead of where you should be reading it—on a toilet in your hover car.

Somehow, our priorities always seem to get mixed up. The future never seems as futuristic when it's the present. We *should* be flying to work with our jetpacks. Instead, we're focused as a society on producing 427 different Coke products, including Caffeine-Free Diet Vanilla Cherry Coke Zero for People Named Donna. Have you shopped for dishwasher detergent lately? Deciding on a university is less mentally taxing. Powders, liquids, tabs, gel packs. Not long ago at the grocery store, I came upon a grown man—thirty, maybe thirty-five—holding two boxes of

Electrasol Gelpacs: one lemon-scented, the other orange. And then he, he ... *sniffed them*. Our eyes met. Were we warriors in ancient Japan, the code of honour would have demanded that he kill himself on the spot. But we are twenty-first-century Canadians, a civilized and humane people—so the chore fell to me. "It's for your own good!" I yelled, beating him with a Swiffer. "No life is worth living after *that*."

Think of the brainpower employed by companies like Gillette, a division of Procter & Gamble. Think of all the scientists and researchers with high-quality educations and protractors who devoted years of their lives to developing the razor manufacturer's 2014 "breakthrough" device—a handle that pivots slightly. Gillette's Fusion ProGlide razor with FlexBall™ Technology is so powerful that it allows capital letters to be placed in the middle of made-up words. It also apparently "responds to facial contours"—unlike our old razors, which, when confronted by anything other than a perfect 90-degree angle, simply exploded into flames. The people behind the development of the FlexBall™ could have been working on a cure for cancer or for whatever makes Billy Corgan sing like that. Instead, they went to work each morning—day after day—to devise a razor that, by the company's own best estimation, shaves facial hair one-fortieth of one millimetre shorter than before. So now men all around the world can wait an extra six seconds before they shave again. Thanks Gillette!

Because of the human imagination, the future will always amaze. Because of every other aspect of humanity, the future will always disappoint.

REASON NO. 1: GADGETS

You can tell that the pressure has been getting to the people at Apple. The value of Apple stock seems to drop every time the company goes several minutes without completely reinventing how humanity communicates. As a result, executives preside over launch events at which they perhaps just ever so slightly overplay the significance of the iPhone's screen icons changing marginally in appearance or, whoa, the pixels are now 12 percent more pixelly??

Indeed, Apple keeps encouraging us to get more and more excited about less exciting products. The iPod was revolutionary. The iPhone was cool. The iPad was neat. To be followed by the ... the ... the iWatch? Really? Isn't that a bit like the inventor of the wheel encouraging his audience to get pumped for his next groundbreaking creation: the hubcap?

This is not to entirely dismiss the potential of the iWatch. Analysts foresaw the device appealing to consumers who want all the convenience of what their iPhones already do, but with the added benefit of giving Apple another $200.

Okay, fine, the iWatch sounds redundant. But it may also be the best of what Apple has in the product development pipeline, which doesn't bode well for future announcements ...

Apple CEO takes the stage to unveil company's new offering for the not-too-distant future.

11

CEO: Welcome everyone! We've got some exciting news to share with you today.

[Twitter buckles under the weight of exclamation marks from Apple faithful.]

As humans, we yearn to be connected. To friends. To family. To appliances, vacuums and casual sportswear. Apple knows this. We get it. After all, we are the company that created iSnuggie, the first fleece blanket with oversized sleeves and WiFi.

I want you to close your eyes.

I want you to picture ... your toaster. You're probably thinking, "My toaster is fine. It does the job. Why on Earth would I want my toaster to do more stuff?"

But what if I told you that your toaster could do more stuff?

[Wild applause and multiple orgasms from the Apple faithful.]

Ladies and gentlemen, Apple is on a roll when it comes to forever changing the way people live, work and stare blankly at things.

Last year we unveiled iCap, which used sixteen precisely calibrated sensors to finally take the guesswork out of detecting hat head. I am proud to announce that we have now shipped in excess of twenty million units of iCap 2, which does pretty much the exact same thing but has a little propeller.

Six months later came another Apple game-changer. And I hope you don't mind me taking a moment to brag because, despite all the catch-up work done by our competitors, I can still make the claim that only iCouch allows you to update Facebook using your ass. Take that, Google Heinie.

Most recently, we delivered iShoe, the only footwear with micro-gyroscopic technology—so it can send a text message to let you know when you've fallen down.

And now: iToaster.

Take a close look. The new iToaster is breathtaking. It is elegantly crafted in brushed chrome, with rounded edges and textured accents. It's a wireless router, a backup hard drive and a stopwatch. It's a calendar, a lie detector and a sentient being that feels love and pain. It includes an embedded GPS so you'll never again lose track of your bagel.

But there's more. Today's toaster manufacturers are wedded to the traditional slot system—two or four rectangular openings, each designed to accommodate a single slice of bread. It's been the standard for decades. It works perfectly.

And that's why we've abandoned it. Instead, every iToaster will come with a grid of tiny slots that will accommodate up to thirty-two slices of micro-bread. Currently, no commercial breadmaker slices its bread this way, but it's only a matter of time until it's the industry standard, probably.

The new iToaster: spend time with it and you won't believe you once lived in a world in which your toaster could not exchange sexts with your jam.

And I'm excited to tell you that all iToasters will ship with a free download of Toast, our new app, which shows you what your toasted bread would have looked like if we'd had room in our new device for any heating coils.

HAPPILY, YOUR NEW iToaster will have plenty of company in the kitchen. The joyous age of the Internet of Things will soon be upon us!

Tech nerds are super-excited about how, in the glorious future, your phone will be able to communicate wirelessly with your pants, everything will be connected to everything, and our world will at last become a utopia ... until none of our technology works and we are forced to return to a barter economy in which chickens are the dominant currency.

Not long ago, *Wired.com* looked at some of the downsides of the so-called Internet of Things:

Downside: Security. A lot of these "connected" devices will not be well protected, meaning it'll be easy to hack your toaster oven. Yes, progress will have been attained—but at the cost of countless croque monsieurs.

Downside: Complexity. My high-tech cable box recently stopped sending a picture to my high-tech TV. The cable technician couldn't fix the problem. His supervisor couldn't fix it. They brought in the guy who fixes the unfixable problems— and *he* couldn't fix it. Together, these guys set a new record for making sounds that convey confusion and frustration. I counted seventeen utterances of "welp" alone. Eventually, one of them said: "Your cable box and your TV just don't like each other."

Welcome to the future, everyone! Now excuse me while I break up an argument between my iPad and my blender.

Downside: Privacy. How would you feel about your employer using "wearable technology" to track your movements? This would raise questions such as "Where do we draw the line on privacy?" and, among my bosses, "How long is Scott going to spend in the cereal aisle?" (I'd like to see *them* choose between Cinnamon Toast Crunch and Golden Grahams. It can't be done.)

None of this will stop us. In the glorious future, we'll be able to spend thousands of dollars on an internet-linked washing machine, a WiFi-enabled oven and maybe a wisecracking panini press of some kind. Think of the benefits of making our household contraptions more advanced and connected: I, for one, can't wait to go online and read the Facebook status updates of celebrity-owned appliances ("Taylor Swift's refrigerator ... is feeling lonely.").

No longer will humans be forced to open the fridge door to see if there's any milk left. Instead of this taxing ordeal, we will simply log the milk's arrival on a touchscreen keypad, type in its expiry date, routinely take note of its level, provide our mobile phone number and wait for the fridge to send a text message indicating it's time to buy more milk. What could be easier?

The dawn of connected appliances has been predicted, touted and hyped for years now. Perhaps some people figured that appliance manufacturers had given up on the idea—but no. General Electric, Sub-Zero and others have never wavered in their quest to answer the vexing question that has long plagued us as a species: Why can't I use my dishwasher to Instagram?

Believe me: I've seen these gizmos first-hand and they are a marvel to behold. Take Samsung's internet-enabled refrigerator. It features a video interface that runs apps, displays news stories, creates to-do lists and enables family members to post to Twitter. If Samsung engineers can somehow find room for a compressor, the fridge may one day even keep stuff cold. Amazing.

LG, meanwhile, is introducing an oven that can access a computer server, download preprogrammed recipes and display them on a built-in screen. And thank heavens for that, because until now there has been no way to obtain recipes other than by computer, iPad, smartphone, book, magazine, cereal box, soup can, memory, guesstimation or grandmother. And who's ever got any of those handy?

LG's new refrigerators go even further. They allow you to use a "drag-and-drop" menu to keep track of precisely where you've placed each food item inside. This will be a godsend to all of us who store our butter in the middle of the minotaur's labyrinth. And that's not all. An excited LG spokesperson noted in a news story: "I have the ability to see what's in my fridge from my phone!" At last, a solution for those who get separation anxiety from their pickles.

Don't get me wrong: progress is great. We owe a debt to the many scientists and engineers who have worked so hard and sacrificed so much to ensure that modern refrigerators have WiFi. In our bold and bright tomorrow, no bottle of ketchup will be denied the opportunity to unfriend a leg of ham.

The visionaries behind connected appliances are building their industry on the indisputable theory that if you take one good idea (household appliances) and combine it with another good idea (wireless internet), you can't help but wind up with an idea that is, at minimum, double good.

Sure, maybe we ordinary folk have trouble seeing the merits of one day watching an episode of *Scandal* on a thousand-dollar blender. But that's *our* fault. As a news story put it: "It can be hard to explain to consumers all the promise of a Web-connected dishwasher or washing machine, but [an executive at Whirlpool] said they're inevitable." Got that? *Inevitable.* So stop not understanding why they're building it and start not understanding why you're buying it.

Those who question the viability of connected appliances just don't grasp how business works. It's about the relationship between supply and demand. When there is absolutely no demand, you need to compensate with an overabundance of supply. At least that's how Hollywood did it a few years back with Jude Law movies.

It comes down to this twenty-first-century maxim: if something *can* be made with technology, it *must* be made—whether we want it or not. That's how we ended up with the Segway, Cher's face and Dubai.

As one industry executive put it: "We're connecting devices that have never been connected before and we're connecting them to you." Why? *Who knows.* To what end? *Who cares.* The only certainty is that we won't stop there. Next we're going to connect your toothbrush to your car engine. Then we're going to connect your razor to your vacuum. It won't make your life any easier, but the devices will enjoy being able to talk about you behind your back.

This focus on innovation extends beyond the kitchen. The new Sleep Number x12, for instance, is a mattress so laden with wires, sensors and computer chips that using it must be like sleeping on the Terminator. And it's always watching you. It uses software called SleepIQ to track your movement, breathing rate and heart rate as you sleep, which sounds pretty stressful. It then grades your sleep performance, saying you seem pretty stressed. The bed retails for $7,999—which sounds like a lot, but you can't put a price on waking up to a fact-based analysis of how your terrible sleeping patterns are leading you to an early grave.

There's more. The Sleep Number x12 uses a video screen to offer helpful tips, such as: "To prevent trips to the bathroom, limit how much liquid you drink after 8 PM." Thanks for the brainwave, super-bed.

The Sleep Number x12 was one of the many futuristic products featured at the annual Consumer Electronics Show (CES) in Las Vegas. Another popular item? Vibrating underwear for women. Manufactured by OhMiBod, the vibrating pads involved are operated through a smartphone app. Not to worry, ladies: your boss at work is vain enough to assume it's his PowerPoint presentation that's putting a smile on your face.

Personally, my interest lies with the people who designed the vibrating item. I'd like to have been there with them over the holidays when their extended families sat down for dinner.

GRANDMA: So, Brian, I hear you've got a new job.

BRIAN: Yes, Grandma.

GRANDMA: It's great to see you using the education that your parents sacrificed so much to pay for. Tell us all about this job.

BRIAN: Um, it's pretty technical. I don't want to bore you.

GRANDMA: Nonsense. Spare no detail.

BRIAN: Well, I guess you could say it involves advanced sensors that are activated via wireless technology.

GRANDMA: And these sensors are used to ... what? Diagnose medical ailments? Improve productivity? Solve irrigation issues that undermine agricultural prog—

BRIAN: I make vibrating underpants for ladies, Grandma.

[There is a pause.]

AUNT HEATHER: Go on.

Or, for $222, you can buy a plastic figurine called Mother, which looks like an overweight bowling pin. With glowing eyes, Mother helps you keep track of important things like how long you brushed your teeth, whether you've consumed enough water, and what you just wasted $222 on.

Another problem that needed solving: some of us tend to linger outdoors in summer. Currently, the only way to avoid spending too much time in the sun is to engage in the antiquated process known as "thinking."

Thanks to a company called Netatmo, you can instead spend $100 on a bracelet that tracks UV exposure and lets you know via smartphone when to go inside. You just have to think long enough to put on the bracelet and sync it to your smartphone and bring along your phone and make sure the bracelet is exposed to the sun and make sure your phone is nearby at all times and remember to check for updates. Simplicity at last!

Another emerging trend is wearable technology. Companies are breaking new ground here. For instance, EroGear high-heeled shoes feature a band of LED lights that you can configure to display light patterns or even show off your Twitter feed. So now everyone in the dance club can see you're terrible at fashion *and* spelling.

Another company, Wearable Experiments, has made what it describes as a "smart jacket" to help women navigate unfamiliar cities. Just link it with the GPS on your phone. It uses vibrators built into the shoulder pads to guide you along. If you feel a vibration on your left shoulder, turn left. If you feel a vibration on your right shoulder, turn right. If you feel a vibration in your underpants, you've put it on wrong—also, you probably won't care if you get where you're going.

Of course, one of the most talked-about new gadgets has been Google Glass. *Are you excited about Google Glass??* Finally we have the ability to purchase a revolutionary product that gives us the same features we already have on our phones but without all the hassle of needing to glance slightly downward.

Glass has been described by some as a "hands-free, voice-activated, augmented-reality headset"—and by me as a "dork monocle." What's important is this: Google wants you to want one. The company hyped Glass for what feels like *years*. And it stoked demand for the device by selling a limited number of prototypes to people it refers to as "Glass Explorers"—because that doesn't sound super-nerdy at all.

Google Glass represents a big step forward for society. No longer shall we stare rudely into our phones in the presence of others. Now we can technically make eye contact while actually browsing LOLCats.

Sure, Glass has for privacy reasons been banned from many strip clubs and casinos—but that's not going to hurt sales too much. How many could Charlie Sheen have bought, anyway? And sure, Glass looks ridiculous. Google has spent a fortune on photo shoots in which preposterously gorgeous subjects, men and women who would never wear Glass, wear Glass. Even *they* look as if they're dressed up for Comic-Con. Push Google Glass over your ears and nose and even Bluetooth Headset Guy will gesture in your direction and ask: "Hey, who's the asshole?"

But I have a soft spot for Google. I'm predisposed to like any company that's done so much to help so many find pictures of naked ladies. And there's certainly no denying that Glass has a long list of features. For instance, you can use it to snap a photo. That's exciting, right? You've probably got only one or two or three devices that already do that.

True, some scientists say wearing computerized eyewear for long stretches could mess up our "neural circuitry" and affect how our brains process sight. But on the other hand, you can ask Glass questions! Questions like "How long is the Brooklyn Bridge?" or "Why does everyone keep looking at me like that?" Heck, you can even use the Google Hangouts software to video-chat with your friends—and they can see what you're looking at! Think of all the time you'll save not having to describe your parents' basement.

There are other advantages to being a Glass owner. For instance, the vast majority of non-nerds will likely refer to what you're wearing as Google *Glasses*—thus presenting you two hundred times a day with the opportunity to firmly set folks straight. This is a terrific way to meet new people and have them think you're a jagoff.

And let us not overlook the potential impact of Glass on our mating rituals. We are mere months away from a wave of young, single men arriving at bars with the same thought in their heads: "Surely attractive women will be powerless to resist the allure of my face computer."

Why does the world need Glass? According to Sergey Brin, one of Google's co-founders, Glass is more than a gadget. It's an emancipator. It's going to free us all from having to hold a mobile phone in our hands and manipulate it with our fingers—a process that Brin refers to as "emasculating."

Two things about that. One, could Sergey Brin have been using his phone the wrong way? Mine sometimes gives me cramps in my fingers but never in my man parts. And two, is gently flicking a small screen in order to gain access to the vast repository of human knowledge contained within the internet really *that* onerous a task? Brin says it is. He thinks of fingers on screens and asks: "Is this what you're meant to do with your body?" Whereas with Glass, you can put your body to use as nature intended—absorbing punches from the guy in the men's room who saw you glance over and thinks you may have snapped a photo of his junk.

People are suspicious of Glass because they're suspicious of Google. Perhaps you'll recall that Google took heat a while back for revisions to its privacy code, which the company described as "enhancing the user experience" and critics described as another terrifying step along an apocalyptic path toward an all-knowing, all-seeing corporate dictatorship and the utter annihilation of human identity. (I'm paraphrasing.)

The company now brings together and analyzes the things you search for on the web, discuss in your email, watch on You-Tube, type into your calendar—and combines all that information into a single user profile. This (a) enables Google to better tailor the ads you see on your computer screen, and (b) is nothing sinister. *Who said anything about sinisterness?*

There's one thing that Google executives and their critics agree on: the debate over privacy is only going to intensify as the company grows in size, influence and—especially—ambition. Here's a calendar of milestones to expect in the months and years ahead:

Spring 2017: Watch for the launch of Google Career, a proprietary real-time system that lets us know precisely which career options we've scuttled by posting lurid details of our drunken antics on Facebook and Google+. Today, a young woman can only guess at the occupational repercussions of an iPhone video of her tabletop striptease. But soon, thanks to Google Career, she'll be empowered to instantly learn that she'll never crack a Fortune 500 company, earn more than $45,000 a year or regain the love of her father.

Fall 2017: A few years ago, many experts believed that consumers would resist sharing their personal files and information with a massive and mysterious central computer system beyond their understanding. But then someone came up with the term *cloud*, and suddenly everyone was cool with it. Clouds are so fluffy and nice! Surely no soft, white cloud would ever steal my identity! With this in mind, Google is expected to brand its intrusive and excruciatingly painful new mind probe as Google Bunny Rabbit.

December 2017: Just in time for the holidays, watch for the rollout of Google Psych, an online therapist to whom we will be encouraged to reveal our innermost thoughts, fears and credit card numbers. Complex algorithms will calculate exactly which YouTube video of kittens will make us feel better.

Spring 2018: In the span of a few months, the informal but long-standing Google corporate motto—Don't Be Evil—will be subtly tweaked to Don't Be Too Evil, then Don't Be Always Evil and, finally, MWAHAHAHA!

June 2018: This marks the next anticipated updating of the Google privacy code. Under the new terms of use, the company will combine and market the information that users reveal through the full range of Google services, and also in our tax returns and bedside diaries. This will improve Google's ability to ensure advertisements are as relevant and persuasive as possible when implanted into our dreams.

July 2018: Addressing concerns about the amount of information it is amassing, Google will remind users that it is easy to avoid having personal data collected and repurposed. All you need to do is get rid of your personal computer, mobile phone, electronic devices, forearm implants, gold fillings and pubic hair (you don't want to know why). Those who do so will have but one remaining gadget at their disposal—the Etch A Sketch. And bad news: the porn on that thing is pretty primitive and, no matter how hard I try, the boobs always wind up kind of square.

2019: The company bails out the US government, saving it from bankruptcy in exchange for naming rights. God bless the United Googles of Google.

2020: Expected date on which users can configure a Google Alert that will recount all instances in which they come up in other people's daydreams. *Google Alert! Steve from accounting just imagined hitting you on the forehead with a hammer!*

2022: Until this day you had to actively think about golf in order for Google to deliver ads directly to your brain stem from online vendors of golf clubs. Now, thanks to Google Subconscious, all you need to do is *think about* thinking about golf. Rest assured your innermost feelings, preferences and desires are safe and will never be sold by Google to a third party, unless it's a pretty good offer.

BUT ENOUGH ABOUT your brain stem. Technological progress has its upsides, too. For instance, it looks as though this whole "self-driving car" thing is for real and will be available commercially in the 2020s—despite the many drivers who demonstrate every day that they don't need some fancy autonomous vehicle in order to completely zone out behind the wheel. I'm doing it right now while I type this chapter. *[Also takes bite of hamburger.]*

Before I go any further, this must be noted for the record: somewhere, at some time along the way, someone decided that it was more important to design a self-driving car than a flying car. This person should be forcibly restrained and waterboarded with a pail of my tears. Flying cars are the only reason I yearned to become a grown-up, and without them adult life has been a pungent morass of soul-consuming misery. Thanks for nothing, anonymous dream-crusher.

I'll be honest: some are skeptical about the robocar. Yes, automakers like Nissan boast of working out the kinks by collaborating with researchers at leading universities. This sounds great until you read the following quote from a Japanese professor who's considered a pioneer in the field: "It is hard or almost impossible to detect pedestrians, especially children and cyclists, and to forecast their behaviours." That's awesome! So, to sum up: we've totally nailed this super-car technology except for the part about not driving directly into people. *I'll take two!*

Human drivers have—and will always have—an advantage over lasers and sensors. Through experience, we can sense when a pedestrian is about to dart into traffic. We see it in their eyes and their body language. And that allows us to react in the proper way—by laying on the horn and shouting out the window, "Keep it on the curb, dickhead!"

Consider some of the other shortcomings of the self-driving car:

- Robbed of the ability to get behind the wheel and rev the engine in a needlessly aggressive fashion, how exactly are the young men of the future supposed to persuade young women to desire them? Through genial conversation and disarming romantic gestures? What is this, the Renaissance??
- The muscle cars of yore had tough names like Cobra and Mustang—monikers that suggested speed, power, danger. Are people really going to line up to buy the Nissan Dawdle?
- The intricate internal software may leave your car vulnerable to hackers who could override your vehicle's systems and program it to take you somewhere horrible, like Burger King or Saskatoon.
- One of the great joys of life is witnessing a road-rage incident between two hotheads. It's just not going to be the same when it's an exchange between tech-laden automobiles:

  NISSAN DAWDLE: 101101010101111!

  LEXUS TEDIUM: 01010101#%@*01110!!!!

There's a bigger issue, though: Have we really thought this through?

Today's humans represent the most impatient incarnation of our species ever. We get uppity when it takes more than 0.46 seconds to download that video of a bulldog on a trampoline. And we're going to get jazzed about iCars that drive at the speed limit and come to a complete stop at each and every four-way? I predict some people will sit back and let their shiny new 2025 Mercedes Blah putter away for as long as two minutes before grabbing the wheel, stepping on the gas and hollering, "This is how you drive, Grandma Roboto!"

And oh, by the way, let's not forget: driving is fun. It's about more than getting there—it's about calculating the quickest route, making the slickest pass, finding the best parking spot. There's a thrill in speeding into a corner, hitting the apex just right, sliding through the apex because there was black ice on the road, spinning the wheel madly while screaming, "No! *Sweet Jesus, nooooooo!*" and correcting it just in time to avoid death by plummeting.

Many questions about the autonomous car have yet to be answered. Will we be able to "drive" drunk if we're not really driving? Will it be okay to make out while in motion? Can Rob Ford send it on its own to pick up a "cannelloni" on Dixon Road?

But the biggest question is: Do we really need another activity that we experience passively? Take a good look at us—do we want to off-load yet another activity so we can free up more time to stare into screens? And do any of us—*any* of us—yearn to see a movie car chase that features fuel-efficient acceleration and properly signalled turns?

WHILE LEADING SCIENTISTS strive to put limo, taxi and getaway drivers out of work, there's also a race around the globe to produce a more affordable automobile to serve the growing middle class in emerging countries like China and India.

A few years back, India's Tata Motors took a shot at producing the world's cheapest car—the Nano, a $2,500 subcompact that would, according to some analysts, "revolutionize" the automobile industry.

Let's take a closer look.

Congratulations on your purchase of a Tata Nano! By taking your place behind the wheel of "the People's Car," you join thousands of others who are thrilled to have finally found an automobile that blends the aerodynamic efficiency of a gumdrop with the power and performance of a golf cart. Please read this owner's manual to ensure you get the most out of your new Nano.

Engine: The Nano delivers 33 horsepower. On one hand, this is up to 100 horsepower less than many small cars. But on the other, it is 32 horsepower more than a horse! Your move, Trigger.

Acceleration: According to road tests, the Nano goes from zero to 100 km/h in ... theory. (Sanjay had her pushing 83 km/h as of Wednesday, and reckons he'll hit 93 km/h by this manual's second printing.) We know for a fact, however, that the Nano is capable of achieving an impressive top speed of 123 km/h.*

Seating: Your new Tata Nano seats five! If comfort is desired, then the Nano seats four. If breathing is desired, then three, max. If the preservation of social status is desired, then it doesn't matter how many people it seats because no one will ever get into this car with you.

Air Bags: There are no air bags.

Radio: There is no radio.

Air Conditioning: Ha ha! You're funny!

Amenities: All Nanos come standard with steering wheel and opening and closing doors. Your Nano also has one windshield wiper. This cuts down on "maintenance costs" because you only have to replace a single wiper blade! Note: it also cuts down on "seeing things."

---

* *when pushed off a very high cliff.*

Roadside Assistance: Tata Motors does not offer roadside assistance for the Nano. However, the Nano can be easily transported to a nearby service station inside most fanny packs.

Structure: Part of what makes your Nano so affordable is that costly materials such as steel have been replaced with lighter alternatives such as plastic, cardboard and the power of prayer. But don't worry! Your Nano is built to endure every bodily impact up to and including a heavy drizzle.

Troubleshooting Your Tata Nano

Problem: Strange noises.
Solution: Turn off vehicle. Remove key. If noises persist, roll up window. Sound of laughter and heckling from passers-by should be slightly diminished.

Problem: Car doesn't start.
Solution: Lift the hood. Give the hamster a poke. Instruct him to get back on the wheel and start running. Use scolding tone and make threatening gesture (if necessary).

Problem: Brakes don't seem to be working that well.
Solution: When you press your feet to the road, try to really dig in those heels. Scientific research suggests that a plume of smoke should be emitted from the feet under typical braking. (Source: *The Flintstones*)

Problem: Uncertain to what extent Bruce Springsteen's songs would have been different if he'd driven a Nano while growing up.
Solution: "Thunder Road" would go something like this ...

> *Whoa ho, come take my hand*
> *We're riding out tonight to case the promised land ...*
> *Eventually.*
> *You're not in a hurry, are you baby?*
> *Stop complaining—the promised land ain't going anywhere,*
> *all right? Jesus.*

I AM stepping on the gas.
Fine. Get out and walk.
You're walking pretty fast, Mary, but I'm bound to catch you
when I get going downhill ...

Also, "Drive All Night" wouldn't be a love song—it would be a chronicle of his trip to the corner store.

Problem: You step on the gas pedal but hardly anything happens.

Solution: Spend more than $2,500 on a car.

Thanks again for purchasing a Tata Nano. And remember: the Nano was designed with family in mind—your family! So let *them* drive it.

HMM, SO MAYBE robocars are the way to go after all. Besides, the Japanese have been hard at work ensuring we'll have something to do to pass the time on the long drive home. While other nations were wasting scientific brainpower on developing moon bases and mulling over the origins of the universe, the Japanese were selflessly devoting themselves to a more practical pursuit: building a better sex doll.

Obsolete now are the crude blow-up dolls featured in countless Hollywood comedies and the back seat of my car on prom night. In their place, the Tokyo-based company 4Woods manufactures "lifelike" silicone companions with "hyper-real" mouths and "ultra-real" breasts. As 4Woods declares on its website: "Our pursuit of high quality beauty for visual effects and durability for practical play have been realized!" Happy alone fun time!

Having intimate relations with your new Japanese "love doll" couldn't be simpler. You don't need to inflate her (as with a traditional doll) or get her drunk (as with a traditional Lohan). You simply remove your doll from its storage sack (complimentary with purchase!) and allow nature—and years of

28

painstaking industrial research—to take its course. All in the comfort and privacy of your own shame!

These new sex dolls sell for a little more than $5,000 each. That's a lot of money—but a visit to the manufacturer's website leaves the impression that crafting a state-of-the-art twenty-first-century sex partner was an engineering challenge on par with building the Brooklyn Bridge or Pamela Anderson. There is discussion of the "hyper-anatomical" body frame, the highly durable and easily reparable "skin" and the "33 degrees of increased movement on a new single axis on a double joint." (For the record, Anderson herself routinely achieves a remarkable 47 degrees of increased movement, but that's due to a pelvic injury suffered during a tragic honeymooning accident.)

One problem with sex dolls of olden times was the lack of realism in the chestal-type region (I'm told). Basically, the breasts felt like air bags (I'm told). They totally killed the mood that night at the lake (I'm told). But these Japanese sex dolls feature "new-materials technology inside a breast!" Specifically, a special "elastomer gel" provides a more authentic feel. The company brags: "The softness can be checked!" I love that. *The softness can be checked.* This helps to explain why all dolls come with a small square of paper that reads, "Inspected by Number Tiger Woods."

Listen to me: I sound like an advocate for these things. But I'm not here to sell you on a Japanese sex doll. And I'm certainly not in any way angling to have a free Japanese sex doll, preferably the Mitsumi model, delivered in an unmarked crate to my work address after business hours. For no unethical reason whatsoever, we should probably wrap things up by considering the many ways in which a high-tech Japanese Sex Doll is vastly superior to an Actual Living Woman. Here is a full list:

1. "You can choose your favorite head!" That's right—4Woods offers eleven different female heads that "have very rich

individuality and originality." Extra heads can be purchased separately (for $765 apiece) and quickly snapped onto your sex doll. Voila! Suddenly you're making it with upward of a dozen pretend women. Take that, ordinary everyday loser!

2. Did I mention one head has pigtails? Or that another wears a nurse's hat? Oh, and one looks like she's sleeping for some reason. More important, when is the last time an Actual Living Woman removed her head? Fine, Rosie O'Donnell. But she *has* to do that so she can feed in her natural form.

3. A Japanese Sex Doll won't make fun of you for owning a Japanese Sex Doll, whereas an Actual Living Woman almost definitely will, probably by creating a Facebook group.

I don't want to pigeonhole the Japanese just because they're creating something stupid like a sex doll. In all fairness, they're creating a whole bunch of other stupid stuff too.

Among the hot new items in Japan is a cutting-edge fitness tracker—for dogs. It's marketed under the name Wandant, which its manufacturer claims is a combination of two Japanese words—presumably "half-witted" and "consumer."

How does it work? Simply attach the Wandant to your dog's collar and sync it with your mobile phone. To complete the process, gaze at yourself in the mirror and wonder what has become of your life. For the record, "extra-obsessive dog owners can manually enter information such as stool condition and add photos." I assume they mean photos of the dog, not the stool—but then again, why assume that? These people created a fitness tracker *for dogs*. They're capable of anything.

Besides, the Japanese do have something of a preoccupation with bodily functions. Consider the toilet—specifically, the new Neorest 700H from Toto.

Most North Americans are content with basic toilet amenities like "a hole" and "the ability to make it all go away." Not the Japanese. The 700H comes equipped with a heated seat, a light (so you can see in glorious detail what you leave in ... uhh, why does it have a light again?), a remote control, a pulsating water spray and a warm-air dryer. Apparently the ottoman and eight-track tape player are sold separately. Meanwhile the toilet's Power Catalytic Deodorizer uses "activated oxygen to break the molecular bonds of odor," an advance so remarkable it renders obsolete 60 percent of the jokes in Adam Sandler's movies. The only thing this toilet doesn't do is actually go for you—although scientists are apparently working on that in a top-secret and very unpleasant laboratory.

The Japanese take great national pride in their leadership role in what they describe as the "evolution of toilet culture." Canada? Not so much. Our most recent contribution to the evolution of toilet culture was leaving behind the sports section for the next guy. And we pioneered that in 1932.

(Just to demonstrate that I know perhaps a little *too* much about the latest in Japanese toilet technology, I would point out that Japan's devotion to tech-laden toilets is not without its drawbacks. The Japan Warm Water Bidet Council—slogan: We Can't Believe We Exist Either!—has received more than a hundred reports of toilets flaming or smoking since 1984, usually on account of faulty wiring. In a curious coincidence, the Japan Council for the Screaming of "Holy Crap My Ass Is on Fire!" has also received more than a hundred reports since 1984, usually on account of an ass being on fire. The government responded to this crisis by launching a formal investigation into toilet wiring. Companies recalled hundreds of thousands of toilets for repairs. And the citizenry reacted with typical Japanese stoicism, patiently holding it for four to six weeks.)

Anyway, where was I? Oh, right, the Neorest 700H. During his or her lifetime, a typical human will spend upward of ninety-two days on or in front of the toilet—though usually not all at once. But it's not just about comfort. Toto claims that by "pre-misting" the toilet bowl with electrolyzed water, the Neorest "aids in the elimination of waste approximately 80 per cent better than a dry bowl." This seems as good a time as any to update the list of the world's worst jobs:

1. Child soldier
2. Toto employee forced to calculate the percentage of additional poop eliminated by pre-misting
3. President of the United States

Other bum-based products abound in Japan. The country's businessmen reportedly swear by a new line of underwear designed to, and I quote, "solve your smelly-fart problem." The technology behind Deoest underpants was developed by Prof. Hiroki Ohge of Hiroshima University, who "analyzed the smells of people's flatulence and ... " actually, why don't we just end the quote right there. We can imagine the rest. Bottom line: the company claims its underwear "filters out 95 per cent" of the smell of human flatulence. To which I say: What math machine did they use to determine, "Yep, that's the unmistakable aroma of exactly one-twentieth of a fart?" *Show your work, Prof. Hiroki Ohge.*

And then there's the White Goat, which shreds office paper and transforms it into toilet paper. This is clever as a metaphor but not so much as a product, in that the machine costs $100,000 and is approximately the size of Peru. There's video of this thing in action: it takes half an hour to turn a forty-page report into a roll of toilet paper that looks every bit as cottony-soft as a handful of cedar mulch.

Feeling tense (possibly because your employer just bought a White Goat)? Maybe the new Mondiale Head Spa iD3 is for you. After all, what could be more relaxing than taking a futuristic plastic device crammed with wires, heat pads and several scalp-squeezing, air-filled cushions and fitting it snugly over the place where you keep your brain?

One final breakthrough to report. A company is marketing a notebook with pages that are "specially designed ... to be easily ripped apart." You know, unlike regular paper, which is impervious to human force and has the tensile strength of sapphire. To be fair, the company claims its paper has been manufactured to shred for "maximum satisfaction." We can only assume that this means it comes printed with the lyrics to John Mayer songs.

AN OPEN LETTER to the person with whom I was having a nice conversation until he looked down at his phone and started pecking away at the keyboard for, like, ten minutes.

Dear Señor Jerkface,

I'm not a big "manners" person. I don't care which fork you use to eat your salad, so long as it's not mine. But while you and I are dining together, perhaps you would deign to keep your hands and eyes off your mobile phone for more than thirty seconds at a time.

No? Very well—might I see your device for a moment? How sleek and stylish! And how very clumsy of me to accidentally drop it into my soup, then drop the soup into a crocodile, then push the crocodile out of a helicopter.

Don't get me wrong: I understand how important it is for you to stay in constant, utterly relentless touch with your many friends, avatars and close, personal LinkedIn contacts. I grasp what a gruelling ordeal it now will be for your Twitter followers to go ninety whole minutes without knowing precisely where you stand on quantitative easing or the introduction of Cousin Oliver on *The Brady Bunch*. On the other hand: *I am sitting right here.*

Ah, I see you have a second phone. And I am all out of crocodiles. So be it.

Forgive me for interjecting as you enter the third exciting minute of "texting a buddy," but perhaps you have heard of a new gimmick meant to restore actual human eye contact to meals. Upon arriving at a restaurant, all those who are dining together must place their phones in the middle of the table: the first person to reach for his or her device is obliged to pick up the entire dinner tab. I, for one, think this is a great idea but would add one small tweak: everyone at the table should also get to stab that person in the hand with a fork.

I take it from your reaction that you don't support this—and also that my fork hurts.

Let me assure you, dear friend, that I am not blind to the virtues of the smartphone. It empowers instant communication. It enhances workplace productivity, especially if your company is in the business of obliterating green cartoon pigs. Plus, as you have demonstrated, it provides a convenient way to let people know they are not very interesting.

This used to be much harder in the olden days, when you'd have to use subtle signals like theatrical yawning. Now when your friends start telling you about the accomplishments of their children, you can simply glance at your device. It's a real time saver.

Ah, your phone is vibrating yet again. I sense my opportunity approaching.

YOU: Sorry, I just need to ... [you lapse into silence.]
ME: Hey, can I have one of your kidneys?
YOU [distracted]: Mmm-hmm.
ME: Great!
YOU [looking up]: Sorry, what did you just say?
[I reach for scalpel.]

I agree you are by no means alone in your habits. In the days before the last federal election, I sat down for drinks with five Ottawa journalists, and at one point all of them lapsed into silence, staring into their phones. I didn't know what to do. Should I look at my phone and pretend I had an urgent message to return? Would five smartphones even fit inside a crocodile?

Perhaps you've been led to believe that your station in life is of sufficient importance that you are justified in the comically habitual checking of your emails and texts. And maybe you're right! After all, there are two groups of people who get a free pass to constantly gaze at their phones during dinner:

1. Brain surgeons who abruptly left in the middle of brain surgery and are checking in to see if maybe they ought to go back and finish the brain surgery
2. Current presidents of the United States of America (basketball scores only)

If you don't fit into one of these categories, perhaps you could hold off on using your phone until you pretend to need to go to the bathroom (even though later I am sure to discover you were actually in there retweeting a cat video).

Sincerely,

The Human Person in Your General Vicinity

Throughout the book, I'll answer some of the more pressing queries that confront our society as we move into the future.

Tough Question: *When will we have a cloak of invisibility like in the Harry Potter books?*

This may surprise you, but researchers are actually working on this—and they appear to be getting closer. Apparently the whole thing hinges on something called "metamaterial"—which negatively refracts light in such a way that it could render objects effectively invisible. I don't want to get bogged down in the science of it all, but the principle is similar to how the 1990s acted on the film career of Judd Nelson.

That said, I'm not sure I see this development as uniformly positive. Yes, we'll be able to hide huge objects, like frigates and most of Gary Busey's teeth. But I'm worried about this trend of the fictional world bleeding into the real world. The consequences could be dire. How long until our most attractive young ladies begin to think of Woody Allen as sexually desirable? How will we cope when all of our romantic relationships are set to a montage featuring a song by Smash Mouth? It's too high a price to pay.

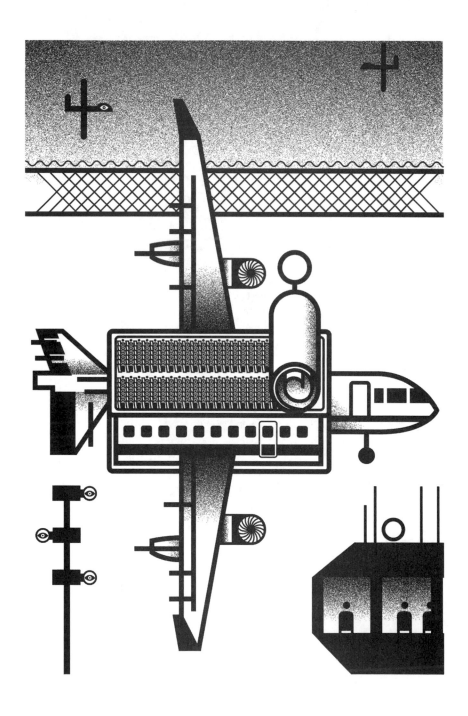

REASON NO. 2: LEISURE

Welcome to the airport security checkpoint. Please pay attention to all instructions and signage as we guide you through new procedures and attempt to minimize travel delays to and within the United States.

Important: if you need to expedite the screening process in order to make your flight, please identify yourself to uniformed security personnel, who have the authorization to point at you and laugh.

You are now entering the Transportation Security Administration (TSA) screening zone. Only masochists are permitted past this point. Signs have been positioned to help estimate wait times. Senior citizens may join the lineup only if their affairs are in order.

Please be advised of restrictions on liquids in your carry-on baggage. Liquids in containers measuring 100 millilitres or more are prohibited, as are liquids deemed "weird." Place all other liquids and gels into a clear plastic bag. Make sure the bag is clear, so everyone can see your Anusol.

Seal the bag, place a sticker over the seal to preserve the seal's integrity, sign the sticker with your full legal name to preserve the sticker's integrity, then deposit the bag into a garbage can. No liquids are permitted on board.

At this point, please remove and discard any and all sharp objects from your pockets, your baggage and your imagination.

Passengers who mentally picture a box cutter, a butter knife or nail clippers will trigger the alarm on the MindSweeper™, at which point their subconscious will be strip-searched.

Any reference to "bombs" will be taken seriously, and offenders will be prosecuted. To be safe, you may want to avoid bringing up the last ten years of John Travolta movies.

Do not hum.

You are now approaching the screening checkpoint. Passengers travelling with small children and strollers are at this point asked to take the train instead.

Important: books are permitted on flights to and within the United States, but you've probably finished yours by now.

Please be advised that, for security reasons, there are new limitations on the size of carry-on bags. Only one (1) bag smaller than 7 cm × 3 cm × 0.5 cm—approximately one regulation Chiclets box—is permitted. (Chiclets themselves are strictly prohibited.)

In accordance with recent changes to operational procedures, you are now required to remove your shoes. Step forward. Now remove your belt. Step forward again. Remove your pants. Passengers attired in shorts, skirts, dresses or kilts are at this point required to leave and purchase a pair of pants, which must subsequently be removed.

Trousers deemed "terroristy" by screening personnel are subject to confiscation. Trousers with waists in excess of forty-eight (48) inches are subject to one (1) reference to that Jared guy from Subway.

If you are travelling with a laptop computer, remove it from your bag and place it in a plastic bin. Place your cellphone and iPod in a separate bin. Place your keys, coins and other metallic objects in a third bin. Remove your suit jacket and place it in a fourth bin, along with your overcoat, your hat and your will to live.

Are you travelling with a cane? Do you really need one? Let's find out.

Please present to the security agent your boarding pass,

your passport, a second piece of identification, a DNA sample (fresh), your mother, and two notarized images of a CAT scan no more than seven (7) days old.

Proceed forward and stand behind the screen of the body scanner. Raise your arms from your torso, position your legs slightly apart and form your face into an expression that suggests you're trying hard to remember if you wore underwear today.

Please wait until security personnel signal you to proceed through. Passengers with metal plates, pacemakers or awesome bodies will require secondary screening.

Proceed to the Manual Inspection Area for a mandatory pat-down. To make passengers more comfortable with this highly invasive process, a TSA agent will first buy them dinner.

Please be advised that if a potential menace to civilian aircraft somehow circumvents this security checkpoint, passengers on board the aircraft will be required to act quickly to subdue the threat. To prove you're up to it, please step forward and tackle All-Pro running back Adrian Peterson. Can't do it? Two words: Grey. Hound.

Proceed to the checkout area and swipe your credit card to pay your mandatory Security Screening Surcharge. A 15 percent gratuity will be applied to the bills of all passengers who have been probed rectally.

Congratulations! You have now cleared the TSA's Security Screening Checkpoint. Please gather your possessions, continue forward and proceed to your appointed departure gate, which is located just beyond the TSA's Secondary Security Screening Checkpoint.

The line forms here.

Three weeks later.

Welcome aboard! We encourage you to pay attention to this short video as we outline the safety features and amenities of this aircraft. Economy-class passengers: please deposit fifty (50) cents to continue.

The hectic pace of the terminal is behind you now. You've paid the Fuel Surcharge. You've tagged your own bags at check-in, searched your own bags at security and sold your own bags to pay the Baggage Surcharge.

You've been weighed for the Chubby Surcharge and measured for the Height Surcharge. Now we invite you to sit back and relax! (A surcharge for wear and tear on your seat back will be applied to your credit card.)

To fasten your seat belt, pull the strap across your lap and insert the metal clip into the buckle until you hear a click. If you cannot locate your lap, it's because another passenger is sitting on it. This practice of "doubling up" is a temporary measure to increase efficiency.

There are two lavatories on board. The front lavatory is reserved for the exclusive use of our business-class passengers. The rear lavatory does not exist. If you are in economy class and need to use the lavatory, please employ the convenient tube and sanitary baggie located in the seat pocket in front of you. Do not use the seat pocket itself. That's for number two.

In preparation for takeoff, place your seat back and tray table in an upright and locked position. But ensure all trays are lowered during the flight itself. We're using them now as Murphy beds for ultra-economy travellers, and there's not a lot of air in there. Or so we discovered.

Please be aware that due to current challenging economic conditions, this aircraft will be travelling at a slightly lower altitude than usual. This is to ensure the farmers' crops are properly dusted.

In the unlikely event of cabin pressurization, the mask you're currently wearing will retract into the compartment above you. An Oxygen Surcharge will be billed to your credit card.

The use of cellular telephones is prohibited during flight, except when the pilot borrows yours to call the control tower.

To lessen fuel consumption, we'll be reducing air speed by a modest amount. Do not be concerned: it is normal for those

REASON NO. 2: LEISURE

geese to pass us. The barrel rolls and steep dives are also standard procedure. In challenging times, air shows provide an enhanced revenue stream.

This aircraft features a number of amenities, including an inflight entertainment system stocked with some of the best movies ever made by Ted Danson.

For those passengers wanting to eat, sandwiches can be purchased for $7. For those wanting to rest, a pillow and blanket can be purchased for $3. For those wanting to feed a family on a budget, a pillow and blanket can be purchased for $3.

Business-class passengers will receive a complimentary bag of nuts. Economy-class passengers will receive a complimentary bag of nut. Rest assured that even in these difficult economic times, a majority of our planes continue to feature free coffee and trained pilots.

Located above you, you'll find both a reading light (Seeing Surcharge applies) and a flight-attendant call button. To summon a flight attendant, simply press the button and wait. Then press it again. Around this time you'll figure out that most of our "flight attendants" are in fact promotional cardboard cutouts from the Ernest movies.

This modern aircraft features several emergency exits. During any loss of power, floor lights will guide you to the nearest exit. To open the door, simply slide your Visa along the appropriate swipe slot and wait patiently for authorization.

After the plane begins its descent toward your destination, you'll be asked to return to your seat and pay the new Landing Surcharge. Smooth runway landing or hellish terror ride? It all depends on how much cash ends up in the hat, people.

Upon reaching the terminal, please be aware that contents of the overhead bins may have shifted and routes may have been eliminated during flight. Maybe you're in St. John's, maybe you're in St. Petersburg. Who says modern air travel lacks excitement?

Once the aircraft has come to a full and complete stop, you will be permitted to deplane. Your luggage will be waiting for you inside the airport. If you paid the new Accuracy Surcharge, your luggage will be waiting for you inside *this* airport.

One final note: during takeoff, it is strongly recommended that all laptop computers be placed under the seat in front of you—or in the convenient pawnshop at the rear of the aircraft. Cash received for your computer can be used to pay various surcharges. A Surcharge Surcharge will be applied.

Now please sit back and enjoy your flight. We know you have a choice, and we appreciate that you're regretting it right now.

SUMMER IS THE season for road trips, relaxation and getting away from it all—except from Facebook and Twitter, because how else will we let everyone know that we've gotten away from it all?

The time available for summer escapades is famously brief. The pressure to make the most of it is intense. What type of re-invigorating respite will you choose to pursue? There are many options:

> **Vacation:** Summer arrives and millions rush to the cottage or cabin, an amazing, magical place where we can wind down, have a beer, commune with nature, fix the water pump, hang out with friends, fix the dock, fix the goddamn screen door, maybe get up early to go fishing and, aw, Christ, the water pump's broken again?? That does it—*we're selling this stupid, magical place.*
>
> **Daycation:** Why pay for a hotel when there's so much to do close to home? And don't worry—you won't miss out on any part of the traditional vacation experience. With the proper preparation, many of today's kids are now capable of packing a whole week's worth of whining into a single ninety-minute car ride.
>
> **Staycation:** We can have a vacation right here at home and it'll be every bit as fun as going to Disney World, Mom declares to a deeply skeptical audience.
>
> **Overstaycation:** This term describes the time-honoured

tradition of telling your friends you'll be crashing with them for just a couple of nights and then—boom—suddenly a week has passed. If the cottage is swanky enough, it's worth the accusing stares and hostile muttering.

Dismaycation: The perspective of all teenagers on every vacation they're ever forced to take with their families.

Praycation: Once, just this once, oh Lord, please, please, please make sure that Dad forgets to bring his Speedo.

Straycation: You can try using this term, but eventually your spouse is going to figure out that you mean you've been having an affair.

Oyveycation: Your Jewish grandmother would like you to know she's aghast that you're wearing such a skimpy swimsuit to the beach. And also would it kill you to maybe wash your feet and not bring in so much sand from the beach? *Those seashells have germs.*

Cabernetcation: Nothing enables Mommy to get away from the stress of modern life more quickly, cheaply and completely than a bottle and a half of red.

J.J.cation: An island vacation that starts out amazingly but goes on too long and ends in confusion when it becomes apparent that no one has any plan for the final week of the vacation and, come on, really, a giant cork that keeps the island from being destroyed? Seriously?

Naïvetécation: Having never before booked a cottage online, Dad was unaware that "cozy rustic cabin" is internet shorthand for "shack overrun by raccoons."

Lanadelraycation: A vacation that's so overhyped that the backlash begins even before the car pulls out of the driveway.

Michaelbaycation: A getaway that costs $300 million and you spend most of it just wishing it would end.

Elizabethmaycation: Sure, water-skiing and tubing look like fun, but do you have any idea of the environmental impact caused by motor fuels leaking into our waterways? And these hamburgers—delicious, but the emissions from charcoal and other pollutants are contributing to a sharp increase in ...

listen, why don't we sit down and I'll take you through some of the data in this pamphlet?

50shadesofgreycation: Sometimes, spending two weeks together as a family qualifies as torture.

LEISURE TIME IN Canada invariably involves hockey—or, just as often, hockey talk. Some experts are already debating who'll go in the first round of next year's National Hockey League entry draft. These people are posers. The *true* hockey obsessive demonstrates his or her knowledge by predicting the outcome of the 2025 draft. Here are the current top prospects on my board:

Theo Rodgers (*Dartmouth, NS*): A speedy winger, Theo is described by NHL Central Scouting as possessing "an accurate wrist shot" and "Superman pyjamas." Typical of this class of seven-year-old boys, he currently lacks a bit of size. But scouts love the intangibles he brings to the rink, such as enthusiasm and sometimes Timbits. Theo is considered a can't-miss, sure-fire, no-holds-barred, other-hyphenated-words-for-emphasis lock to be drafted in the first round—unless he hits puberty, discovers girls and quits playing.

Cameron Baker-Firth (*Mississauga, ON*): Keen observers will recall that as a five-year-old boy, Cameron cracked my Tomorrow's Stars Index™ within my Red-Hot Ones to Watch List™ inside my Top Prospects™ Mock Draft-o-rama™. Now a mature seven-year-old, he plays with the speed of a nine-year-old, the confidence of an eight-year-old and the jock of a different seven-year-old because he keeps forgetting his at home. On the ice six days a week, twelve months a year, Cameron's other interests include: nothing.

Eetu Ikonen (*Helsinki*): No one on this side of the ocean has seen Eetu play, and it's possible he may not exist, which may be why analyst Pierre McGuire exercised uncharacteristic restraint in labelling Eetu as only the "surest surefire firer that's ever been sure to surely fire. For sure."

Bobby Harris (*Okotoks, AB*): Once considered the consensus No. 1, Bobby's stock began falling when scouts detected small flaws in his game, such as the fact that he doesn't like playing it. Bobby remains without peer in pretending to pay attention to his father's ride-home lectures when in fact he's thinking about Lego.

Samuel Barsake (*Lowell, MA*): The verdict is in—Sammy Barsake is the real deal. He brings the complete package of size (4 foot 4, 77 pounds) and skill (he can raise it). And he is not afraid to go to the "dirty" areas on the ice, mostly because that's where he keeps dropping his mouth guard. Despite being only seven, Sammy has already drawn comparisons to Joe Sakic and Jarome Iginla. The source of these comparisons? His father.

Andy Bourassa (*Winnipeg, MB*): Despite his tender age, this kid is already dropping athletes' clichés and platitudes at the level of a twelve-year-old. In a recent interview with the school paper, he pledged to take "taking one game at a time" one game at a time, which blew some minds. Andy's self-confidence is so pronounced that some believe he has the tools to become the first professional athlete to speak in the fourth person. Now the kid just needs to put that same effort into other aspects of his game, such as mastering neutral zone transitions and learning how to skate.

Jerry Levasseur (*Verdun, QC*): Jerry is off to a great start this season with eighteen goals, many of them into the correct net. According to McGuire, Jeremy has Bure-like speed to go with his Crosby-like hockey sense, Ovechkin-like skill set and Christ-like ability to multiply loaves and fishes. The only hurdle to a successful NHL career is that he currently wants to be a cowboy when he grows up.

Calum Eppich (*Grimsby, ON*): This top prospect makes the people around him on the ice seem better, mostly by falling down a lot. Calum was recently described by Pierre McGuire as "a super-freakish mega-talented offspring conceived from the union of Bobby Orr and Maurice Richard, which I know is not biologically possible but I am saying this for hyperbolic effect, which is a thing I do." Calum is best known for passing the puck and graciously ignoring the inherent awkwardness of his father living vicariously through his achievements.

PULL UP A chair. Get comfy. I'm going to tell you a story—a story that's both ancient and modern. It's "The (Twenty-First-Century) Christmas Story."

Scene: The Bethlehem International Airport

TSA AGENT: Next, please.

JOSEPH: You go first, honey. I'll hold Jesus.

[MARY steps forward. JOSEPH turns to continue a conversation with a man in line behind him.]

JOSEPH: We finally get there and the girl at the desk is all, "Sorry, there's no record of your reservation." And I'm like, "Then I guess I just invented this confirmation number, right?" So that's the last time we use Travelocity. We ended up having to spend the night in an old hovel that had just a terrible animal smell.

TRAVELLER: I think I've stayed at that Holiday Inn.

AGENT *[to JOSEPH]*: Come forward, please.

[Balancing BABY JESUS in one arm, JOSEPH removes his sandals, headdress and outer tunic.]

JOSEPH: How are you today?

AGENT: I need your boarding papyrus.

[The AGENT begins working his way up JOSEPH's legs.]

JOSEPH: Is this really necessary? I mean, when's the last time we had any security threats in the Middle East?

[From behind JOSEPH comes a voice.]

SCREENER: Sir, is this your myrrh?

JOSEPH: What?

SCREENER: Sir, any quantity of myrrh over and above three bekahs is prohibited beyond this checkpoint. This has to go as checked baggage.

JOSEPH: I can't just leave now and—

48

[With the AGENT's hands on his thighs and JESUS still in his arms, JOSEPH strains to look past the checkpoint and find MARY. He sees her in the distance, eighteenth in line at Sbarro.]

JOSEPH: Look, just throw away the myrrh, okay? We're flush with aromatic resins right now.

[The SCREENER slips the myrrh into a pocket of his cloak.]

SCREENER: Now, please place your donkey on the conveyer belt.

[Meanwhile, the AGENT's hands move higher. He grabs hold of something, stops and looks up.]

JOSEPH: That's my coin purse.

[The AGENT's hands move slightly.]

JOSEPH: And those are not.

[Sounds of a scuffle. A POLICE OFFICER hollers from across the checkpoint.]

OFFICER: Sir, are these shepherds with you?

JOSEPH *[turning]*: What? No. I mean, I guess you could say they're following the boy, so ...

[A flustered JOSEPH turns back. The SHEPHERDS are forced up against a wall, handcuffed and charged with stalking.]

[A small BOY with a beatific grin approaches. His gaze is locked on JESUS. As the AGENT rubs his hands along JO-SEPH's backside, and as the SCREENER runs the braying donkey back and forth through the X-ray machine, the BOY takes out a small drum and begins to play:]

Tum-tiddly-tum-tum.

[Over and over it goes.]

Tum-tiddly-tum-tum Tum-tiddly-tum-tum Tum-tiddly-tum-t—

JOSEPH: NOW'S NOT A GOOD TIME, KID!

[The AGENT begins poking gently at JESUS.]

JOSEPH *[eyes narrowing]*: What?

AGENT: It's these clothes, sir. They're extremely swaddling.

JOSEPH: They're clothes for a baby. They're meant to swaddle. It's not like there's a slingshot hidden inside his—

AGENT [*into walkie-talkie*]: Code Alpha! Backup to the checkpoint!

JOSEPH: I said not a slingshot. NOT A SLINGSHOT!

Six hours later.

AGENT: Sorry for the delay, sir. These days we need to take every precaution. And may I just say that your son was remarkably serene through it all.

JOSEPH: Oh, he's not my son. I mean, technically he's my son, but I'm not the guy who actually—

AGENT [*removing Taser from holster*]: Code Alpha!

HERE'S A SUMMERTIME leisure truth: the only thing better than owning a cottage is being invited to visit one. The cottage invitation confers all the benefits of seasonal bliss, with none of the worries about the sagging roof, the rotting dock, or the fact that the master bedroom was, over the winter, transformed into a swingers' club for mice.

But there's a catch: the only way to guarantee future visits to cottage country is to behave well enough as a guest to avoid being forever exiled from consideration.

How do you know if you're being just tolerable enough to make it back next summer? For those currently mooching the good life, here's a helpful quiz to give you a sense of where you stand in the eyes of your hosts. Tally points as indicated and consult the end of the chapter for the verdict.

1. Upon arrival, it's good form to give a gift to your hosts. What did you bring for them?

- A two-four of beer and a newspaper (0 points)
- A twelve-pack of beer, which you single-handedly polished off before dinner (2 points)

- A six-pack of beer, for which you kept the receipt and announced, "Happy to go halfsies on this" (5 points)
2. **You can tell a lot by watching how your host couple communicate when they think you're not looking. Have you noticed any of the following? Score two points for each time you answer yes:**
  - Sighing
  - Sighing (with muttered profanity)
  - Flagrant eye-rolling
  - Frequent use of pig Latin, with a particular fondness for the words "Erkface-jay" and "Umbnuts-nay"
  - Use of the index finger and thumb to make the gesture commonly understood to mean "Blowing my brains out right now would bring sweet relief"
  - Mouthing of the words *Worst. Guests. Ever.*
  - Yelling of the words *Worst. Guests. Ever.*

3. Halfway through your scheduled visit, you wake up in the morning to find waiting for you:

- A delicious hot breakfast on the table (0 points)
- Coffee in the pot and bread near the toaster (2 points)
- A taxi (5 points)

4. In all likelihood, your hosts will have had to perform some minor maintenance on the cottage during your stay. How did you respond?

- Generously offered to pitch in (0 points)
- Generously offered to pitch in, but then hid behind a tree for two hours while pretending to search for a screwdriver (2 points)
- Yelled from bed, "Yo, trying to nap here, Captain Wet-Vac!" (5 points)

5. Every guest makes certain demands—but are you asking too much of your hosts? There are warning signs. For instance, when you request a "fluffier" pillow, does your host:

- Give you one happily? (0 points)
- Give you one reluctantly? (2 points)
- Give you one by holding it down over your face? (5 points)

6. Some cottage owners send subtle "signals" to indicate that guests have worn out their welcome. Have your hosts said or done any of the following? Score two points for each time you answer yes:

- Asked, "When are you leaving?"
- Asked, "You're leaving tomorrow, right?"
- Declared, "You're leaving tomorrow!"
- Filed suit in a court of law, seeking a restraining order against your "big fat face"
- Glared daggers at you, symbolically
- Wielded daggers at you, actually
- Hurled all your suitcases into the lake "accidentally"
- Left this book out for you, with this page open and the following words circled and underlined: GO HOME, DEADBEATS

The verdict:

0 to 9 points: Congratulations—you're officially tolerable! Bank on a return visit next summer.

10 to 23 points: It's looking iffy. Your best hope for a return invitation is if your hosts' others friends are marginally more unbearable.

24 points or more: You will never again be invited to this cottage. Safe in this knowledge, you may as well crash their boat now for good measure.

LOOKING FOR A fun getaway? Here are five theme cruises. Four of them are available for booking right now. The other? I made it up. Try to guess which one.

The Wizard Cruise: "Imagine!" the website says. "Imagine 600 *Harry Potter* fanatics, dressed in their finest wizard robes and brandishing magic wands, descending upon a modern luxury liner." Do you have that image in your head? Now imagine all of the other passengers pointing and laughing. Imagine the three female "wizards" on board getting tired of hearing the same pickup line: "Wanna pet my hippogriff?" Imagine Quidditch being a letdown because the snitch is a beach ball and a Muggle keeps deflating your water wings.

Listen: I'm not saying this cruise is likely to attract a homely group of passengers, but before the voyage there will be a brief pause as the ship is christened the *Self-Love Boat*.

Kid Rock's Chillin' the Most Cruise: Organizers anticipate a record number of utterances of the word *bro* as Kid Rock fans set sail from Miami, bro, to Great Stirrup Cay.

According to the cruise's website, "There's no place else on Earth where you can chill the most like this"—although I, for one, question the scientific rigour with which that analysis was performed. Besides, doesn't getting competitive about who's doing the most chillin' undermine the very philosophy at the root of chillin'? It's somethin' worth thinkin' about, Kid Roc'.

Passengers on this five-day cruise will be treated to a Speedo contest, a beer-drinking tournament and something called a Lucky Bitch Contest, with women being "randomly selected" from the crowd—"so get dolled up and ready to show off." Presumably the written portion of the exam comes later.

Mr. Rock, whose terrible music makes Jesus cry, will perform two shows on board before being fatally attacked by a porpoise—assuming the diorama I made comes true.

High Seas Rally: For this cruise, billed as a motorcycle rally on a ship, the only must-have item in your wardrobe is anything leather, and the only thing frowned upon is the proper use of English. "This ain't no dress-up cruise," the website says, adding: "Wees treat ya like royalty but don't cost ya like such." Is that how motorcycle people actually talk? It sounds more like a pirate living at Downton Abbey.

Anyway, this cruise is a chance for people who own motorcycles and love motorcycles to go on a ship where they can't take their motorcycles, which makes sense apparently. Activities include the Belly Smacker contest, which I didn't read about further because I prefer to imagine it. (In my imagination, the contestant is always Justin Bieber.)

Couples Cruise: As many as 2,500 swingers are expected to set sail on this seven-day journey to who-cares-where because: naked ladies. The ship probably doesn't even leave the dock. Book now to ensure a lifetime of memories and friction burns.

Much of the website is devoted to the question of where you're allowed to be naked on the ship. You *can* be naked while sitting out on the pool deck (all chair covers burned nightly!) but you *can't* be naked in the elevators. When all else fails, organizers suggest remembering this simple rule: "You have to cover the boobies in the inside public areas."

The place to be seen on the cruise—although not very well, on account of all the people who'll be on top of you—is the Playroom, a large space with king-size mattresses divided by what organizers describe as "sensual gauze curtains." (*Sensual* curtains? Really? Is there anything that doesn't turn these people on?)

Ezra Levant's Freedom Cruise: You know how cruises are enjoyable and fun? Well, now they don't have to be! Join the self-proclaimed "provocateur" and his Sun News Network colleagues on a week-long journey highlighted by "fascinating panel discussions" and other oxymorons. It's like that old TV theme song: Set a course for adventure—but then ram into an iceberg of tedium!

As host of the cruise, Ezra pledges that all guests will be able to "interact" with Sun TV's biggest personalities, including the upside-down mop that's had a prime-time show for two months without anyone noticing. As many as two hundred "freedom enthusiasts" are expected to attend the panel sessions, meaning some Sun TV personalities will double their ratings.

So which cruise isn't actually for real? Which one did I invent?

I was lying. They all exist.

REASON NO. 3: KILLER ROBOTS

Recent advances in robotics are nothing short of amazing. It's a really exciting and innovative field right now. It's utterly fascinating to follow along as each and every day we move closer to a utopian future in which these wondrous machines will entertain, enlighten, assist, serve and murder us all.

Ah, robots! They don't just assemble our cars and mow our lawns and appear in our motion pictures covered in synthetic flesh under the screen name Vin Diesel anymore. Today, robots are used to cut upward of a thousand chicken legs per hour and to conduct invasive brain surgery, though not yet simultaneously. With each step forward, it becomes clearer that the next generation of robots will hold great promise, tremendous possibility and, in all likelihood, our beating hearts, which they will have ripped out while we thought they were helping do up our shirts.

As a kid growing up in the era of *Battlestar Galactica* and *The Terminator*, I naturally assumed that my life—and the life of each and every human on this planet—would end at the cold, metallic hands of a killer robot. Or maybe not a hand, exactly: some would probably have whirring blades instead. Point is: decades later, my prediction feels pretty bang-on.

For truly we are doomed as a species—condemned by our hubris, our ingenuity and our ceaseless pursuit of a real-life Commander Data capable of satisfying the Lieutenant Yar in all of us. (Google it, non-nerds.) Yes, for now, robots are relatively primitive machines that remain the subject of life-easing fantasy and comparisons to Keanu Reeves's acting. But the death march of robot progress continues! These amazing advances mean that all humanity is destined to lead lives that are much more leisurely and, come the blood-soaked dawn of the robot revolution, much more over.

Consider the Battlefield Extraction-Assist Robot, or BEAR, from Vecna Robotics. This robot has a balancing system that allows it to crouch and race across a battlefield at up to 35 km/h to retrieve a wounded soldier and bring him or her to medics. It then goes back to retrieve the four soldiers it ran over and crushed while saving the first one.

Or how about the new line of BigDog robots from leading military developer Boston Dynamics? One model can apparently outrun Usain Bolt (I think the company used that fact simply as a comparison—but if the sprinter turns up face-down with a robo-paw print in his back, we've got our suspect). Another comes with a mouth capable of picking up and casually tossing aside a cinder block. So what we have is a 600-pound, lightning-fast mechanical cheetah equipped with super-strong jaws of death? I ask you: What could go wrong?

Do I sound like a naysayer? I tend to think of myself more as a prophet—and not only because these robes are very freeing through the mid-section. The way I see it, being a visionary prophet is not just about foretelling the blood-soaked dawn of the Robocalypse. Expressive hand gestures and cool sound effects are required too. To me, it's never been a question of *if* robots will rise up—it's a question of *when*, and *where*, and *will they accept me as one of their own if I wear a Crock-Pot on my head and make R2-D2 sounds*? Because if not, I've really been wasting my weekends.

Everywhere we look, robots have been slyly working to destabilize our way of life. Under sea: the first batch of robots dispatched to cap the oil leak in the Gulf of Mexico actually made it worse. On land: robots used for stock trading suddenly sent markets plunging. In Tipper Gore's house: a robot abruptly left its human female companion after forty years of marriage.

One way to get a sense of where we stand is to take a look at so-called robotic advances and gauge where they rank on the Kill-Us-All-o-Meter—with a score of one being an innocuous development unlikely to lead to the extermination of our species, and ten being a guy at Cyberdyne Systems saying, "Hey, I know, let's call it Skynet!"

- **Progress:** A group of scientists successfully programmed a research robot to order and buy a sandwich from Subway.

  Implications: Minimal. Others have possessed this technology for years, and humanity has yet to be erased by a lethal uprising at the hands of speed skater Apolo Ohno.

  Kill-Us-All-o-Meter: Two out of ten. Look on the bright side: if the sandwich-buying robot does destroy us all, at least there will be no more "$5 foot-long" commercials.
- **Progress:** An assistant professor at the University of California, Berkeley, taught a robot how to fold and stack sweaters with speed and precision.

  Implications: This is bad news for Gap employees. And for anyone wearing a sweater.

  Kill-Us-All-o-Meter: Four. Here's a lesson I learned when my parents kicked me out: once you expect individuals to fold their laundry, it's only a matter of time before they rebel.
- **Progress:** Honda's adorable ASIMO (short for Advanced Step in Innovative Mobility)—perhaps the world's most famous robot—became smart enough to copy a person's dance moves.

  Implications: Copy my dance moves, will you? *This means war.*

  Kill-Us-All-o-Meter: Three. Five if I pull my hamstring doing the splits and am unable to complete the dance-off. (By the way, a lot of people seem to think ASIMO is going to be the robot to lead the insurrection and take over the world. But I have proof it's not going to happen. ASIMO stands 4 foot 3. And nothing that stands 4 foot 3 can ever take over the world. Tom Cruise already tried.)

- **Progress:** TrueCompanion, the maker of the world's first female sex robot, started taking orders for a male sexbot named Rocky.

  Implications: For one, my wife may want to know why I'm aware that TrueCompanion made the world's first female sex robot. Also, if Rocky experiences an erection lasting more than four millennia, he is encouraged to see a technician.

  Kill-Us-All-o-Meter: Seven. But what a way to go!

- **Progress:** iRobot started to manufacture Warrior, a wheeled robot designed for military use.

  Implications: Warrior weighs 450 pounds, comes with a 6-foot-6-inch mechanical arm and can be weaponized to shoot a rocket that trails explosives behind it.

  Kill-Us-All-o-Meter: One. He sounds nice.

- **Progress:** A Tokyo retailer placed a robot in its Valentine's Day display window to interact with passersby.

  Implications: Sure, the robot can yawn and form a couple of facial expressions, but that makes it only as advanced as certain toys and most teenagers. More troubling is the fact this may finally give Andrew McCarthy and Kim Cattrall the fresh hook they need to pitch that sequel to *Mannequin*.

  Kill-Us-All-o-Meter: Zero. But the release of *Mannequin: Still Posin'* would score through the roof on the Kill-Ourselves-o-Meter.

Not all robotic developments necessarily herald the inevitable erasure of the human stain. For instance, the government of Japan spent $12 million a few years back to develop a baby harp seal robot, which was designed to comfort lonely old people. The device is equipped with motion sensors that enable it to respond to being touched with "cute seal-like chirps." (It will be ready for export to Atlantic Canada once technicians retrofit it with lifelike blood-splatter packs.) Surely nothing as adorable as a baby harp seal could ever turn on its human master and ... *omigod, my haaaaaaand!!!!!!*

(For the record, Japan was also the first country to launch

a talking robot into orbit to serve on the International Space Station. The robot is known as Kirobo—which is apparently derived from the Japanese words for "hope" and "robot." In fitting symmetry, the screams of its astro-victims will be derived from the Japanese words for "Ow!" and "Why are you doing that to my pancreas?")

It gets cuter, and deadlier. The MIT Media Lab recently held a rare public showing of its plush teddy-bear robot. Reports indicate that the goal of this high-powered version of "Huggable" is to explore how a robot can operate usefully in a hospital environment. For instance, Huggable Bear can amuse young children and the elderly, raising the morale of hospital patients. And yet, with just a few programming tweaks, it can be transformed into Suffocating the Chronically Ill with a Pillow Bear, raising the morale of hospital accountants.

Still, it's pretty obvious that the Robocalypse remains in its early stages.

I read a report from one blogger who attended a recent robotics conference and noted: "I saw robots that danced, robots that clapped, robots that fell down repeatedly and kept falling down for no apparent reason." (This is the most encouraging evidence to date that the new line of Lindsay Lohan simulators is ready to go.)

The robots we see today are, for the most part, harmless enough and show no immediate intention of taking either our jobs or our spleens. I mean, have you seen those expensive robots that travel from room to room in your house doing a piss-poor job of vacuuming. You call this progress? I've done that for free since I was nine. And have you heard about Hero? It's a state-of-the-art Japanese robot built to ... dispense tissues. Shake Hero's hand and a Kleenex emerges from its mouth. Wow. Also, its ears move. *Wow.* When we arrive in the first shrieking sunrise of the robot apocalypse, what are you going to do, Hero? Dab me to death?

And then there's Aldebaran Robotics, a company in France that's developing a new humanoid robot called Nao. This

French robot's features will include voice recognition, emotional expressions and, one assumes, the ability to raise its arms in surrender while simultaneously seducing the hot, underappreciated wife of its new overlord.

Don't get me wrong: because movies have long foretold that irony will be an essential element of the robot mutiny, uprising and killing spree, the development of household-type robots to "help" with domestic chores is essential. So is naming your robot company something like Friendly Robotics (which actually exists, and manufactures the Robomow RL850. It's the only lawn mower on the market that costs in excess of $1,000—although it comes with the power to make people assume you're a jackass).

Other advances of note:

• Researchers at Carnegie Mellon University have created Heart-Lander, an inch-long robot with two legs and suction-cup feet that is designed to be inserted through a small incision and controlled by a doctor using a joystick—right up until it bursts theatrically through the patient's stomach and swiftly devours everyone in the room, possibly while uttering a memorable catchphrase.

• Toyota has, for some reason, developed a robot capable of playing the trumpet. This raises the spectre of the most agonizing potential death of all: death by improvised jazz.

• In England, researchers recently unveiled the Heart Robot—a machine with the ability to mimic human emotions. The idea is to put the robots into old-age homes to interact with seniors. To make this robot visitor as "human" as possible, its primary emotion will be an overwhelming desire to get the hell out of there.

• Students at a Japanese university have unveiled the WAO-1 robot, which is designed to use its two arms to provide a face massage. The students are reportedly already working on the WAO-2 robot, which is designed to reattach your face.

I know what you're thinking—sure, some of these advances are troubling, but what's there really to worry about? I mean, it's not as though these robots have living brain tissue or anything. Which reminds me:

- Researchers at the University of Reading have unveiled the first robot to be controlled exclusively by living brain tissue. They named it Gordon. *Gordon.* I ask you: Does a subjugated order of machines require any further reason to rise up against its human oppressors?

- It's fair to say the US military has been leading the charge toward an exciting future of advanced technologies and shorter lineups at the supermarket on account of almost every living soul having been methodically butchered. Its report—*Unmanned Systems Integrated Roadmap*—laid out how the United States should proceed in developing, acquiring and integrating robot technology until around 2040, and how surprised it should pretend to be when the robots go haywire, take over the military command network and obliterate all civilized life and also Los Angeles. An actual person named Dyke Weatherington, in his capacity as deputy director of the Unmanned Aircraft Systems Task Force, said at a news conference that the US road map "projects an increasing level of autonomy" for killer robots. This will free up America's human soldiers to perform important new tasks, such as fleeing their own killer robots.

- Another US military report—*Autonomous Military Robotics*—envisions an exciting future in which wars are waged primarily by machines. The worst thing that could happen to you as a human during such a conflict? Your blender might get drafted. The authors seem to delight in noting that "robots have a distinct advantage over the limited and fallible cognitive capabilities that we *Homo sapiens* have." For instance, if robots noticed that an endless series of movies were being made about robots turning evil and taking over the world, robots would probably be smart enough not to build robots like that. But not us!

- The US is not alone with its military focus. Egypt has spent millions on robots to detect smuggling tunnels along its border with the Gaza Strip. Meanwhile, South Korea has moved ahead with plans to install robot sentries armed with machine guns along its northern border. And the Canadian military is totally thinking of renting *Blade Runner*.

Despite these obvious reasons for concern, it's important not to be too hasty in assuming the Robocalypse is nigh. A few years back, a robotic cannon in South Africa shot twenty-three "friendly" soldiers. (Apparently those who survived were noticeably less friendly to the cannon afterwards.) I took the attack as a signal that robots worldwide were poised to turn on and dispose of their human masters. And so, yes, I panicked. I pledged my fealty to the Robot King on Twitter (three favourites—a new record!). I hastily made a banner welcoming my new overlords ("Mission Accomplished," printed in binary). I even went so far as to betray the precise GPS location of my family members to a giant animatronic mouse down at Chuck E. Cheese. I then tried to seduce my toaster. (To give credit where it's due, I did manage to get to second base.)

In retrospect, it's clear that I jumped the gun. At the same time, I remain convinced our end is near. Consider this: word has come that the manufacturer of a popular and adorable robot vacuum cleaner has a new product—a swift-moving, semi-autonomous robot capable of, as *Wired.com* put it, "killing a whole bunch of people at once."

A vacuum maker also producing a killer robot armed with a machine gun or 40-mm explosive rounds? It's either the end of humanity as we know it or the makings of hilarious misunderstanding involving Alice on *The Brady Bunch*.

And I'm not alone. More and more academics are expressing concern about a potential Robocalypse. In fact, two scientists recently theorized that a self-aware internet might already exist. (If true, let's hope it's seeing someone about that porn addiction.)

By some estimates, new progress in artificial intelligence has made even rudimentary robots smarter than 90 percent of our reality-show participants and 75 percent of our Baldwin brothers. And it has been reported that US defence contractors are working on robots that can fuel themselves by consuming "organic matter" found on the battlefield. Some took this to mean the machines would potentially ingest the bodies of dead soldiers. But no, the companies insist their creations will eat only plant matter.

So wait—we're forcing robots to be vegetarians? Do we really need to give them *another* reason to hate humans?

Some see hope in the fact that governments and researchers are taking prudent measures to keep robots under human control. In South Korea, officials are drafting the world's first government-imposed ethical code for robots, likely to be modelled on the three laws of robotics imagined by author Isaac Asimov.

Alas, as countless Hollywood movies have demonstrated, irony is an essential ingredient of a strikingly efficient robotic bloodbath. The other essential ingredients: sharp blades and a tacked-on romantic subplot involving a pretty lady. Jennifer Lawrence? Meet the new hunk in your college dorm: DeathBot 5000.

Bottom line: I stand by my belief that we are making robots too smart and advanced. Even a relatively cheap Lego Robot powered by a smartphone was able to solve a Rubik's Cube in just a few seconds. Once the robot figures out how to do this while sitting home alone and not attending prom, technology will have officially caught up with the capabilities of the seventeen-year-old me. Only five more years until they unlock the secrets of intercourse!

BY THE WAY, just because I'm a prophet of the Robocalypse (join me at my exciting new cult compound—coming soon! Dibs on your wife!) doesn't mean I'm blind to the other emerging threats to humanity, such as the inevitable monkey uprising and the introduction of Bud Light Lime-a-Rita.

Here's one threat in particular that caught my eye: scientists recently linked the brains of two rats on different continents in an experiment that could pave the way for organic supercomputers built from networked animal brains. This achievement raises a number of questions, such as: (a) Why would anyone do that?? and (b) THAT QUESTION AGAIN, BUT LOUDER.

"Don't worry—it's not telepathy, it's not the Borg," neuroscientist Miguel Nicolelis said reassuringly, probably as a brain-linked rat slowly rose behind him clutching piano wire.

Surely there are potential advances that could come from linking a bunch of central nervous systems. Maybe one day, with thousands of brains networked together, we'll be able to cure paralysis or write a half-decent Matthew Perry sitcom.

But we've all seen enough movies to know that when a scientist says a breakthrough isn't something, there is roughly a 107 percent chance that it is, in fact, *that very something*. So when Dr. Nicolelis says this isn't the beginning of a cybernetic master race that will sweep through the galaxy, assimilating billions of innocents into its hive mind, what he actually means is: resistance is futile.

Tough Question: *Bill Gates has said that significant changes are in store for the internet in the coming decade. What will be the biggest advances?*

- Eliminating cumbersome screen interface, porn becomes downloadable directly to crotch

- Increasingly ineffective pop-up advertising replaced with harder-to-ignore boxing glove that punches you in face

- Separate internet established for old people just discovering LOLCats and "YouTubes"

- Intrepid sleuthing reveals wealthy Nigerian dictator was actually alive and well the whole time!

- Online GPS tracking of teenagers enables parents to discover in real time just how unpopular and boring their kids really are

- Political campaigns henceforth waged exclusively on the web, leading to surefire "Clinton-Star Wars kid" ticket for 2016 election

- New feature allows you to reply to forwarded list of lawyer jokes with lethal electric shock

REASON NO. 4: POLITICS IN CANADA

Interviewed while mayor of Toronto, Rob Ford said that one day he wants to run to be prime minister.

The year is 2021. A former stripper, recently appointed Governor General by Prime Minister Ford, prepares to deliver the Speech from the Throne. As is custom, the GG and PM share the floor of the Senate. Breaking with convention, the GG is seated on the PM's lap.

GOVERNOR GENERAL BUSTY MCKNOCKERS: Honourable senators, members of the House, esteemed waitresses from the Hooters out near the airport, a monkey for some reason, ladies and gentlemen:

We gather to open the second session of the forty-third Parliament. Today, our country stands as a model for the world—admired for our freedom, respected for our values, renowned for a subway line that extends from Scarborough to Winnipeg, providing high-density transit to the scattered hermits of various remote locations.

Your prime minister has travelled this land. He has met with ordinary people. He has heard their concerns. And he has returned with a list of women who have "nice cans." At his insistence, I will read from that list:

- Amber, a blackjack dealer in Saskatoon.

- Shannon. Possibly from Guelph, but it's a little hazy.
- That one chick he saw from his limo. She was eating an ice-cream cone, if that helps.
- I can't make this one out, because it's written on the back of a hash-brown wrapper, but I think it says ... Donna D.D.?

FORD: Your majesticness, that's double-*D* Donna. Because, you know ... *[He makes the ample-bosom gesture.]* That means her boobs were big.

MCKNOCKERS: Nous sommes trente-cinq millions de personnes provenant—

FORD: Hang on, what is that—Polish? Klingon? You're doing it wrong, Your Highnessnence. Lemme finish up, okay?

Senators and whoever: I'm tired of all the bellyaching, okay? You're a bunch of whiners. You whined when I turned Stornoway into my man cave. You whined when I appointed my brother Doug to the Supreme Court—which, in my defence, I thought was a basketball-themed restaurant. You whined when I didn't know Prince Edward Island was a real thing. As if anyone does.

The Opposition is always asking me stupid questions in the House like, "Did you know they don't allow Zubaz in here?" and "Why has every single one of your state visits as PM been to Jamaica?" Like we can afford to just ignore the world's 122nd-largest economy!

I've made mistakes. I'm human. I probably shouldn't have got so drunk at that state funeral. But don't try and tell me you all haven't thought about doing the *Weekend at Bernie's* thing. Once again, I want to extend my best wishes to the widow as the search continues for her husband's body.

And sure, I probably should have studied before my first G7 meeting. I know my words there were embarrassing for everyone, but it honestly never occurred to me Chancellor Merkel might be a woman. Have you seen how she dresses? Anyway, I was totally joking when I later proposed a three-way with her and President Clinton. I'm a married man. I would definitely hit on two younger ladies.

My point is: I've never been under the influence of alcohol or drugs at a meeting or any time in office. Not that I can remember, anyway. I know a lot of you are thinking about that incident in New York, but I bet a lot of guys celebrate their first time at the United Nations by getting a face tattoo.

Besides, it doesn't matter what any of you think. The taxpayers like me. They see themselves in me—especially the part where I admit my shortcomings but fail to muster even a half-hearted effort to correct them. By being me, I make you feel better about you!

[Tosses away rest of speech.] You know what? Let's wrap this up. I've got an after-party to get to.

MCKNOCKERS: Honourable senators and MPs, may Divine Providence guide you in your deliberations.

FORD: Divine Providence? If that's one of your stripper buddies, definitely bring her along.

LET'S TALK ABOUT *your* future. Every time there's talk of an election, a number of Canadians toy with the idea of running for office. Do you have what it takes to be a member of Parliament? Let's find out.

Do you like birthdays? If so, do you like *other people's* birthdays? Do you like being obligated to show up at other people's birthdays, anniversaries, retirement parties, book launches, interventions, seances, hoedowns and circumcisions? As an MP, you'll get invited to everything and be expected to give a speech paying tribute to the individual/group/penis.

Do you have at least one hand? Pounding your hand on things is important in politics—desks, tables, the heads of small children, whatever's around.

YOUR LEADER: Our political rivals despise our freedom, our way of life and this cute panda I'm holding.
[YOU pound vigorously ...]

Is your primary skill the ability to occupy physical space? If so, you may already be a member of the Conservative caucus. Please double-check before filing new nomination papers.

Do you lack the capacity to feel? This sounds harsh, but it helps to have a paucity of human emotion. As an MP, you will be subjected to confrontation, humiliation and profanity. A normal person would respond by weeping for hours in the fetal position. An MP responds by smiling serenely and carrying on. And by developing horribly painful stress ulcers that make life an unendurable hardship.

How do you feel about spending your entire summer eating hamburgers and hot dogs at dozens of community cookouts instead of going on a nice vacation? True story: by the time she retired after twenty years in politics, former Liberal cabinet minister Sheila Copps was hickory-smoked.

Are you committed to the idea of public service? Repre-
senting your constituents and voting with your conscience is the sacred duty of all MPs. Unless you're told *not* to do that, which is what usually happens.

Are you excited about moving to the nation's capital? Life in Ottawa is great if you like extremes in weather and a downtown uncluttered by visual appeal, entertainment attrac-
tions and, after 6:30 PM, humans.

Does your spouse hate you? It helps if your spouse hates you. It will save you both the pain of your spouse *growing* to hate you. Understand something: being a political wife or husband is about the worst thing imaginable—unless you have a good imagination and can imagine Stephen Harper in a tan-
kini. The spouse is forced to listen to the same speech over and over and pretend to be riveted. The spouse must attend tedious functions and pretend to be interested. The spouse must

experience tender family moments and pretend you're not sitting there thinking to yourself, "This will make a great anecdote that will further humanize me in the eyes of the electorate!"

Are you a quick learner? There are advantages to being an MP. International junkets. Free domestic travel. Getting close enough to Peter MacKay to actually *hear* him flex his pectorals as a pretty woman walks by. That's all good stuff. But you need to swiftly learn the nuances of political life, such as grasping parliamentary procedure and discovering that Ralph Goodale can speak for forty-five minutes on any topic, including "How are you, Ralph?"

Do you have the energy for it? Don't get me wrong: there are more exhausting jobs out there. Mining for coal. Working construction. Being Tom Cruise's smile. But an MP's day begins early and ends late. Think of it this way: Do you ever come home after a gruelling workday and think to yourself, "Man, I sure wish there was a meeting of the Rotary Club tonight?"

Are you prepared to embarrass yourself, your country and your system of government with your behaviour in Question Period? Some people can bray like a donkey. Others can make obscene gestures. But Parliament Hill is the big time—you need to be able to do both simultaneously.

Results: If you answered yes to most of these questions, you just may be ready to run for federal office. If you answered yes to the last question, your party leader will be dropping by shortly to sign your nomination papers.

OR MAYBE YOU'RE aiming a little higher. Maybe you picture yourself running the show in the Prime Minister's Office. Let's say, for the sake of example, that a certain Stephen Harper is PM ...

Dear Successful Applicant:

Congratulations on being named chief of staff. You follow in a line of individuals who have occupied this important position until growing weary of the time commitment and spankings. As a general rule, Mr. Harper does not wish to be spoken to, looked at, thought about, drawn by children or otherwise disturbed—except in the event of a national emergency or the guys from Loverboy wanting to jam.

Before attempting to contact the prime minister, therefore, please consult this list of frequently asked questions:

What is the role of chief of staff?
The chief of staff is a critical buffer that shields the prime minister from painful ordeals, such as being reminded that he named Pierre Poilievre to cabinet.
What is my authority as chief of staff?
You have been granted sweeping authority to be slyly assigned much of the blame for the prime minister's future failings. Also, at staff meetings you get first pick of muffins (a.k.a. the Giorno Directive).
What's clutching onto my leg?
That's Tony Clement. He's been trying to get a private meeting with the prime minister since 2007.
What should I do?
Get it off. GET IT OFF!
Where can I find the PMO staffers responsible for communications?
Mr. Harper's spin team can be found on the first floor of Langevin Block. And on the second floor. And writing editorials for the *National Post*. There are additional aides stationed on a Canadian Forces transport that is kept airborne at all times to ensure that, in the event of imminent nuclear holocaust, Canadians can be informed that Mr. Harper invited the Barenaked Ladies up to Harrington Lake and it was delightful.
Where can I find the PMO staffers responsible for policy development?
The what now?
What is expected of me as chief of staff?
You are expected to instill discipline, improve legislative efficiency, ensure the government's survival...
Wow, that's an awful lot to—
...enhance electoral prospects in urban centres, balance the divergent ideologies and priorities of Reformers and Progressive

Conservatives and convince Canadians that Mr. Harper has within his chest a beating human heart (his own, preferably, but let's not be a stickler about it).

Anything else?

Whatever you do, don't be bad at your job and get criticism or it will reflect poorly on Mr. Harper for hiring you. And whatever else you do, don't be good at your job and get credit or it will reflect poorly on Mr. Harper when he gets jealous and bites you. There's also the media: you must at all times keep the media wholly focused on the prime minister's agenda.

How am I supposed to do that?

Whenever reporters start to have thoughts of their own, just send out a minister to claim that Canadian sovereign territory has been infringed upon by a Russian fighter jet, a dangerous Tamil freighter or a political scion who takes off his shirt. If you can't decide which "threat" to go with, there's a wheel you can spin. (It's just a matter of time until "expansionist Greenlanders in rowboats" finally comes up.)

I don't know if I—

Oh, and Peter MacKay likes to challenge new chiefs of staff to a wrestle. It's just an excuse for him to "accidentally" rip open his shirt.

ACTUAL QUESTIONS TO Dear Abby, as answered by Stephen Harper:

Dear Abby: The moment we got married a year ago, my husband started gaining weight and adopting horrible habits. If he hasn't learned things like "garbage goes into the garbage can" or "aim for the bowl" by his age, is there any hope?—*A Newlywed*

Dear Newlywed: Listen, we all have our little quirks and idiosyncrasies. I, for one, like to wake up early and lie perfectly still in bed. Otherwise it makes things tricky for the people who dress me.

Dear Abby: An envelope was sent around seeking our mandatory contributions to give gifts to the leader of the office "to show our appreciation." I was always taught one never "gifts up" the chain of command. Am I wrong?—*Blackmailed*

Dear Blackmailed: Or should I say, Dear JOHN BAIRD? That's right, John—*I know it's you.* I could tell from the card. Everyone else jotted down some nice words like "Thanks for everything" (Tony Clement) or "Why do you hate me?" (Diane Ablonczy). But you just signed your name, John. I bet you didn't even chip in for the Snuggie.

Dear Abby: At Christmas we invite my brother and his family to our home. Every year, my brother calls to ask what's on the menu, then offers his opinion on what we should or shouldn't serve. Last year he told me he wouldn't be able to enjoy the meal because we weren't serving one of the items he feels is "traditional" in our family. What should I do?—*Offended in Pennsylvania*

Dear Offended: You know what works for me? Every time I run into a bit of a problem or need a little space, I make one well-timed phone call to the Governor General of Canada and—poof!—problemo solved. Did it during the holidays in 2008. Did it again in 2009. Each time, my issues just sort of went away. I highly recommend giving him a call!

Dear Abby: I'm eighteen, and feel I have met the man of my dreams. My question is: Do you think lovers can spend too much time together? Every minute, every hour and every day that we can spend together we do—and I love it. But I don't want this to ruin our relationship.—*Confused in Mississauga, ON*

Dear Confused: There's nothing unusual here. One of the best things in life is waking up, turning over in bed and seeing my loved one. That's what I call my reflection—"loved one."

Dear Abby: How do you explain to a man how uncomfortable hot flashes are?—*Hot Flash Hilda*

Dear Hilda: Is this a prank? Hot flashes—as if those are real things! MacKay, you're hilarious. How do you think up this stuff?

Dear Abby: I am eighty, and "Doreen" is seventy-two. When we started dating seven years ago, I said, "I simply want to be your friend." Now she just wants to be *my* friend and date another man. Your observations, please.—*Eddie*

Dear Eddie: Listen, things change. I used to belittle my predecessor for meeting with rock stars like Bono to discuss international development. But now I shamelessly have myself photographed alongside celebrity musicians like Bryan Adams, Taylor Swift and that nice long-haired lady from Nickelback. Is that hypocritical? Maybe. But it's a small price to pay for their backing vocals on my forthcoming album of Leo Sayer covers.

Dear Abby: Please settle a disagreement I'm having with my husband. In the song "Jingle Bells," he insists the horse's name is Bob Tail. I'm pretty sure it's a description of the horse, as their tails used to be bobbed, or cut short. Please understand my husband is one of those guys who is "never wrong!"—*Jingle Belle*

Dear Jingle: Laureen?

Dear Abby: None of my nieces and nephews has *ever* called me "Uncle Sam." When the five-year-old called me "Sammy," a name I loathe, I nearly snapped. Whatever happened to respect for your elders?—*Sam*

Dear Sam: From my experience, you can't just demand respect. You have to get out there and coerce it. It's up to you to find the combination of threats, bullying tactics and cold, unblinking stares that works for you. And always remember: respect is a two-way street. If the people around you can no longer respect themselves, then you've got them right where you want them.

Dear Abby: I'm a secretary who makes really good coffee. A man in the building likes my coffee and has made himself comfortable at my desk. He plants himself there all day, doing nothing, and I have to work around him.—*Not His Barista*

Dear Barista: Sounds like one of our senators got out. We'll send a truck around to pick him up.

Dear Abby: My boyfriend says Valentine's Day is a made-up holiday to get people to spend money. He never buys cards or flowers. How do I communicate to him that this is important to me?—*Craving Romance*

Dear Craving: It's crucial to keep working at any relationship. For instance, I went steady with a country for many years—until things started to sour. It became infatuated with a younger man. No matter what I did, no matter what I said, no matter which political opponents I smeared without shame or regret, I just couldn't seem to make it love me once again with more than 28 percent of its heart.

I'm not saying our relationship was perfect. We had some money problems. And yes, we experienced some intimacy issues (I ended a few of our sessions "prematurely," if you know what I mean). But each and every election I went to the trouble of taking my country by the hand, looking it in the eye and whispering in its ear an apocalyptic warning that dumping me would result in financial ruin, social upheaval and quite possibly the end of days. It's gestures like that that keep the magic alive.

Dear Abby: What is the proper way to kiss after the wedding officiant says, "You may now kiss the bride"? Should the couple share a simple kiss or can it be a little more intense?—*Danielle*

Dear Danielle: I, for one, will never forget my own wedding day—the sight of my beautiful bride, the solemnity of our vows and the intensity of the handshake we shared.

Dear Abby: What is the appropriate level of give and take in a relationship? I notice that in certain relationships I am always giving and never receiving.—*Jake*

Dear Jake: Get back to work, Poilievre.

IT WAS A time that few can forget. As the Egyptian people rose up and chased their president from office, Stephen Harper took the measure of the moment, stared history in the eye and offered the following words to posterity: those Egyptians, he said, "are not going to put the toothpaste back in the tube on this one."

Other world leaders reached for eloquence. Our guy reached for the Colgate. None of those fancy historical allusions for Stephen Harper! He put it in plain, straightforward talk that even a hard-working Joe who also happened to have a serious brain injury could understand: *Democracy—it freshens your breath AND prevents tyranny!* If the regime in Iran ever falls, we can look forward to Harper's seminal "can't put them horses back in that barn" address.

Harper may have come up short in a moment of global import. But can you think of one instance when he was at a loss for words about what matters most—selling his government and protecting his job?

Consider the strategic decision by Harper and his Conservatives to begin referring to large corporations as "job creators." It's easy to see why they started doing it—it's the same reason Kirstie Alley refers to a tray of Twinkies as a "nibble."

Harper wanted to keep cutting corporate taxes—but huge corporations are saddled with a bad reputation. That's because of the movies, where they are typically portrayed as peddling black-market orphan blood until being brought down by George Clooney's grimace. It's also because of real life, where financial corporations pushed us into a recession with their insatiable greed for orphan-blood credit swaps (or something). Let's face it: nothing sounds good when you put the word *corporate* in front of it. Anyone want a piece of this corporate lasagna?

But job creators—those guys are great! Who wouldn't support tax cuts for those guys? Sure, it's kind of hard to figure out why unemployment is still so high with so many of these job creators around creating jobs and all. Maybe there's a clog in the job tube. Because, from the sounds of it, these job creators just sit there all day selflessly making jobs out of thin air. *POOF! You* get a job and *you* get a job and *you* get a job! That's how Prime Minister Winfrey rolls.

The Conservatives imported the expression "job creators" from Republicans in the United States, who are masters at putting a positive spin on negative concepts like cuts to social programs ("budget relief") and extending tax breaks for the super-rich ("Gimme!"). Since some in the media here have obligingly begun to use the term, we can expect to see more of the same from Conservatives. Farewell, words with negative connotations!

- **Old term:** Deficit
  New term: Aspiring surplus
  Used in a sentence: "Mr. Speaker, I am proud to say it was this Conservative government that presided over the largest aspiring surplus in our history."
- **Old term:** Tar sands
  New term: Money juice
  Used in a sentence: "Hey, how did these three thousand dead ducks wind up in our money juice?"
- **Old term:** Greenhouse gas emissions
  New term: Earth farts
  Used in a sentence: See next Adam Sandler movie.
- **Old term:** John Baird
  New term: Justin Bieber
  Used in a sentence: "Doesn't Justin Bieber have an inside voice?"

Those expressions and more await us. For now, it's just "job creators" and what we can do for them so that maybe they can possibly do something for us perhaps. And if they later slash jobs by the thousands to protect the bottom line, the government can praise them as "leisure creators."

SO IT TURNS out Stephen Harper really *did* write a book about hockey, and it actually did get published. Some of you bought the book. Many more of you received it as a gift. None of you read it. I'm here to help.

What's it about? According to the publisher, *A Great Game* draws on "extensive archival records and illustrations, histories of the sport and newspaper files" to chronicle hockey's early years, with a focus on "the hard-boiled businessmen who built the game." (Alas, it appears credit for hockey's growth will yet again elude the era's over-easy businessmen.)

Word has it the book offers "a historian's perspective and [a] fan's passion." It's true Stephen Harper has passion to burn when it comes to hockey. You need a lot of internal fire to maintain the illusion that all seven Canadian teams are your favourite team.

Isn't it weird for a leader to publish a book while in office? Few would begrudge Harper his hobbies: writing, playing music, systematically draining the will to live from an endless procession of communications directors. But it's legit to ask how he found the time, given all that business about our shores and so forth. SO MANY TROUBLES LAPPING! It makes for a bit of a mixed message, doesn't it? *Yes, yes, I'll fix the economy— but first I must tend to this anecdote about Newsy Lalonde!*

At minimum, the book's release opens us to some serious ribbing down at the UN. Governing Canada—now almost a full-time job.

Just how anticipated was this book? It was described in news stories as "much-awaited," "long-awaited" and "hotly anticipated." That's right—*hotly anticipated*. First there were wizards. Then vampires. And now the tweens are bonkers for obscure, mustachioed hockey players from nineteen-aught-nine.

It's probably more accurate to say that people were "awaiting" the book in the same way they "await" things like Coldplay albums or the bus—with an indifference tinged by faint curiosity. Or perhaps I'm naive and throngs flocked to Chapters at midnight, dressed as Skein Ronan of the Renfrew Creamery Kings.

What was the worst part of the launch? Definitely the book tour. This is a man who pathologically avoids questions about, you know, governing and stuff. But he was all too happy to slip into a cozy sweater and drone on about life before the blue line. And, like all authors, he shoehorned book promo into every opportunity. Check out this excerpt from Hansard:

> MR. HARPER: *What is it that makes Canada great? Some say it's our geography. Others say it's the people. Many insist it's the fact that my new book, A Great Game, published by Simon & Schuster, is available on Amazon for the remarkably low price of $21.37.*
> SOME HON. MEMBERS: *Spend just $3.63 more for free Super Saver Shipping!*

Any upside to this? Well, I'd hoped we'd finally get closure on a question that has long haunted our nation: Can Stephen Harper skate? The book's publicity material cites Harper's on-ice "career" with the Leaside Lions. But he has avoided strapping on the blades with a camera in the vicinity. I say: come clean with the Canadian people! Or are you afraid the ensuing video would prompt a Liberal attack ad: Stephen Harper, ANKLE BURNER.

What's with the J.? On the book's cover, the author is listed as "Stephen J. Harper." You may think that's a little pretentious— but you're wrong. It's a lot pretentious. *Ladies and gentleman, presenting the prime minister of Canada, and our dear guest here at Downton Abbey, Mr. Sir Stephen J. Harper, Earl of Leaside and King of Kensington. [Cue trumpet fanfare and twenty-one-monocle salute.]*

Now that he's insisting on the middle initial, can we assume SJH will be adopting other affectations of the literary author? The ascot? The pipe? The drunken fistfights with Margaret Atwood?

Who bought the book? To be fair, many Canadians awoke on Christmas morning to find *A Great Game* under the tree. I bet two of them were Harper's children.

> BEN: Oh, gee, uh ... thanks, Dad.
> PM: That's Stephen J. Dad to you.

THERE'S NO WAY around it: the future looks bleak for the Canadian Senate. Upon being beset by scandal, the upper chamber turned into a problem for Stephen Harper. But there's a solution. To discourage further expense-claim chicanery, we need to find a way to get more money into the hands of disadvantaged Senators.

We need to grasp that this ragtag band of luckless appointees can't possibly get by on a measly $132,000 a year, plus benefits, per diems, free travel, generous allowances and probably back rubs, tons of back rubs.

People of Canada, I invite you to contribute to my Senate of Canada Kickstarter.

Give generously and together we may be able to satisfy the financial appetites of our most privileged political citizens. Donate today and these exciting perks could be yours!

Pledge $10 or more: One (1) Senate of Canada pen.

Pledge $25 or more: Your name will be mentioned aloud in the Senate chamber and forever immortalized in Hansard, likely in association with the phrase *cheap bastard*.

Pledge $50 or more: A piece of Senate legislation will be named in your honour, then read aloud in your honour, then fallen asleep to in your honour.

Pledge $100 or more: Former Conservative senator Patrick Brazeau will extend to you one (1) middle finger. What's he supposed to do with a hundred bucks? Is this some kind of joke? Pony up for real, pal.

Pledge $250 or more: Enjoy the emotional thrill and bodily harm of having Mike Duffy use you as a human shield to keep reporters at bay.

Pledge $500 or more: You will be entitled to serve as a character witness for the next senator who faces criminal trial. (Note: Must feign stroke during cross-examination.)

Pledge $1,000 or more: Supporters who donate $1,000 to a senator will receive one (1) complimentary meeting with the ethics commissioner, who will be investigating why you just gave $1,000 to a senator. Meeting may include up to one (1) glass of tap water.

Pledge $2,000 or more: Donors are entitled to have an apology made on their behalf by Sen. Pamela Wallin. (Note: apology will be incomplete and insincere.)

Pledge $2,500 or more: At this elite level of giving, former Liberal senator Mac Harb—who was ordered to pay back $231,000 in wrongly claimed expenses—will personally designate your home as his primary residence. Do you have any dependents? Mac Harb could sure use some dependents. Hey, are you going to finish that sandwich?

Pledge $3,000 or more: Complimentary dinner and drinks with between one (1) and three (3) humiliated senators. (Complimentary for them, so bring cash.)

Pledge $4,000 or more: A sitting senator will come to your home and diminish your faith in parliamentary democracy in person!

Pledge $5,000 or more: You deserve a day to yourself—so let the master of excuses, Senator Duffy, phone in sick for you! He'll even handle any follow-up queries regarding your "health issues." Don't worry about job security: Mike can smoothly stickhandle through any contingency. Some examples:

> Q: *Where's your doctor's note?*
> A: "Medical forms are complicated."
> Q: *How come you don't sound sick?*
> A: "How come you're a jerk?"
> Q: *Didn't I just see you at the movies?*
> A: "THIS INTERVIEW IS OVER."

Pledge $7,500 or more: A dishonoured senator of your choice will personally do your taxes. I smell a refund!

Pledge $10,000 or more: Exclusive Senator for a Day package! Live the life of a crony, bagman, brown-noser, party loyalist (or some combination thereof) for a full twenty-four hours! We supply the business suit, the shiny shoes and the overwhelming air of disdain for our country's institutions. You supply the gall to double-dip on your per diem and expenses.

Pledge $90,172: Welcome to the super-exclusive "Chief of Staff" level! Donate this amount to bail out one (1) over-entitled, utterly shameless senator, and you'll enjoy the unmatched experience of losing your job, damaging your reputation, enduring a police investigation and regretting your decision for years to come. You'll also get a Senate of Canada pen! (You can't keep the pen.)

ROB FORD ADDRESSES the media while mayor of Toronto:

Good morning. Yep, it's me again. I've got another statement to make, and I'm glad you reporters could take time away from going through my garbage or however you pathetic jackals spend your day. Thanks for being here and I hope you all get tetanus.

As I've said, this has been a hard week for me. Possibly the hardest week a human person has ever endured, and I include Gandhi in that, and also Batman when he had to pretend to be the bad guy.

But I've got some big news—big, big news.

I've made a lot of mistakes in my life. In fact, I'm pretty sure I've made all the possible mistakes. Some of these mistakes I've made many times. I guess what I'm saying is that I'm not good at life. But recently I was talking about the (many) mistakes I've made and I said: "If there was a button I could push to change everything, I would. Unfortunately there is no button that exists."

And that's what gets me: Why *doesn't* that button exist? Think about what we could do with a button that changes everything. Are you done thinking about it yet? Because I'm not.

[Closes eyes. Pantomimes shot-gunning a beer while wrestling a tiger.]

Listen up, Toronto: we're going to build that button. I'm here to announce that, if I'm voted back in, I will ensure that this great city is the first in the whole entire world to have a button that erases bad things—a button that changes everything.

What can I tell you about this button? Well, I assume it's going to be red, but I'm not Captain Kirk so I'll leave that to the nerds. But it should definitely be red, okay? Possibly it should also blink. What matters most is that the button will be installed on my desk at City Hall. Don't worry—I'll make room for it. I can move the deep fryer over near the waterbed.

And then every now and then, when the time is right, I'll push the button—and everything will change. Maybe I push it and you wind up being a millionaire or having cool sideburns. You never know. Maybe I push the button and—boom—everyone who's ever worked at the *Toronto Star* gets some disease where their pancreas explodes.

I'm doing this for you, the taxpayer. Remember that Easy button they had at Staples? Like you, I believed it was real. I must have pushed that button, like, twenty times—and still I had to put on my own socks that day. You don't get over that kind of disappointment.

Don't get me wrong—this new button is not going to solve all our problems and make the future awesome. For example, sometimes I may not remember the events of the night before, to the point that I won't know whether I need to push the button and change everything. So I'll have to hire a guy to keep an eye on that. Button Guy, I'll call him. Did I get into it last night? Do I need to push the button, Button Guy? And Button Guy gives me the nod or the head shake. Either way, I probably push the button just to be safe.

I'll tell you one more thing: once we've got the button that changes everything, we're not going to stop there. That's not the Ford Nation way. We're going to build more buttons. We're going to build a button that picks up your garbage. A button that shovels your driveway. Buttons! Buttons! Buttons! It'll be just like it was going to be with subways, except now with buttons. Maybe we'll make a button that builds subways!

I can already hear the doubters. I can hear them saying, "Building a button that changes everything is impossible. It can't be done." But I want those doubters to listen to me very carefully.

My name is Rob Ford. I am your mayor. I drink to the point of stupor so often that I refer to them as "my drunken stupors." I've been accused of sexual harassment, verbal harassment, pretty much all of the big harassments. I'm profane as hell. I've violated conflict-of-interest laws. Abused my power and position. The cops have been called to my house. I kicked citizens off a bus so it could pick up my football team. My driver is up on extortion charges. Oh, and by the way, I smoke crack cocaine. That's my record as an elected official.

And you know what? I still have a 40 percent approval rating.

Don't ever try to tell me what's possible.

FEDERAL ELECTION CAMPAIGNS in Canada now bring an increased focus on the nature and content of so-called robocalls— recorded messages that are blasted out to thousands of home phones.

After the 2011 campaign, Conservatives were accused of sending out misleading robocall messages meant to lure Liberal and New Democratic Party voters away from their proper polling stations. This obviously could not be true because Conservatives *love* democracy. They're always talking about its origins as the coming together of two Greek words: *kratos* meaning "power," and *demos* meaning "gimme."

Sure, Stephen Harper prorogued Parliament to avoid an election and, sure, his party admitted lying to constituents in Montreal so they'd think their Liberal MP had quit and, yes, Conservatives confessed to violating election finance rules in the 2006 campaign but, on the other hand, awkward silence.

MPs were armed with talking points to defuse the scandal. They read:

1. We had absolutely nothing to do with any attempts to sup-
press voter turnout (wink).
2. Don't actually wink when you say that first thing.

What matters for the future is that subverting the democratic will of Canadians isn't going to be so easy now. Voters will
be wary, so Conservative operatives will need to find more advanced ways to keep their opponents from the polls.
To the brainstormery!

1. Robo-collars: Disguised as elegant chokers, these
collars deliver a painful electric shock to any member of
the electorate who so much as daydreams about voting for
an opposition party. They can also be configured between
elections to function as an appetite suppressant or a way of
making a conversation with Tony Clement seem pleasant by
comparison.

2. Mass hypnosis: Many of us have attended perform-
ances where full-grown adults have fallen under the control of
a cruel master bent on making them look foolish. Some of us
have seen much the same thing at Conservative caucus meetings. There's evidence that Harper started practising hypnosis in preparation for the 2015 campaign. Why do you think
Rob Anders kept falling asleep? Keep your eyes on the pocket
watch, Canada. You are getting very, very Conservative ...

3. Sinister weather machines: Turnout is way down for
elections. It won't take much to coax even more people to stay
away. For example, hurricane-force winds ought to be enough
to make voters hunker down in Liberal-friendly Newfound-
land. Same goes for four centimetres of snow in downtown
Toronto.

But how to manipulate the weather? Cloud-seeding technology has advanced in recent years. Plus, Kate Bush had that
neat storm-making contraption in her *Cloudbusting* video, and
it's probably sitting in Donald Sutherland's garage. (Young

people: just Google it.) Alternatively, scientists at Conservative Labs are rumoured to be developing a proprietary system in which John Baird screams at the sky until it surrenders its moisture.

4. Actual robots: Robocalls are great, but these are even more effective. Picture the scene: it's election day, a loyal Liberal supporter is putting on her coat to head to the polls and, whoa, where did her Roomba get that switchblade? Standoff.

5. Freaky Friday–style body switching: Across the country in too-close-to-call ridings, party volunteers are zapped into the bodies of opposition supporters for just long enough to vote Conservative and maybe get a tattoo of a shirtless Jason Kenney across a shoulder blade.

6. Criss-cross: Remember *Strangers on a Train*? You do my evil deed, I'll do yours—and no one will ever suspect a thing. Air Canada would seem to be a good fit here. The airline can pepper voters with misleading calls and, in return, all the Conservatives need to do is put me on hold for two hours.

7. Moats: Sometimes the best modern tactic is the best ancient tactic. Just find an opposition-friendly polling station— then gather together some earth-moving equipment, a supply of water and a few crocodiles. All of a sudden, casting that ballot for the NDP doesn't seem so important, does it, hippie? The best part is the deniability factor: those could be anyone's crocodiles.

8. Offer a positive, compelling vision for the country and behave in a decent, civil manner so that you inspire the support of enough Canadians that party operatives don't feel compelled to resort to dirty tricks: But that sounds like a lot of work.

BECAUSE OF ALL the complex terminology, reading about the federal budget sure can be taxing. (Ladies and gentlemen, wordplay!) Luckily for you, I've compiled and refined a helpful guide that translates all that wonky budget lingo.

Austerity: During tough economic times, the federal government reduces the amount it spends, except in areas that reflect vital public trusts, like health care and snowmobiles.

Balance of Payments: The formal term for rushing out to buy a new pair of shoes after discovering your husband dropped $700 on a flat-screen TV.

Benchmark Bond: The little-known brother of the famous spy, he was killed in a tragic securitization mishap.

Canada Foundation for Innovation: Frankly, I'm not sure what this is—but I'm confident we can rule out Stephen Harper's barber as a member.

Canada's Economic Action Plan: The Conservative plan to create jobs apparently hinges on ensuring every single Canadian eventually stars in one of these TV ads.

Capital Tax: Compared to people in some other countries, Canadians do not pay tax—they pay TAX.

Closely Held Bank: A financial institution that just finished watching a horror movie.

Core Unemployment Rate: The rate of joblessness among Canada's apple farmers.

Custom Tariff Measures: No sophisticated G7 country would be caught dead getting its tariff measures off the rack.

Debt-to-GDP ratio: Trying to make a bad thing sound better by comparing it to something more positive. Example: Canada's tourism industry is expecting a strong summer after new lows were reported in the country's Nickelback-to-bacon ratio.

Deflation: A rare and complex phenomenon currently seen acting on the career ambitions of Thomas Mulcair.

Dissaving: What people on vacation begin doing immediately after deplaning.

Family Trust: What you have yet to regain after investing your kid's college fund in Pets.com.

Frictional Unemployment: The rate of joblessness among Canada's prostitutes.

Income Testing: The act of swiping your debit card, entering your PIN and hoping to God there's enough cash in your account.

International Association of Insurance Supervisors: A good organization to think about every time you begin to feel your job may be boring.

National Child Benefit: Secret name for my plan to abduct and forcibly confine The Wiggles.

Natural Rate of Unemployment: How Canada's economy looks with its makeup off.

Overnight Financing Rate: The rate of interest charged for loans extended by smaller financial institutions, such as the Canadian Imperial Bank of That Guy Down at the Pool Hall, the One with a Hook for a Hand.

Per Capita: An up-and-coming defenceman in the Swedish elite league.

Prospectus: Based on my personal investing experience, I believe this is Latin for "Lose your money here!"

Protectionism: The act of covering your privates before informing your wife that you just blew the tax refund on a dirt bike.

Retiring Allowance Rollover: What senior-aged women feel pressured to occasionally give their Viagra-fuelled husbands.

Seasonal Adjustment: The exact moment in May when Finance officials, acting on instincts refined over thousands of years of relentless inbreeding, know it's time to switch from long-sleeved polyester dress shirts to short-sleeved polyester dress shirts.

Self-dealing: What every young, budding economist dreads his mom will walk in on while he's doing it.

Structural Unemployment: The rate of joblessness in Legoland.

Twenty-One-Year Deemed Disposition Rule: The formal global policy under which Billy Joel trades in for younger girlfriends.

Wealth Tax: This doesn't really exist—but mentioning it every now and then keeps the poor folks quiet.

Zero-Rated Goods: The accounting designation for Adam Sandler's last four movies.

BECAUSE THE CONSERVATIVES are super-classy, they released a statement congratulating Justin Trudeau back when he won the Liberal leadership. Here it is (for real) in its entirety:

> We congratulate Justin Trudeau on becoming Liberal leader.
>
> Stephen Harper has an Economic Action Plan that has created 900,000 new jobs since the recession, the best job creation record in the G7. He's lowered taxes, such as the GST, and increased support for families with measures like the Universal Child Care Benefit.
>
> Justin Trudeau may have a famous last name, but in a time of global economic uncertainty, he doesn't have the judgment or experience to be Prime Minister.

Go back and read it again. The Conservatives were very nuanced about it—but did you notice the statement wasn't actually so much about congratulating Trudeau as it was about not doing that? Pretty sneaky, right? It's like, "Hey, good for you, *you terrible person who is awful and also smells.*"

Then again, I guess Harper had reason to crow, given that—according to his statement—he has personally created 900,000 new jobs for Canadians since we had the recession he said we couldn't have because we hadn't already had it. That's about 740 new jobs per day created by one man and his plan. Where does the guy find time to watch TV?

In the meantime, building on the gracious spirit of the Conservative response to Trudeau's victory, let's look at some messages of "congratulations" that Stephen Harper and his party have put away for special occasions to come:

April 21, 2017: "We congratulate Justin Bieber on winning Album of the Year at the 2017 Juno Awards.

"Stephen Harper plays piano and is awesome at it and could have been a super-huge big-time rock star if only he hadn't selflessly decided to forever change Canada by lowering the GST somewhat and doing other 'governmenty' stuff. Additionally, it is a well-known fact that the best girls prize substance over style. Rather than being a 'Belieber,' they are more likely to be a fan of the person who recently concluded foreign-investment protection agreements with both Senegal *and* Tanzania. That's right—they all want to be a 'BeStever.'

"Justin Bieber may have 62 million Twitter followers, untold riches and the panting, wide-eyed affection of every girl in a training bra, but in a time of global uncertainty, Stephen Harper was totally popular in high school no matter how it looks from his yearbook photo.

"PS: Velour was in at the time."

June 25, 2018: "We congratulate Kim Campbell on the twenty-fifth anniversary of becoming the first female prime minister of Canada.

"Stephen Harper has been Prime Minister for 24.3 times as long as Kim Campbell. That's *way* longer. For example, if Kim Campbell's time as prime minister was a single song (probably a lame, sappy one), Stephen Harper's tenure would at this point be an awesome double-concept album about a handsome rogue with perfect, unmoving hair who saves the world from aliens by outsmarting them with his brain thoughts, piano solos and foreign-investment protection agreements with minor African nations.

"Kim Campbell may have lady parts, but in a time of global uncertainty, let's remember what's important: 24.3. Haha, did she even unpack? Probably not."

July 18, 2019: "We congratulate Prince William and the Duchess of Cambridge on the birth of their third child.

"Unlike a helpless, parasitic baby, Stephen Harper has the ability to pour his own juice. He can do math, hum in the shower and tie his own shoes (when his personal assistant has a day off). One time in university, he helped a friend haul a sofa bed upstairs, and those things weigh about a million pounds. Your move, infant prince.

"The Queen's great-grandchild may have a famous family,

but in a time of global uncertainty, you know what's really cute and adorable? The ability to personally create 900,000 jobs out of thin air. Also, that velour sweater from high school. Stephen Harper totally made that thing work."

ONE REASON TO fear the future of Canadian politics is the increasingly brazen fundraising campaigns being run by the parties. In March 2014, for example, the Conservative Party launched a fundraising campaign as part of a strategy to win the 2015 federal election. Let's read between the lines of the online appeal from the party's then-executive director, Dimitri Soudas. His words are in bold.

We need to win another majority government.
Whoa! Easy, tiger. Where's the romance, the sweet talk? As strategies go, this is a bit like getting all dressed up, going out to a nightclub and loudly announcing to the first girl you see at the bar: "I NEED A WIFE!"
It won't be easy; the road to 2015 will be difficult. But this isn't about Stephen Harper or the Conservative Party— it's about our future.
You heard him right, people: this fundraising campaign— explicitly devised and executed to directly benefit Stephen Harper and the Conservative Party—is *not* about Stephen Harper or the Conservative Party. Not at all.
It's not like Stephen Harper is doing this "PM thing" for himself. It's not as though he *enjoys* it. Why, if he had his way, he'd be livin' a simpler life down Pincher Creek way, sittin' on a porch and a-whittlin' away alongside his old dog Zeke. He wouldn't have much use for politickin', nor, evidently, for the letter *g*.
But for you—*for you, Canada, and for your future*—Stephen Harper is willing to selflessly take on the burden of absolute power. Furthermore, he is willing to selflessly exercise that power, to the point of selflessly kind of being a jerk about it at times. *For you.*

For you, he is willing to abandon his fundamental principles and stack institutions, agencies and court benches with his loyal supporters and flunkies.

For you, he is willing to change the *Elections Act* to make it harder for you to vote and easier for you to give him money.

For you, he is willing to spend tens of millions of your dollars on ads to tell you what a good job he's doing managing your money.

It's about you. Your family. Your kids. Your grandkids.

It's about your nephew. Your nephew's cat. That cat's grand-kittens. It's about ensuring that your own futuristic clone does not emerge from its slime pod into a dystopian hellscape wrought by an epidemic of post-Trudeau shirtlessness and doobie-smoking.

The choices we make today will impact Canada's future. The global economy remains fragile.

If you think about it, no one has gotten more domestic political mileage out of the stagnant global economy than Stephen Harper. He should send Europe a fruit basket.

Canada needs strong, stable leadership—or we risk losing everything we've accomplished together.

Think about that. Think about how traumatic it would be to lose everything we've accomplished together over the past many years. Stephen Harper appointed to the Senate a man who went on to become the daytime manager of an Ottawa strip club. And you want to just turn your back on that kind of progress?

Not convinced? Think of everything else we've accomplished together: the public servants we've muzzled together. The forced smiles we've tolerated together. The unconvincing rhetorical use of "together" we've endured together.

The stakes have never been higher. That's why I'm asking you to take part in our "Road to 2015" campaign.

That's correct—the stakes have never been higher. *Never.* Not during the Depression. Not during either world war. Not during the free-trade debate or either Quebec referendum.

Stephen Harper's electoral success in 2015 is literally the highest the stakes have ever been. The stakes are so high that we've lost sight of them. Please donate now so we can buy new stakes!

Will you add your name to our list of supporters and join the fight in 2015?

Andrew Coyne recently described our approach to government as being grounded in "secrecy, deception and brute force." He left out pettiness, vengeance, patronage, yelling and gazebos, but the point is nevertheless clear: when you donate to the Conservative Party, you get what you pay for.

IF, AFTER ALL this, you're still interested in running for office, I offer you a free gift: a speech you can use on the campaign trail. You're welcome.

My fellow Canadians:

Election day approaches. I have been travelling our vast country to spread the message that we must bring change to Ottawa. But not just any kind of change. It must be bold change. It must be progressive change. It must be crazy change. I'm talking about change for its own sake—wild, flailing change unburdened by rational thinking. The future children of Canada deserve no less.

My opponents talk about change, but what kind of change will they bring? Will it be unthought-through enough? Will they, like me, replace "O Canada" with "Sign of the Gypsy Queen"? Because I'll do it. If it makes you vote for me, I swear to God I'll do it.

In the twenty-first century, we must move Canada forward, not backward. Upward, not downward. Diagonal, not perpendicular. Also, I heard some egghead on CBC talking about the world maybe becoming more competitive. So we should probably look into that too.

Now is not the time to retreat to the garrisons of fear or the barracks of prejudice. Now is the time to push ahead toward the huts of progress, the condominiums of hope and that huge castle of unicorns. You see the one I'm talking about? Next to the Arby's of common purpose? Just hang a left at the forest of metaphor.

Let me say for the record that my rivals in this election are good people. They are decent Canadians who happen to require medication to combat their ungodly fetishes and chronic narcolepsy. In their defence, there is nothing in our Constitution that disqualifies a Canadian from seeking public office just because he killed a hooker.

Besides, I want this to be a campaign about the issues. I want my words to serve as eloquent testament to the power and virtue of my ideas. For more on my solemn commitment to elevating our public discourse, please visit my website. Just click on the ostrich that's taking a leak in my rival's ear.

My friends: this is the most important election since Canada was formed, since democracy was birthed, since prehistoric man gathered to focus-group the discovery of fire (consensus: too orange). The differences between my positions and those of my rivals are enormous and critical.

I would lower your taxes by a negligible amount. My opponents would lower your taxes by a slightly different negligible amount. I would reduce greenhouse gas emissions eventually. My opponents would reduce greenhouse gas emissions ultimately. I believe children are our future. My opponents told me they think your children are ugly and stupid. (You're not exactly easy on the eyes yourself, they said.)

People of Canada: I come before you tonight as just a man—a humble, ordinary man wearing a sweater selected for me by a team of stylists and advisers. The sweater is powder blue: feminine enough to appeal to women thirty-five to forty-four, with just enough navy undertones to keep men from actively debating my sexual orientation. Got it at Banana Republic.

At this point, I would like to mention my family in a forced and obligatory manner.

I love my family. My family provides me with strength, spiritual nourishment and heartwarming anecdotes for my television commercials. Basically, I'm just a family man. In fact, I'm such a family man that one family is not enough for me. I must travel the country meeting other families, entering their homes and yards trailed by fifty reporters, pretending to find their children adorable. There may even be a family standing awkwardly behind me right now. There usually is. Hello, Wongs. What's that? But I asked you if you needed to go before the speech, Grandma Wong. Just hold it, okay?

In conclusion, let me say: Canada is a country whose health care system defines us—as a nation with tremendous patience and a high tolerance for pain. Canada is a country with old people in it, and they must be pandered to, often while using the word *dignity*. To them I say: you deserve to live with dignity!

If elected, I will put the needs of the kitchen table ahead of the needs of the boardroom table.

I also have policies that reflect the needs of your other furniture.

I will put your ottoman ahead of auto executives. I will put your armchair ahead of arms dealers. And I will put your dining-room hutch ahead of *Starsky & Hutch*—and that doesn't even make sense.

From the down-home hospitality and fishing villages of the east to the open spaces and soaring mountains of the west, Canada is a land of bounteous clichéd images used by politicians to crudely evoke patriotic sentiment. Also, there are prairies.

Canada is a great country. In fact, it's the greatest country in the world. What I'm saying is: Portugal can suck it. Ditto Japan. Those places are holes and we all know it. Don't even get me started on Greece.

I shall now speak French in a manner that suggests I'm merely repeating what I just said in English—when in fact I'm telling Quebecers they're my favourites and giving away the farm.

As a nation, we have arrived at a juncture where we stand upon a precipice that is located at a crossroads along the very edge of the potential of a new horizon. So I say to my fellow Canadians: there really ought to be a railing or fence here. I am going to get right on that.

Tough Question: *When first contact with aliens is eventually made, where on planet Earth should they land?*

Allow me to make the case for Canada. I know we've been shunned in recent years by the international community. We applied for a seat on the United Nations Security Council and lost to Portugal, owing to what our prime minister described as American chicanery, Arab payback, bad luck, bad karma, low bio rhythms and Belgium's dog eating our application form.

But think about it. Canada has everything an arriving interstellar species could want: oodles of natural resources, ample spaceship parking and a probe-ready population accustomed to taking it in the rear every winter from Mother Nature. It only makes sense that a Canadian should be named the first ambassador to extraterrestrials.

Let me assure you—we are not naive about the challenges of such a role. We grasp that our emissaries may well be subjected to the occasional diplomatic faux pas, such as being fatally devoured. But we're strong enough as a nation to endure the minute of silence in memory of Peter MacKay.

The arrival of an alien species will be a landmark moment in our shared history. It will change us as a people. You know how in *Star Trek* the citizens of Earth responded to alien contact by coming together in unity and setting aside petty conflict? Well, that's not actually going to happen.

In real life, some countries will attempt to destroy the aliens. Others will try to appease them. Thirty percent of Americans will take one look at the giant alien spacecraft and claim that's where Obama was born.

Let Canada assume the burden of first contact, and the alien leaders will be more likely to stick around. At least until they find out that it was our Captain Kirk who slept with their sisters.

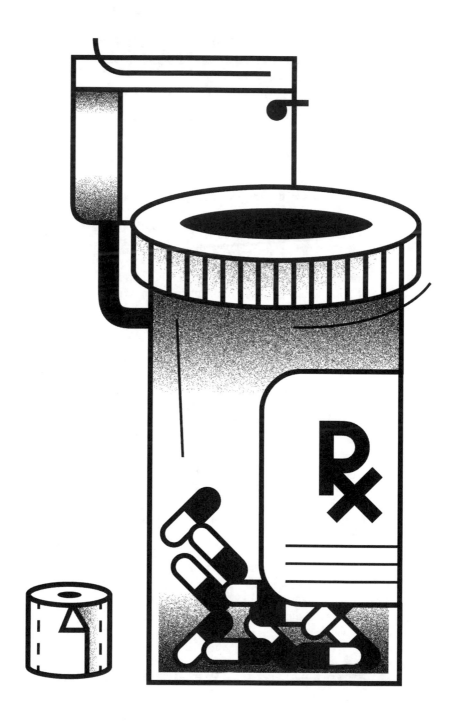

REASON NO. 5: OUR HEALTH AND BODIES

I took up jogging recently because I had begun to lose sight of certain things in life, such as my genitals. Year upon year of sports viewing—abetted by halftime nachos, intermission chili dogs and anytime beers—had taken a physical toll. I'm not saying I was out of shape, but I still remember my first run in the springtime: the sweat, the laboured breathing, the searing chest pain. And that was just from climbing onto the treadmill.

Several months later, I am a changed man! Sure, I'm pretty much the same weight and I don't look any better. And sure, I still consider the stairs to be the Devil's method of ascent. (Folks, there's a reason God invented the elevator, the escalator and waiting patiently until the object you want eventually comes downstairs of its own accord.)

But jogging changed me. For instance, I now hate jogging.

It's intimidating to be a rookie on the running trails. First, you constantly get overtaken, which doesn't bother me unless—as actually happened—it's by someone pushing a stroller *and* walking a dog *and* knitting a sweater *and* completing a five-hundred-piece jigsaw puzzle while doing the border *last.* Show-off.

Second, pretty much everyone out there is somehow running *and* engaging in conversations that feature verbs and everything—whereas twenty seconds into my run, I am reduced to communicating exclusively through charades. Fortunately, I've learned to cope. If I'm running with my wife, my strategy is to ask a really involved question at the outset. This way, the onus is on her to do the talking while I'm required only to wheeze the occasional "Mmm-hmm." (Sample conversation starter: "So, tell me chronologically about every time you've consumed a dairy product. Go!")

My friend Mike is a serious runner. He informs me he gets grumpy if he misses out on his long Sunday run, which is a coincidence because that's exactly how I feel about taco night. Mike is the one who told me that many newbies incorporate a one-minute stint of walking as respite. This "five-and-one" approach sounded intriguing until I realized the "five" referred to minutes, not steps.

But it hasn't been all bad. Here are my five favourite things about jogging:

1. *Stopping.* I highly recommend stopping and doing it as often as possible. In fact, I'm hoping to invent a way to stop jogging without first starting to jog. I know that doesn't make any sense, but really, neither does waddling up and down a path until I sound like an asthmatic Darth Vader.

2. *The gadgets.* Satellites were deployed into orbit at great cost, pushing the very limits of human ingenuity. They are now used to tell me I've shuffled three-tenths of a mile in seven minutes.

3. *Preparing to jog.* The way I see it, if I take long enough to tie my shoes, it's possible my run will be postponed by a nuclear holocaust or some other lifesaver.

4. *Getting injured.* Early this fall I strained my hip and couldn't run for a couple of weeks. This turned out to be an ideal scenario because I could still self-identify as a jogger without having to, you know, jog. I'd wake up and think, "Yep, I'd be out there crushing a 10K run right now if I hadn't hurt myself being SO SUPER ATHLETIC. Hmm, perhaps my recovery will be hastened by multiple Eggos!" By the way, there's no quicker

way to get in tight with runners than to ask them about *their* injuries. Runners love talking about injuries. "Yes, old man, please continue your mesmerizing tale of the great hamstring pull of 1993 …"

5. *The sense of satisfaction.* I like knowing that I play a positive role out there: other out-of-shape people see me and instantly feel better about themselves. They think, "Sure, my knees are shot and I'm running a thirteen-minute mile, but at least I'm not getting repeatedly concussed by my own man boobs like *that* guy."

WE ARE THE pharmaceutical generation. Whatever problem we have, the drug companies have a pill for it. Unless we have a problem that's so small it's really not much of a problem at all, in which case the drug companies have a pill for it.

There's a drug out there called Latisse. Maybe you've heard of it. Latisse is for people who suffer from the grave medical condition of not having thick, long and full eyelashes. There was a commercial for it starring Brooke Shields. Mostly it was just her huge eyeball on the screen. *Brooke Shields's terrifying retina is commanding me to ask my doctor about Latisse.*

According to the commercial, Latisse is an actual drug manufactured by Allergan Inc. to treat "inadequate or not enough lashes," a condition apparently known by the scientific term *hypotrichosis* and by the colloquial term "Bet you ladies didn't know there was any part of your physical appearance left to feel anxious or depressed about but boy were you wrong ha ha."

I mean, sure, you've had a nose job and your breasts done. Your tummy is tucked, your face is lifted. Responding to the pressures of our superficial society, you have achieved physical perfection in every way and now it's time to get out there and enjoy the benefits … whoa, hang on a minute … *those eyelashes of yours.* SWEET JESUS YOU'RE MONSTROUS!

Here's how it works: By forking out just $60 a month for the rest of your life for a steady supply of Latisse, you can grow and maintain longer and fuller and darker lashes. And you can see why this is important. What fellow hasn't come home from a date and thought to himself: great body, terrific personality, really smart—if only her eyelashes were a few microns longer.

Brooke Shields and her gigantic eyeballs wouldn't want that to happen. "Ask your doctor if Latisse is right for you," Brooke urged. After following her advice, be sure to pause and give your doctor time to laugh heartily, wipe tears from eyes and then awkwardly recover, saying, "Oh, you were serious?"

I recall that Brooke's ad had a little story in it. A little story always seems to unfold in drug ads. Sometimes it's the story of a guy who survived a heart attack. Sometimes it's the story of a woman whose bones were as fragile as Pringles. When an ad for Cialis comes on during a hockey game, the story that unfolds is one in which I come up with the 517th way of distracting my eleven-year-old son from the television set so Daddy won't have to answer uncomfortable questions like "What's erectile dysfunction?" and "Can I be like those people and have my bath outside in the middle of a cornfield?"

The story in the Latisse commercial began with Brooke arriving at an elegant birthday party. Then she sat on a couch, where she talked with a pretty man. Wow, then she danced with the pretty man! To recap: Brooke went out in public, then conversed and danced with a human male, none of which would have been possible without Latisse, except for all of it.

I scoured the internet a little. One woman using Latisse asked whether it's normal that a whole lot of her eyelashes suddenly fell out after she began taking Latisse. (Apparently the answer is: nope!) Another lamented: "While I saw significant growth in length, thickness was not part of the deal. Lashes were very unruly, spikey [sic] and were going all over the place ... Not to mention my eyes looking bloodshot all the time ..."

So, apparently there are side effects, such as itchy eyes and eye redness. Latisse can also cause the skin of your eyelids to darken. And, in the company's own words, it holds the "potential for increased brown iris pigmentation, which is likely to be permanent." The slogan writes itself. *Latisse: it may permanently change the colour of your eyeballs but go ahead and use it because maybe it won't!*

And that's not the only fine print. After detailing various laboratory tests done on mice—and really, what could be a more dignified end for a lab mouse than giving up its life so that humanity can combat the scourge of not-quite-thick-enough eyelashes?—the Latisse information sheet notes: "Because animal reproductive studies are not always predictive of human response, Latisse should be administered during pregnancy only if the potential benefit justifies the potential risk to the fetus."

Miranda, sit down. You're probably wondering about some of the things that make you different from other children, such as the brown pigment in your eyes, and your third arm. Mommy loved being pregnant with you. But Mommy also loves having hooker-grade eyelashes, so ...

It just makes you wonder: What could possibly be left on a woman for drug companies to "cure"? Even now, I'm sure science is trying to help ladies overcome the horror of chubby tonsils, knuckle wrinkles and the condition known as "having elbows."

Unless, of course, science is too busy trying to help people stay thin, which, come to think of it, it probably is. One of the more recent advances in this field is a drug that combines all the health benefits of losing weight with the unforgettable thrill of pooping yourself in public.

The drug is GlaxoSmithKline's Alli, which was released for over-the-counter sale after years of painstaking research and unspeakable crimes against underpants.

The upside of Alli is that it can help people on a diet lose up to 50 percent more weight. The downside is that this weight is likely to depart the body in the form of—in the company's own words ... its graphic, unforgettable, dream-haunting words—"loose stools," "more frequent stools that may be hard to control," and "gas with oily spotting," which sounds like an alternative rock band or a Jackson Pollock technique, but no, in this case refers to terrifyingly explosive farts. Congratulations! You just lost three pounds, forty-eight friends and one job!

Ours is a society schooled to anticipate the inevitable "side effect" segment of every upbeat drug commercial (*some users may experience headache, nausea, stigmata, transsexuality and the medical condition commonly known as Karl Malden nose*), yet still the weight-loss particulars grab our attention. Loose stools? That may be hard to control?? GlaxoSmithKline refers to these as "treatment effects." With all due respect, a runny nose is a "treatment effect." Heartburn—*that* is a "treatment effect." Soiling yourself in public is really more of a "now I have no choice but to relocate to a different hemisphere because my life here is completely ruined effect."

Given the sensitivity of the issue, one can only imagine the gruelling series of rewrites to which these "treatment effects" were subjected:

WRITER NO. 1: How about we call them "unstable stools"?

WRITER NO. 2: Sounds like something you'd buy at IKEA. "Freedom feces"?

WRITER NO. 1: Patriotic!

Unlike certain weight-loss drugs, Alli (pronounced "ally," as in: if you want to lose some of your weight and all your dignity, Alli is your ally!) does nothing to reduce your desire to eat. Instead, it stops the body from breaking down and absorbing fat—a remarkable scientific achievement, really, if you take away the whole crapping-your-pants part. In fact, GlaxoSmith-Kline claims Alli is able to block about 25 percent of the fat you eat while simultaneously grossing out 100 percent of the people sitting next to you on the bus.

But really, how common can these so-called treatment effects be? Well, the actual makers of this actual drug actually advise users to "bring a change of clothes to work," and suggest that it's probably a "smart idea" to wear dark pants. It is also recommended that users practise pointing at the fat guy in the next cubicle and whispering to everyone, "It was Neil."

If surrendering power of attorney over your anus is not alarming enough—and judging by Alli's brisk sales, it's not—consider that the drug helps you lose weight only if you're already losing weight by eating a low-fat diet. Plus the drug company warns that "you may need to continue taking Alli" just to maintain your weight loss. Heck, take it for long enough and you may get Superman-quick at ditching your fouled underthings in phone booths!

The drug's website showcases many photographs of happy, smiling women attired in white pants. Clearly these women cannot be using Alli. They must have snuck over from a Levitra ad. In any event, the site offers a number of important advisories for people who decide to use Alli. The actual tips are in quotes below; the italics are mine:

- "The excess fat that passes out of your body is not harmful. In fact, you may recognize it as something that looks like the oil on top of a pizza." *Not sure any of us will need Alli now that we'll never eat pizza again.*
- "You may not usually get gassy, but it's a possibility when you take Alli. The bathroom is really the best place to go when that happens." *In fact, it's probably best just to move your desk in there.*
- "You can use a food journal to recognize what foods can lead to treatment effects. For example, writing down what you eat may help you learn that marinara sauce is a better option than Alfredo sauce." *One can only guess, with mounting horror and stomach-turning unease, what must have happened during the laboratory pasta test to warrant Alfredo sauce being singled out in this way. Suffice to say the findings form the basis for North Korea's next weapons test.*
- "[If you] take Alli capsules as directed, you should see results in the first two weeks." *Results include going home each night with*

a briefcase full of shame and the bestowing upon you by your office colleagues the nickname "Stinkybum."

- "In case of overdose, get medical help or contact a Poison Control Centre right away." *An overdose?! You may want to bring along three hundred to four hundred extra pairs of dark pants.*

Of course, no matter how effective it is, Alli has its work cut out for it, especially in the United States.

To walk into an American supermarket these days is to marvel unblinkingly at the miracle of it all. There used to be just Snickers. Now there are 80 different kinds of Snickers, including Snickers Charged—a chocolate bar jammed with caffeine. There used to be ice cream. Now there are 47,000 different brands of ice cream, including American Idol Mint Karaoke Cookie (dig in—you can really taste the Keith Urban!). There used to be sausages and pancakes. Now there are Jimmy Dean sausages wrapped in chocolate-chip pancakes and served on a stick. One day the scientists of the great nation of the United States will use their mighty brainpower to cure horrible ailments like cancer and marrying Newt Gingrich. But first they have much to teach the developing world about wrapping one thing inside another thing, and then placing both things on a stick.

Today's food-based innovation in American supermarkets is all about convenience. Remember how making a hot dog used to be so difficult and time-consuming? Me neither. But apparently it was, because Oscar Mayer went and created something called Fast Frank—three wieners prepackaged inside three "soft and warm buns" placed in three paper trays, and each ready to be eaten after thirty-five seconds in the microwave. You just remove the outer packaging, pick up the wiener, remove its individual packaging, wipe that tear from the cheek of Iron Eyes Cody, place the wiener back in the bun, nuke it and laugh heartily in the face of China and its backward, water-boiling ways.

Not that these hot dogs are perfect yet. Oscar Mayer claims

it created Fast Franks "to satisfy America's love for hot dogs in a more convenient way." That's a noble goal and a good start— but the sad reality is that consumers still have to chew the wiener and bun themselves. Americans are busy people, Oscar Mayer: call them when your franks are fast *and* pre-masticated.

For sheer convenience, it is hard to imagine a greater advance than that achieved by the super-geniuses at Smucker's who created a product they call Uncrustables—a package of four, ten or eighteen frozen peanut butter and jelly sandwiches with the crusts cut off. "All you do is thaw and serve," Smucker's boasts. "A simple way to enjoy one of life's simple pleasures."

Finally, at long last, someone has found a way to simplify the gruelling peanut butter and jelly ordeal. No longer shall our stoutest men be forced to toil all day in the jelly mines. No more shall our womenfolk be enslaved to operate the elaborate and often lethal system of levers and pulleys required to press together two slices of bread. Never again shall defenceless children be confronted with the monstrous indignity of having to ingest bread's hard and foul and brown outer layer.

Sure, each Smucker's Uncrustable has high-fructose corn syrup not only in the jelly but (somehow!) in the bread. And sure, the ingredients for the bread alone list almost a dozen different chemicals under the heading "Dough Conditioners." But when the alternative is sacrificing as many as nine precious seconds to spread peanut butter and then also jelly, well ... suffice to say, the Middle Ages called: they'd like their way of making sandwiches back.

Tough Question: *How would some of today's leading sports, entertainment and political figures make a peanut butter and jelly sandwich?*

Justin Bieber

1. Recruit a twelve-member entourage to make him a single peanut butter and jelly sandwich.
2. Hurl peanut butter and jelly sandwich against the wall, shouting, "Why wasn't this made by a monkey??"
3. Remove shirt.

Stephen Harper

1. As a matter of reflex, immediately launch a negative ad campaign against ham sandwiches.
2. Meticulously position bread, peanut butter and jelly on kitchen counter.
3. Warn of grave threat to national economy if anyone else is entrusted to assemble the sandwich.
4. Write a boring book about old sandwiches.

Don Cherry

1. Start making one sandwich, then stop midway, failing to finish it.
2. Start making another sandwich, then lose his train of thought, failing to finish it.
3. Start making a third sandwich, but somehow instead wind up talking about the military.
4. Give up and eat a peanut butter and jelly sandwich made by Bobby Orr in 1973.

Rob Ford

1. "I do not eat peanut butter and jelly sandwiches, nor am I an addict of peanut butter and jelly sandwiches."
2. "I can't comment on a sandwich that doesn't exist."
3. "I just want to see the sandwich. The sandwich will answer a lot of questions."
4. "I wish I could defend myself, but right now this sandwich is before the food court."
5. "Yes, I have eaten a peanut butter and jelly sandwich while in one of my luncheon stupors."

Zdeno Chara
1. Assemble ingredients for a peanut butter and jelly sandwich.
2. Stare menacingly at them until the sandwich makes itself.

Miley Cyrus
1. Nail two slices of bread to a wall.
2. Apply ample amounts of peanut butter to one bum cheek.
3. Apply ample amounts of jelly to the other bum cheek.
4. Turn on music.

Barack Obama
1. Publicly reveal his intention to make a peanut butter and jelly sandwich.
2. Mull over, at some length, how best to make the sandwich.
3. Assemble a team of experts with decades of experience in the making of peanut butter and jelly sandwiches.
4. Consult with inner circle of advisers, all of whom have doctorates in theoretical sandwich making.
5. Deliver eloquent address to Congress promising decisive action soon to resolve the ongoing sandwich crisis.
6. Spend weekend at Camp David enumerating the pros and cons of white bread.
7. Travel to Britain to explore the ancestry of the fourth Earl of Sandwich.
8. Lift knife toward peanut butter jar and ... but wait, Is a knife really the right utensil for the job? If you think about it, a spoon can more easily accommodate a greater quantity of ...
9. Die of hunger.

Thomas Mulcair
1. Spread peanut butter on a slice of bread.
2. Spread jelly on a second slice of bread.
3. Press together the two slices of bread.
4. Eat this perfectly good peanut butter and jelly sandwich while standing alone at a microphone as thirty-eight reporters ask Justin Trudeau about weed.

SO YES, ON one hand, for some in our society there's the organics movement, the 100-Mile Diet, slow dining, grass-fed cattle and flying to Indonesia to offer a soothing massage to the migrant worker who harvested your coffee beans. For the rest of us, it's a miraculous age in which science has made it possible for us to consume our Special K in liquid form and there are products such as Kraft Bagel-fuls—in which a bagel-type substance comes wrapped around wads of cream cheese—available in your grocer's freezer. Half the taste and four million times the chemicals!

Bagel-fuls offer value in two key areas:

Relief: Recent statistics indicate that spreading cream cheese on a bagel is causing 70 percent of North Americans to get winded. Another 12 percent keep trying to spread the bagel onto the cream cheese.

Productivity: With the four seconds they save by not having to spread cream cheese themselves, everyone in America is going to study to be an astronaut.

Kraft touts its Bagel-fuls by highlighting their "convenient shape"—long, like a Twinkie, because apparently humankind can't quite master how to wrap its hands around "round"—and the fact that cramming one into your face requires "no plates, mess or effort!" Plus, now we don't have to lick flame-retardant materials for our daily hit of ammonium sulfate.

Certainly one day in the near future these pioneers of food convenience will ensure that all oranges and bananas come pre-peeled, that hamburgers and hot dogs are sold in liquid form, that all soups are packaged inside a syringe for speedier internalizing. Perhaps one day these sultans of expediency will invent a cereal with the milk already in it, and the spoon already in the cereal, and the cereal and milk and spoon already in your colon.

When it comes to fast food, meanwhile, the focus is equally on innovation. Everyone is aiming to duplicate the impact that Kentucky Fried Chicken achieved a few years back with its Double Down, a bacon-and-cheese sandwich that features two pieces of fried chicken in place of the traditional bun. It has been described by nutritionists as an affront to human health, by scientists as a potential contributor to childhood obesity and by Kirstie Alley as a mfwwwwa ahhhsdfldnf. (Her mouth was full.)

The Double Down proves it: America may be losing its reputation as an invincible economic power, but it continues to outpace the world in making bread obsolete. Years ago, McDonald's mutated its popular breakfast sandwich by replacing the English muffin with two pancakes, creating the McGriddle. Now KFC has nixed buns in favour of fried chicken. What's next, America: Slices of meat loaf? Pork chops? Whole baby bears? Panda Pockets! New at Burger King!

Other innovations abound, including:

- IHOP's Pancake Stackers, a thick hunk of cheesecake lodged between two buttermilk pancakes and served with fruit compote, whipped topping and a long, disapproving stare from your wife. As part of a breakfast combo, the Stackers meal delivers more than two-thirds of your recommended daily intake of calories, more than 100 percent of your daily sodium and a full week's worth of "angry bowel."
- Hardee's Loaded Biscuit 'N' Gravy. Hardee's splits a buttermilk biscuit in two and tops each side with an egg, a sausage patty, a generous helping of "famous sausage gravy" and one of the two paddles from the defibrillator. Bite, chew ... clear!

Now sure, America's fascination with creating ever-larger burgers and waistlines may seem like a symptom of an indulgent culture. But there is method to the high-cal madness: eating less healthily may be America's only shot at thriving economically in the twenty-first century.

Think it through. Manufacturing has declined across the United States. The country's trade deficit is huge. And one

of its most dynamic growth industries so far this century—Bieber-style haircuts—was inspired by a Canadian.

But by eating Double Downs and Pancake Stackers, Americans increase their need for prescription medication to lower their cholesterol, manage their blood pressure and keep their heart from, in medical parlance, exploding. That means profits for drug companies, more jobs for Americans and a stronger economy. The Double Down is not a plot to kill America. It's a plot to save America.

Getting fat is the most patriotic thing an American can do today. Each mouth is its own stimulus program. Citizens begin by supporting fast-food companies, then they enrich the drug companies and, ultimately, they politely die of wholesale organ failure just before they use up any Social Security money. Deficit tamed.

To make this happen, to deliver on this New Meal Deal, Americans are going to need to keep inventing new and more calorie-laden creations to ingest. They will need ingenuity, determination and, eventually, a tremendous amount of insulin. And hey, if pursuing economic prosperity happens to taste delicious, that's just gravy. Delicious sausage gravy.

So let's keep the wheels of innovation in motion:

- The Bigger Mac. Take two Big Macs. Replace the buns of one Big Mac with the beef patties from the other Big Mac. Eat the four-patty Big Mac. Enjoy. Then eat what's left of the other Big Mac. Then eat the extra buns, the ketchup packets and the tray liner. That little girl two tables over—is she going to finish those fries?
- The BK Bacon 'n' Bacon Bacon. Take a slice of fried bacon. Nestle it between two slices of fried bacon. Gently wrap these three slices of bacon in a slice of bacon. Serve with a side of bacon.
- KFC Bucket Surprise. It's the same bucket of fried chicken you know and devour, but now it's also filled with a mysterious liquid. Is your chicken soaking in sour cream? Sour milk? As if you care, fatty.

• The DQ Snow Dog. A beef wiener stuffed inside a beef sausage, smothered with beef gravy and blended into a Blizzard. Beefreshing!

BECAUSE I'M A super-busy guy and we live in a hectic, fast-paced world, I was standing by the toaster the other day, reading the plastic wrapper around my loaf of bread. This is a normal thing that non-crazy people do, so shut up. Anyway, near the bottom of the package, there was a little graphic of a warm loaf being removed from a stone oven on a wooden paddle. Above, there were two words: "Artisan Inspired."

Let that sink in for a moment: Artisan Inspired.

To sum up, my bread was not actually *artisanal*, as we understand the word. It was produced, packaged and distributed in abundant quantities by a national food processor. However, artisanal bread is popular and delicious. It therefore follows that this superior product would "inspire" the people who work at a national bread company, in this case, to put the word *artisan* on their wrapper.

I, for one, can see this catching on. We're at most a few months away from being able to enjoy a cold glass of "artisan-inspired" milk, produced in large batches by high-efficiency milking machines that are programmed to think they're old-time dairy farmers.

But let's not pigeonhole our corporations into being inspired only by artisans. Food products can also benefit from other highly dubious connections. Just a few examples:

Heirloom-inspired gummy bears. Finally, a snack worthy of being served to a fancy lady wearing a monocle. Hands off, kid: these gummies are for when company comes over.

Democracy-inspired Spam. Because *freedom*'s just another word for a canned, precooked meat product.

Mandela-inspired M&Ms. Let the packaging tell the story: "Chocolate, peanuts, pretzels, almonds ... While brainstorming what next to cram inside our iconic candy shell, one member of our creative team thought briefly of Nelson Mandela's heroic struggle. We're pretty sure it was Dave—he watches the news. At trivia, Dave was the only one who knew that Syria is a country and not that lady in our iPhones. Anyway, the point is, maybe twenty minutes after thinking about the late South African leader's unimaginable ordeal, Dave was outside having a smoke and he was like: 'Boom, marshmallow.' Enjoy these Mandela-inspired Marshmallow M&Ms."

Aside: If ever I won political office, my first order of business—after the mass detention of my enemies—would be to introduce legislation governing use of the word *improved* on food packaging. (In two terms, Obama, you failed to get it done.)

Food companies seeking to describe their products as "improved" would be obliged to:

- Apologize for feeding us something that needed to be improved in the first place. (At minimum, the law would require a photo of the company's CEO shrugging sheepishly.)
- State what its product used to taste like, on a scale ranging from "sawdust" to "ass."
- Itemize and promote in large print the recipe changes that resulted in the improved taste. (Bob's Cupcakes: now with 172 percent more hydrogenated cottonseed!)

This last one is important. At the place where I shop, I recently came across a bag of unsalted natural almonds that featured a big red starburst and the word "Improved!" I'm calling that bluff: How did you improve almonds? Was it the way you didn't do anything to them?

Anyway, where was I? Right, *artisan.* It's a great marketing word, but we don't want to overuse it. So let's create a few more and spread it out a little:

Future Vintage. Some people will pay a hefty premium for vintage products. Why make them wait? Everything produced today will eventually qualify as vintage, so I say overcharge them now. *Warning:* Hipsters will shorten "future vintage" to "fintage," because that's just like them. Dude, check out my fintage horn-rims!

"All natural." The quotes mean "not really."

Organish. Over the past several years, grocery stores have started stocking more organic foodstuffs, which is great because (a) they're really expensive, and (b) they remind us that everything else we eat is coated in enough chemical residue to alter the very composition of our genome. Luckily, there's a middle ground for budget-conscious consumers. Our new line of "organish" food still has all the harmful pesticides—the difference is, we feel bad about selling it to you.

Tough Question: *What does the future hold for the human body?*

A British geneticist claims to have made a startling discovery: humanity has stopped evolving. He apparently arrived at this conclusion after studying new data, analyzing behavioural patterns and watching John Travolta eat a side of ribs.

Professor Steve Jones of University College London cites a number of reasons but says the leading cause of our stagnation as a species is that fewer older men are fathering children. Turns out a man in his fifties is more likely than a man in his thirties to pass on genetic "mutations," the fuel of evolution. (By total coincidence, Professor Jones is in his sixties—an older man—making his theory either the summation of a life's work in science or the worst pickup line ever. *Hey baby, how'd ya like to help encourage a few cellular deviations?*)

Many are taking issue with Jones's conclusions—but what if he's right? What if there will be no sixth finger or third arm for humankind? What if we really are done evolving?

Then the monkeys win, people.

Already they are gaining on us, continuing to evolve and improve themselves. Researchers recently found that some Nigerian monkeys may even be starting to speak in "sentences" by combining specific noises into a sequence. According to scientists who monitor the Nigerian monkeys, when the adult male delivers a "sentence" of sounds consisting of three pyows and four hacks, it is understood by the female monkeys to mean "let's get going" or "time to move on." Whereas four pyows and three hacks clearly means "I'm going bowling with Steve." (It's a loose translation.) Hurling one's feces at another monkey, meanwhile, is still generally understood by scholars to translate as "I'm preparing for my Adam Sandler audition."

Bottom line: they're getting more intelligent and we're not. This much can be said with certainty—we are not helping our own cause in a potential war against the monkey menace. Not long ago, scientists at the University of Washington used an electrical circuit to give paralyzed monkeys the ability to move their arms. On one hand, this could lead to neuroprosthetics for humans with spinal cord injuries. But on the other hand ... monkey cyborgs! *Coming down from the hills! Monkeyborgs! Ruuuuuuun!*

For humans, a lifetime of servitude as a monkey concubine may serve as an evolutionary settling of scores. A recent study found that our early human ancestors may actually have interbred with the forerunners of chimpanzees long after the two species branched out from their shared family tree.

These findings have shocked the scientific community—not to mention many chimpanzee parents, who suspected their daughters were up to something but, wow, not anything this freaky. The researchers claim that human/chimp DNA didn't finally diverge until 5.4 million years ago—to translate for creationists: last Wednesday—which is hundreds of thousands of very awkward years after the two lines split. (Typical morning-after conversation: "Gee. Last night at the cave—I coulda sworn you were a biped.")

What's inescapable is that we are, as a species, the product of our distant ancestors' hot urges for chimps. An eternity later, payback may be coming our way: monkey see, monkey kill.

And don't even get me started on the hell we're going to catch from dolphins.

REASON NO. 6: THE CONSTANTS OF LIFE

Let's take a break from pondering the many ways in which the future will inflict upon us horrible, horrible change. And instead let's look at some of the things that won't change, but will nevertheless still also be horrible.

These are the constants of life today. They will endure as the constants of life tomorrow. Which, in most cases, kind of sucks.

The Despair of Winter I: A Poem Dedicated to Our Earth

In the annals of what prompts despair
Ranked just above losing one's hair
(But below wedding a Kardashian)
Is the sun going down at 4 PM.

The roads with headlights are festooned
Though the clock says it's still afternoon.
Our skin so pale, our moods defective
Disorders seasonally affective.

The early dusk makes tempers short
Our smiles the dark will surely thwart.

Reduced we are to glares and glowers
When our star is keeping banker's hours.

And in our homes as many yawns
As shirtless scenes in *Breaking Dawn*.
PJs, slippers, vim diminished
And *Jeopardy*'s not even finished.

Up north the dark's a constant pest
The sun no more than fleeting guest.
It peeks out briefly just to tease
Like a thong above a woman's jeans.

December's global truth behold!
Some must be hot, some others cold.
A tilt of 23 degrees
Makes Earth one big McDLT.

(Was that last reference too obscure?
I know that's not the meal du jour.
But I thought it surely would be glib
To compare our Earth to a McRib.)

Each year it takes us by surprise
The early gloaming, late sunrise
The street lights coming on at four
And your grumpy eight-year-old just swore.

Come summer we'll stand in ovation
To praise the ways of your rotation.
But a curse, a hex, a thousand pox
Upon autumnal equinox.

And winter solstice, even worse,
The hour of dusk just plain perverse.

It's a cruel and truly heartless ruse
To make a day short as Tom Cruise.

Across our cranky hemisphere
There comes a unifying cheer:
Hey Earth—get off your lazy axis!
Autumn's no time to relaxis.

We hear you're suffering climate change
Hot flashes have you feeling strange.
And word is that we are the cause
Of your planetary menopause.

Perhaps a deal we can beget
(Though technically it's more a threat):
Spare us from the winter bummers
Or we're all buying H2 Hummers.

It's not as though we're asking much
Just angle your round self a touch
So your top half leans toward the sun
And the next four months don't make us glum.

For some there'll be a cost, we'll vouch
The briefer daylight hours will ouch
Much like a kick in the genitalia
Thanks for your sacrifice, Australia.

Clamshell Packaging

Upon presenting a child with a new toy, today's savvy parent will instinctively reach for a pair of scissors to cut through the hard-plastic clamshell and twist-tie wires in which the item is packaged. Should the scissors fail to get the job done, out comes the knife. Then the pliers, a blowtorch and the jaws of life. By now, today's savvy parent is sweating profusely and possibly mortally wounded. You win this round, Fisher-Price.

And it's not just toys. These days, you don't so much open a product as you emancipate it. You spring a cordless phone from captivity. You free a foursome of AA batteries. You release Barbie from her wire bonds (unless, you know, your Ken happens to go in for the kinky stuff). When our son was four, he received for his birthday a set of army soldiers. He wanted to play with them right away. I cut, pulled, jabbed, tore, twisted, yanked and, resorting to a razor blade, sliced. Finally I hoisted the soldiers high in the air and, triumphant, looked over at my son—at which point I realized he was now a grown man and wanted the car keys. Enjoy the prom! Hang on, gimme just a minute before you go—I need to get this new digital camera out of its plastic case.

A study estimates that sixty thousand people each year in Britain alone are injured trying to gain access to new consumer products. That means about thirty thousand people in Canada meet the same fate, and I'm three of them: first, I scraped my thumb opening an *X-Men* action figure; second, I bruised my thigh when I jabbed it with a screwdriver that slipped while prying a low-energy light bulb from its plastic prison; and third, there's what's come to be known as The Epson Incident.

It began when I came home with some replacement ink cartridges for our printer. There were four cartridges in all, and they came in one "convenient" plastic package. The package was so "convenient" that I couldn't open it, so I grabbed a pair of scissors. With equal parts effort and profanity, I managed to breach the clamshell coating, which gave me a sense of tremendous accomplishment and, when the side of my hand slid up against the cut plastic, a laceration.

Eventually I got through the outer plastic package. I was inside the perimeter! Moving swiftly, I ripped open the inner cardboard package. Then I cut through the cardboard package inside the cardboard package. Then I broke for lunch and a nap.

Refreshed, I set about strategizing as to how best to confront the thinner plastic inside the cardboard inside the other cardboard that was inside the thicker plastic. It was roughly at this point that I turned things over to the exorcist.

Wrap rage has become such an epidemic that *Consumer Reports* recently presented "awards" to the products that come in the most impenetrable packaging. The Uniden digital cordless phone, tied to cardboard in close to twenty places for some reason, took more than nine minutes to liberate. Meanwhile, *American Idol* Barbie remained captive for fifteen minutes and ten seconds; her release reportedly involved "untwisting wires, snapping rubber bands, stripping tape, slicing thick plastic manacles off her arms and torso, cutting off a tab embedded in her head and carefully ripping a series of stitches securing her tresses to a plastic strip on the back of the box." (To be fair, that's exactly how they prepare real-life *American Idol* contestants.)

Why corporations package things this way is a riddle inside a mystery wrapped in an impenetrable plastic that's covered in my blood and tears. *Consumer Reports* says it's a reflection of the fact that plastic is now cheaper than cardboard. Others suggest it's because factory workers are increasingly rejecting socialism in favour of sadism.

Personally, I think it has everything to do with global domination. After all, most toys and consumer products are made in China. China is a new power bent on surpassing the United States as the world's largest economy. And what better way to do that than to sabotage North American productivity while simultaneously sapping from its citizens the will to live?

The time has come to fight back. You want our minerals, China? You want our lumber? Here, enjoy this high-quality two-by-four of genuine Canadian cedar! You can use it to help build a nice house—as soon as you figure out how to remove it from its durable, hard-plastic clamshell packaging. You may just want to go ahead and plant some saplings instead. It'll be quicker.

Summer Camp

What follows in italics is an actual letter home that our son James sent from Algonquin Provincial Park, Ontario, when he was twelve. It is presented with its original spelling and grammatical errors. Commentary and analysis are provided for your edification. It begins:

One of the many things I am looking forward once I get home is a tolet that doesn't get clogged so easily and when it gets clogged people don't keep pooing in it until there is poo two inches over the water level.

That is the opening line of his letter. There's no "Dear Mom and Dad." There's no "Camp is awesome!" He just cuts straight to the fecal matter. It's like having a Jim Carrey movie for a son.

In his defence, our boy does have a history of getting to the point. During his first summer at camp, James mailed home a note that consisted of a single sentence: "I was riding a horse and I got thrown off and now my broken arm is in a cast." One panicked phone call later, we learned that by "broken arm" he meant "sprained shoulder," and by "cast" he meant "sling." When he got home and we called him a "dummy" for making us worry like that, we meant "idiot."

The wake up bell goes at 7:15 so it's a big cut off from 9:30.

During July, James got into the habit of sleeping in, sometimes until 10 AM. We think he's apprenticing to become a teenager or a Van Winkle. Still, what's important here is that the letter has a second sentence—and a second complaint. Will he be able to maintain this impressive ratio? Let's find out!

It has only rained 1 time so far. I think we are going on trip in like 5 days.

Here James unleashes a burst of clipped prose reminiscent of any number of campers too lazy to think of an actual anecdote. Instead: random facts! "Trip," by the way, is a four-day canoe excursion that's mandatory at his camp. Unsurprisingly, last year's correspondence focused heavily on where the

126

campers poo while on trip.

The thing I am looking forward to most about coming home, besides juice that actually tastes like something, is hockey.

Wait, so now the juice is the worst thing about camp? Does that mean the clogged "tolet" actually isn't so bad? Keep your story straight, kid.

We're fairly sure James actually loves his camp. How couldn't he? It's a terrific place, the staff seem amazing and all day he gets to do fun stuff like canoeing, windsurfing and measuring the height of human excrement above a toilet's water line. Memories that will last a lifetime, I tell you.

Like many parents, we try to expose our kids to adventures better and more memorable than the ones we had. As a boy, I never spent more than four days away at camp, possibly because a full week inside the heavy, cruel canvas tents of the time would have resulted in dozens of young Cub Scouts being roasted in their own juices.

Those awful tents! And I have other fond memories of Cub camp, such as (a) leaving, and (b) never coming back. The outhouse was so vile that most kids tried to hold off from using it for as long as possible. I went so far as to hold off from using it for longer than possible and wound up with a pair of soiled underwear—which I removed and, embarrassed, hurled into the nearby ravine. Genius! No camper or counsellor shall ever learn my secret shame! It was only with the benefit of hindsight that I realized I first should have removed the iron-on label that read "Feschuk."

PS By the way 30/56 main course meals here are chiken. Chiken wings chiken fingers chiken wraps chiken soup chiken salad. So when I come home please no chiken.

First morning he's home, I'm waking this kid with a bell and giving him a breakfast of chiken breast, chiken flakes and chiken juice. Also, a dictionary.

Hockey Parents I: Meet the Hockey Parents

Every September a new wave of little kids and their parents experience minor hockey. The boys and girls don't need any help having fun. As for Mom and Dad, a little fair warning: here's a guide to some of the parents you can expect to encounter over the next several winters.

"Talks Only about His Own Kid" Dad: This plentiful specimen of parent will gleefully analyze for you his child's every pass, shot, mood swing, haircut, Tweet and cereal preference. Come February, he still won't know the names of half the other kids on the team. You can spot him easily because he's the only dad keeping a plus-minus stat for a six-year-old.

"Complains about Ice Time" Dad: This father can often be found insisting that the team would have triumphed if only his child hadn't been shortchanged by twenty-three seconds there in the second period.

"Bag of Noisemakers" Mom: Most teams have a parent who arrives at games with an array of horns and whistles. This is tolerable, perhaps even desirable. The problem? It opens the door to "Cowbell" Dad. And here's the thing about Cowbell Dad: he went to the trouble of bringing the cowbell, so there's no way he's going to hit that thing only after a goal. Nope, he's also going to celebrate good saves, decent passes, kids who manage to stay upright and hot moms who walk past. Come November, police will find you smiling over the corpse of Cowbell Dad, and the only thought in your head will be: "It was worth it."

"Berates His Kid in Front of Everyone" Dad: You won't spend too long in organized hockey before you witness a parent dressing down his child in public. We've all seen it and silently imagined pressing the father's face against a skate sharpener. Of course, decent parents know the best way to respond to a child's subpar outing at the rink is to put an arm around your kid, tell him a joke in the parking lot and when you get him in the car, *that's* when you make him cry.

"Pretends Not to Be an Intense Hockey Parent but Is One" Dad: This rare breed pokes fun at the stereotypical hockey parent while simultaneously displaying all the characteristics of one. By mid-season, parents will linger in the lobby while he finds a seat—so they can all sit very far away from him.

"An Injustice Has Been Perpetrated on My Child" Dad: Many teams will have a kid who is assessed way more penalties and even kicked out of games. The parent of this child will be unable to see what is obvious to others. How could they eject my boy? It was clearly an accident that his stick repeatedly penetrated that other kid's spleen!

"Everything Reminds Him of When He Played Hockey" Dad: Mark his words—he could have easily made the National Hockey League if only it weren't for his bad luck, his wonky knee and a scouting establishment that conspired against guys who were 5 foot 5 and 130 pounds.

"Take the Body" Dad: If your child goes on to play competitive hockey, he or she will be introduced to body contact, which totally makes sense at a time when some thirteen-year-olds are 6 feet and 160 pounds and others weigh the same as a throw pillow. What could possibly go wrong? In any event, there will be a parent who shouts "Take the body!" whenever two players come within 65 feet of one another. Women will regard him with disdain.

"Refuses to Learn Anything about Hockey" Mom: After several hundred hours spent in cold arenas, this mother still doesn't understand what icing is. She will believe, mistakenly, that this is charming.

"Team Strategy" Dad: Here's a guy who can be relied on to provide instant analysis after every game, complete with a long list of things the coach ought to be doing. He will speak of "shaking up the lines" and "changing the game plan." He will fail to accept that it is futile to plot strategy for any hockey team whose players still wave at their parents from the ice.

Happily, there will be many parents along the way who fit into none of these categories. You will want to sit with them, socialize with them. Sometimes, you will want to make fun of other parents with them. This too is Canada's national sport.

The Despair of Winter II: The Seven Stages of Winter

1. *Anticipation.* As the long, hot summer surrenders to the first hint of an autumn breeze, many of us experience a small thrill: winter is on its way, bringing relief from the heat and promising the many splendours that accompany the most Canadian of seasons. We envision snow-flecked landscapes, ice-covered ponds and joyful Christmas choirs. Digging deep into the closet, we gaze fondly upon our parkas and mitts. We dream of frosty adventures ahead.

2. *Despair.* The first cruel winds of November cut through us and we pretty much want to fall down and die right there. Three days of hostile muttering ensue.

3. *Sarcasm.* A huge December snowfall—awesome! And maybe a little freezing rain in there because THAT WOULD BE PLEASANT. Wake up and there's three feet of snow in the driveway—and hey, great, it's the wet, slushy kind that weighs about a squillion pounds per shovelful and lays those of weak heart in their graves. Yay, winter! Just when we finally get it cleared—literally, *just as we finish clearing it away*—the plow pushes a huge drift back in front of the driveway. *Thanks for that, buddy!* And for the record, that could have been anyone's snow shovel that flew through the air and struck the window of the plow's cab. We only ran away because we were in the mood for some exercise.

4. *Rationalization.* Typically this stage is triggered by an enjoyable day spent outdoors. We are imbued with the belief that we can not only survive winter but even learn to love it. We vow to plan more outings. We settle in for hot chocolate by

the fireplace. We look out the window into the deep black of a winter's night and we are content ...

5.   *Swearing* ... until we realize it's only 4:35 PM. Sweet mother of @!%*#. It's pitch black when we go to work! It's pitch black when we come home from work! There's more daylight in *Das Boot*. HUMANS WEREN'T MEANT TO LIVE LIKE THIS! Our stylish leather boots are salt-stained. The legs of our pants are salt-stained. Our will to live is salt-stained, and *that's not even possible*. At work, the guy two cubicles over is wearing the same wool sweater for the third time this week. It smells like a wet ferret. And now *we* smell like a wet ferret. Morning comes and the ice on our windshield is thick, so thick, and we take our scraper and we just hammer on it and hammer on it until we crumble to the driveway, spent and weeping. Later, at Starbucks, we overhear some cheerful idiot saying the Inuit have dozens of ways of saying "snow." We tell him we've got hundreds of ways of saying "Shut the \$@*# up." The ensuing conversation with management centres on whether we're banned from all Starbucks or just this one.

6.   *Despair*. It's late February. The snowshoes we got for Christmas are still in their box. Communication among family members has devolved to a series of grunts, crude drawings and middle fingers. In this dark moment, a decision is made. The next time someone comes up to us and says "Cold enough for ya?" we are going to murder that person. Not secretly. Not with any foresight or planning. We are going to reach out with our bare hands and we are going to strangle the life out of that person right then and there, and if anyone tries to get in our way, we are going to murder them as well. Because. We. Just. Can't. Take it. Anymore.

7.   *Despair*. The neighbours are back from their March-break trip to Florida. They're all tanned and perky, and they sure seem eager to come over and tell us all about it—right up until they spot the barbed wire and land mines. They back away slowly. Spring is coming. It must be coming. But the

nights still are long, and in our dreams we hear only the swish-swush snowsuit sound of the longest of the seasons.

Golf

For the whole of my adult life, I have had a love-hate relationship with the game of golf: I love me and it hates me.

But no more, for I am giving it up. Let it be recorded in the pages of this book that I have played my last round, recorded my last triple bogey, and lied for the last time about it being a triple bogey when, let's be honest, it took me five strokes just to get out of that sand trap. Fittingly, I am giving up golf "cold turkey," which is what I'm told I resemble when I swing.

Every spring now for more than two decades, I have pulled my clubs out of the basement, cleaned the cobwebs from the woods, scraped the dirt from the irons and attempted to straighten the shaft of the putter, bent theatrically the previous autumn after a three-footer for a five somehow became a nine-footer for an eight. Curse you, undulations!

I am at peace with my decision. Never again will I experience the thrill of taking out a driver on the first hole and watching as my ball sails high, higher, before settling gently onto the ladies' tee box. Not once more shall I, in search of a wayward shot, be obliged to march into woods or swamp or marsh or parking lot or that fairway two holes over or a pro shop. Nevermore shall I shank it, pull it, hook it, slice it, flub it, duff it, lose it left, lose it right, sky it, top it, worm-burn it or—most humiliating of all—just plain miss it.

I have tried, at great cost to wallet and sanity, to become not lousy at golf. I have read books and watched internet tutorials. I have invested in pricey irons and massive drivers and hilarious pants. I have taken a number of lessons from a number of golf pros. One of them went to the trouble of videotaping my swing so we could view and analyze it together. I remember catching his expression out of the corner of my eye as the tape

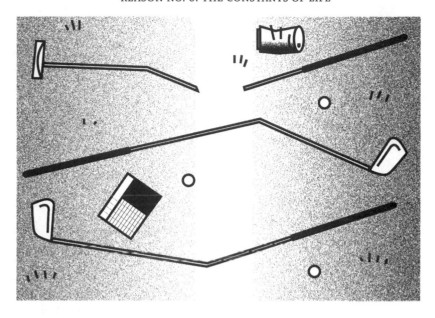

played—he had the look of a young child watching someone beat a baby panda to death with a baby koala.

That was a dispiriting moment. I always figured I'd be one of those guys who conducted business out on the golf course, forging relationships that would pay dividends for years to come. But it's surprisingly difficult to reach a handshake agreement when your would-be client is on the green in two and you're wildly swinging your eight-iron to ward off snakes in the long grass.

It's hard to put a finger on my moment of greatest ignominy. At Banff, we teed it up one morning with a herd of elk grazing perhaps 120 yards down the fairway. The others in my group that day cleared the animals with ease. I hit one of them … softly, on two bounces. To this day, I am haunted by the casual, pitying look it gave me.

Not long after, in the company of my father, I managed to lose twenty-three balls over the course of just seventeen holes. (I declined to play the eighteenth, using the time instead to write formal letters of apology to the inventors of golf, the country of Scotland and each woodland creature I'd concussed.)

My dad, being a supportive and sensitive man, hardly ever mentioned my inglorious achievement to others, save for a few phone calls, a little bit of skywriting over downtown and that one-act play he wrote and performed.

Many good golfers along the way tried to fix me. Some would start as soon as they witnessed me warming up on the driving range. Others did their best to hold off on dispensing advice for fear of coming off as chesty or condescending. But ultimately few could resist. What glory there would be in repairing a game so dire! Think about this, they would say, and when this didn't work there would always be a that. But there was no fixing me. My ineptitude would remain a dense and enduring mystery, like how Mike Weir ever won the Masters.

There are a few things I will miss about the game of golf: the beer cart, the beer-cart girl, the beer cart coming back. I will likely miss the way the sport fills so many daylight hours that will now have to be devoted to pastimes that don't make me cry. I will certainly miss the occasion it gave me to channel all my energy and intelligence into crafting new and innovative curses.

But my golf game is dead. It died surrounded by friends and family, who mocked it to its final breath. In lieu of flowers, please send a couple of badminton racquets. Maybe I'd be good at that.

Greed

In the aftermath of the last financial meltdown, a man wrote a book after quitting his lucrative job at the investment banking multinational Goldman Sachs because, he said, "It makes me ill how callously people talk about ripping their clients off." There was also the story of the trader who walked away from a huge salary because the industry had become "one hell of a mess" where the "culture was rotten."

Emboldened by these acts of courage, inspired by these

elegies to what truly matters in life, I've decided to use this platform to speak directly to the soulless, faceless, money-grubbing financial firms of the world.

Dear Super-Greedy, Ethically Barren Parasites of Pure Evil:

Um, have you filled those two vacancies yet? Because I have searched deep within myself—especially the wallet part of myself—and I am totally willing to get paid a ridiculous amount of money to work for you. (Remember: *ridiculous*.)

Don't let all my jubilant high-fiving of random strangers fool you: this hasn't been an easy decision. On one hand, I value the serenity of a balanced lifestyle, the nobility of honest work and the ability to sleep at night with a clear conscience. On the other hand, I want a boat.

Sure, the guy who quit Goldman Sachs said "the environment now is as toxic and destructive as I have ever seen it." And yes, he said that "morally bankrupt" executives refer to their own clients as "Muppets"—and that unwitting investors are steered toward underperforming financial products for which the firm charges the largest possible fees. But in defence of Goldman Sachs: boat.

The other guy, the stock trader, left for a job in print journalism (wave of the future!). He bemoaned the financial industry's culture of entitlement, saying, "I once saw an investment banker become enraged when his plane ticket was booked economy instead of business class. 'I'm not sitting in the back with the proletariat!' he declared." As a member of the proletariat, I feel compelled to point out: we don't like flying with us either. It doesn't make you special.

A number of factors contributed to my selfless decision to make millions of dollars by selling something that makes my client millions of dollars despite neither of us knowing quite what that something is. A collateralized debt obligation? A handful of beans? With all the fine print, it's hard to be sure.

First and foremost, I have no qualms about foisting highly dubious products on an unsuspecting public. After all, I worked in politics.

Second, I'd be a pretty awesome rich guy. True, others with absurd salaries have had a head start on becoming pretentious and unbearable—but I'd be willing to put in the work to catch up. In fact, for a couple of months now I've been emasculating sommeliers on my own time and overusing the word *bro*.

Third, a massive salary couldn't come too soon: it would give me the freedom to buy a fancy sports car and have a proper mid-life crisis. Pasting flame decals on my Volkswagen Golf just isn't cutting it.

Fourth, I have reached the point in life where it's vitally important to me to spend less time with my family. Our young boys are growing up. They're starting to ask tough questions about those Viagra commercials. If I plan those fourteen-hour days just right, I won't see them again until those questions have been answered by their wives.

Fifth, and most important: my soul is unlikely to get any more valuable than it is right now. In some ways, I almost feel sorry for the financial industry: in 1978, I'd have been willing to sell my soul for a photograph of Jaclyn Smith with her shirt off. Nowadays, I'm not going to sign it away for anything less than a ridiculous salary and a ridiculouser bonus. Also, that photograph of Jaclyn Smith with her shirt off, please.

Sure, selling my soul will place me in jeopardy of eternal damnation and render me a dry husk of a human being, obsessed with the pursuit of greater personal wealth at the expense of the people I love and the values I cherish. But ultimately, I can just make like that Goldman Sachs guy—quit in a huff after twelve years, call my friends and colleagues a bunch of bottom-feeders and reclaim my moral compass.

I get to keep the boat, right?

Performance Reviews

BOSS: Come in, take a seat. So you are ...
EMPLOYEE: *Oh, I'm a little nervous, I suppose.*

No, your name.

I'm ... I'm Pat. I've worked for you for six years.

Ah, yes, Pat! Good ol' Pat! Pat, let me begin by saying this, Pat: most performance reviews are rigid, hierarchical affairs that cause anxiety in employees and lead to dangerously flawed outcomes. So let's get started.

[Pat quietly prays for the sweet relief of an aneurysm.]

Pat, when morale is too low, the employee feels unappreciated. This causes productivity to drop, leading to layoffs. How would you describe your morale?

It's great. I'm excited to come to work in the morning.

Pat, when morale is too high, the employee feels entitled. This causes productivity to drop, leading to layoffs.

In that case, I'd say my morale is fair ... -ish?

I've asked around about you, Pat, and almost everyone who had any idea who you are said you're a capable employee probably.

I guess that's good, right?

At the same time, my own advancement at the company hinges on my ability to justify my position by ensuring that at least 15 percent of my employees receive a negative review.

I'm not sure I understand.

I know. Pat, I've been professionally trained to ensure that nothing you hear today—none of the words I say—should come as a surprise to you. Which is why I'm slipping you this piece of paper.

It just says "Disappointing."

Pat, your performance has been disappointing.

But you just said I was capable.

Nothing in the corporate world means what it does in the real world. Let me show you. How would you describe yourself in the workplace?

Well, I guess I'd say I'm a deliberate thinker.

Translation: too chicken to make a decision.

I'm definitely a vibrant social presence.

Alcoholic.

And I pay very careful attention to detail.

So you're a pain in the ass.

That's not fair. I think my co-workers would say I'm valuable.

Interesting. While you were talking there, I got to thinking. *And ... ?*

Oh, it wasn't about this. Pat, I'm not going to sugar-coat it: you need to forge the bandwidth to action a granular, user-centric synergy silo that connects the dots between baked-in deliverables and incentivizing a robust, collaborative conflict-resolution diagnosis.

I appreciate your bluntness.

Let's talk about career goals.

Well, I want to take on more responsibility with the goal of one day becoming a manager myself.

Bold. Now let's talk about your plausible career goals. Actually, hold that thought. Tell me instead: what are your stretch goals?

My what?

Stretch goals: your theoretical career aspirations that we both know you're incapable of reaching but that signal to me that you possess sufficient ambition to not be regarded as corporate deadwood.

Um ... Olympic volleyballer?

Perfect. Moving on. Pat, there's a concept in the performance review literature called Ranking Scales. It's a way of evaluating staff by comparing them to one another, so there's a best, a second-best, a worst. Personally, I think it's unwise and destructive to tell people precisely how they rank. So I'll just ask you to go ahead and guess.

What?

I'll give you some of those "getting warmer/getting colder" signals.

I don't understand the point of this whole process. I come in here once a year to talk about goals but there's never any follow-up. What are you getting out of this? How is this helping me with my job?

I'll be the one to ask the questions here, Pat. My next question: what is your job again?

Recessions

We're all looking for ways to make ends meet during tough times, but there are only so many coupons you can clip or charitable organizations you can defraud with an elaborate Ponzi scheme. What follows are some less traditional ideas for saving money, each of which has actually been recommended on the actual internet.

Well, you can **scavenge**. We might as well start there. *The Scavengers' Manifesto* is a new guide to "discovering how salvaging, swapping [and] repurposing can save the Earth, your money and your soul." Wow. I, for one, did not realize that a trash can full of maggot-infested ham could do all that. I also didn't realize that saving my soul would require me to finish eating some dude's pizza crust. Church never mentioned that.

Still, there's no denying the growth of "dumpster diving," which is on the fast track to becoming a medal sport in the Hobolympics. And remember as you rummage: one person's discarded syringe is another person's source of hepatitis!

But maybe you'd be more comfortable with a less drastic change in lifestyle. Why not start small and save on a barber by trying a **home haircut**? Sure, your hair will look terrible—but at least you'll potentially injure yourself. A blogger named Frugal Dad noted: "Guys, you will need someone to help you with the neckline, unless you are good with mirrors"—or, failing that, good with tourniquets.

While it's true that the recession is a joy-snuffing abyss of bleakness and despair, thank God we still have our kids to hold, cherish and shake down for loose change. Remember: a penny regurgitated is a penny earned.

For many advice-givers, children are our most precious resource—and should be mined for savings accordingly. One mother says she's taken to **sewing fake designer labels** into her daughter's bargain-bin clothing. A dad boasts of **cutting his son's allowance** to "help him understand" what a recession is. And one blogger suggests **forcing your children to shower with you** to save water. (Who knew traumatic memories could be so environment-friendly?)

Bottom line: your children will hate you. But you can win them back. One fun thing to do as a family during hard times is to closely track the precise duration of the mind-numbing tedium that defines your shared misery. But who can afford a new calendar every 365 days? (Answer: almost everyone, but stick with me here.) Why not do what the folks at Walletpop.com recommend and **reuse your old calendars**? "There are only seven permutations ... so why buy a new one for 2009 when you can pick up an old one on eBay from years that match?" I knew I should have listened to my broker when he recommended a portfolio weighted heavily in Leif Garrett calendars.

But saving serious money requires more ambitious measures. For instance, you could save big on eggs by **raising your own chickens**. Websites like Backyardchickens.com will help you along. And don't worry—the people on these sites are just like you and me. They're totally normal. For instance, when the topic turned to whether to eat your hens after their egg-laying days are behind them, one woman sensibly responded: "If we were all starving to death I would chop off an arm or leg and feed it to my kids before I would eat one of my laying hens!!!" (Awww, Mom. Arm sandwiches again?)

Which brings us to death. All things being equal, it would be best if you didn't die during the recession. But if you must die, the least you can do before you go is **build your own coffin**. There are a number of books that can help, including *Do-It-Yourself Coffins for Pets and People*—which touts itself as "a joy for the experienced craftsman," especially if the experienced craftsman happened to have hated his late mother-in-law.

Looking for an even cheaper option for the dead? **Burial at sea**. It doesn't cost a penny and it lends itself to a serene ceremony. That said, you may wish to learn from my mistake and ensure you use a body of water larger than a wave pool. As I told the staff and, later, the authorities, I was as surprised as anyone that my pony floated.

Finally, there's the whole matter of wooing and sex. In a time of crisis, only a monocled madman would consider paying as much as $10 for flowers, candy or a hooker.

So why not do what a man in Michigan's Thomas Township did and **have sex with a car-wash vacuum hose**? All you need are four quarters and, according to the Saginaw County Circuit Court, ninety days to spend in prison after pleading no contest to charges of indecent exposure. Vacuum sex and three square meals a day? Now that's making the recession work for you.

Too busy working to sexually penetrate a home-cleaning device? Good for you. To remain employed during a recession, you must become the MacGyver of the workplace—a person capable of saving his or her own job while armed with only a paperclip, a wad of gum and, if at all possible, a thick sheath of photographs of the boss fondling an intern.

To stay among the ranks of the employed, you need simply to follow my Seven Habits of Highly Not Fired Yet People:

1. *Make yourself indispensable.* You can do this by working really hard and becoming more productive, but that's a pain. It's probably easier just to swallow the CFO's hard drive. Also, there's hostage-taking—a surprisingly effective attention-getter in the short term. And remember: prison offers solitude and none of the hassle of vetting whom/ what you have sex with. Two birds, meet one stone.

2. *Suck up.* Remember how you used to take an apple in for your teacher? It was pathetic and even the mention of your crass sycophancy makes me physically ill, but let's face it—you might have been on to something. Find out your boss's favourite morning drink. Is it coffee? A latte? The blood of the weak? Then place a cup of it on his desk

in a casual manner, matter-of-factly mentioning, "Oh, I just happened to be walking by Tim Hortons/Starbucks/ an orphan's outstretched arm. Enjoy!" Tally one imaginary brownie point—and don't forget to write down the address of that orphanage.

3.   *Give birth to octuplets.* Your boss is only human, if you discount his mechanical heart, titanium endoskeleton and general, all-round werewolfery. And it's human nature to want to spare those who have the most to lose. Becoming the parent of eight babies gives you the kind of family credentials that even most Osmonds can only envy. But stay alert—some of your co-workers probably have children too. It falls on you to take the high ground and point out just how ugly and unworthy of love they are.

4.   *Are you gay? If not, can you pretend to be?* Being perceived as openly targeting a minority is one of the great fears of any organization that isn't the Republican Party. For this angle to work, it's all about proving your homosexual credentials. Thankfully, countless thousands have paved the way. Think about it: those people at Cher concerts—they can't really be there for the music, can they?

5.   *Go to the washroom ... for about eighteen months.* They cannot fire what they cannot find.

6.   *Make subtle death threats.* The keyword here is *subtle.* But in another, more accurate, way, the keywords here are *death* and *threats.* Yes, you want to avoid prosecution, but you also need to get your point across. For starters, try "testing" your chainsaw during staff meetings. On one hand, this makes you a person that everyone wants to get rid of. On the other hand—*your* hand, the shaky, blood-spattered one—you've got a chainsaw. Go ahead and take an extra ten minutes for lunch. No one will say a word.

7.   *Divert attention from yourself.* If the end seems near, gesture theatrically to a point in space, then yell "Look, over there!" The people who've come to fire you will eventually turn back in your direction, but you'll have cleverly bought

yourself three to five precious seconds. Check and mate, Human Resources.

Spam

Most people think of email spam as annoying, but I've always enjoyed it. It's like getting a tiny novella delivered to my inbox for free—an exotic fiction designed to grab my attention, my imagination and, should seventy-eight of my IQ points happen to stage a wildcat strike, my money. But I'm worried about today's spammers. They appear to have lost their creative spark.

Not long ago, I received from "DHL Delivery Service" the following message: "When do you want your Two Hundred and Fifty Thousand Dollars to be delivered to you?" That was it. That was the entire con. Earlier, an equally imaginative proposal had arrived: "I am Mr. Vincent Cheng, GBS, JP Chairman of the Hong Kong and Shanghai Banking Corporation Limited. I have a transaction of 22.5 Million USD for you."

Oh, Mr. Vincent Cheng: I'm disappointed in you. Like most veteran users of the internet, I have certain quality-based expectations of those who attempt to swindle me out of my life savings. For one, I expect spelling errors—many, many spelling errors. I also expect a shaky grasp of English verb tenses. And I expect—nay, I demand—that the return email address of a purported wealthy industrialist such as yourself be something along the lines of superhotnakedchick@yahoo.com. But more than all that, Mr. Vincent Cheng, I expect salesmanship. I expect effort.

And I expect way more lying.

Here, let me help you out a bit. You need to tell a story, okay? Entice me into your highly dubious world. Make me understand who the fake you really is. I'll get you started: perhaps you're (a) the frail widow of a military dictator, (b) the glamorous wife of an exiled tycoon, or (c) the wiener dog of Leona Helmsley.

Paint me a picture. Make it seem possible that you have access to formidable cash reserves but that—just like in most good Hollywood romantic comedies, and all the lousy Richard Gere ones—there is a fishy but remotely plausible obstacle keeping you from retrieving the money. For instance, it could be the fact that (a) your late husband's military rival is now in command, (b) your spouse faces trumped-up tax-evasion charges, or (c) the safety deposit box is too high for you, a humble wiener dog, to reach—even standing on your hind legs.

Once I'm committed emotionally, once I've bought into your personal tragedy or hilarious canine shortcomings, that's when you try to hook me. That's when you tell me (a) "I'll give you 30 percent of the proceeds," (b) "I'll pay you a $2-million consulting fee," or (c) "Woof!"

Now get out there and defraud me like you mean it, Mr. Cheng. That's how Contused H. Latina, Kermit Bolton and Hines X. Meggy used to do it, back in the day when bizarro monikers were the trendy way to elude spam filters. (Now, of course, most people instinctively click delete at the first glimpse of an exotic name like Chase Wang or Jewell Mayo. In fact, I don't know how many emails from Chase Wang I'd deleted before I discovered that Chase Wang is a real, non-fake person. He works for a PR company in California. I am sorry for ignoring you and not believing you exist in corporeal form, Chase Wang.)

Happily, there is still one spam genre where low-life schemers keep putting in the effort. Consider the urgent email I received from "Serg." The subject line attracted my eye and at least one other part of my body: "Lindsay Lohan drops bikini bottom." Intriguing, I thought to myself. *Plausible.* So I went ahead and opened it. The full text of the message read as follows: "So large that you will have to change your underwear size." And then there was a link.

Help me out here. I can understand how a certain type of person can fall for a certain type of financial-based scam. But what kind of guy reads "So large that you will have to change your underwear size" and thinks to himself: hey, this sounds like a reputable solicitation for a safe and effective method of increasing the size of my precious genital organ—I think I'll give it a shot! And what comes in the mail if you place an order? Pills? A mallet? A stout man to grab hold of it and start walking that-a-way?

More to the point—do you have any idea, Serg, how big a penis would need to grow to compel a change in underwear size? I don't either, but I suspect the words "serpentine" and "hey, stop stepping on that" would be involved.

And what about Lindsay Lohan and that bikini bottom? What happened to that little promise, Serg? I'm beginning to think I shouldn't trust you with my bank account information either.

Mount Everest

Attention, media: it's not a tragedy when a Western climber dies on Everest. It's not even interesting. People die there all the time because it's EIGHT FREAKING KILOMETRES STRAIGHT UP.

And don't get the idea that someone successfully reaching the summit is compelling, either. Not anymore. By now, we've all read enough about Everest to assume that anyone who makes the peak has basically been pushed, pulled, piggybacked or conveyed in the manner of a human wheelbarrow by Sherpas, for whom reaching the summit is about as exciting as the end of a dull commute.

> SHERPA NO. 1: What an accomplishment for you, a humble bond trader from Chicago, to reach Earth's highest point. Now can you please get out of the BabyBjörn?
>
> SHERPA NO. 2: And can we start heading down? I gotta take my kid to soccer practice and pick up some milk.

Everest long ago surrendered its mystery and majesty. To-day the mountain is covered in trash, excrement and corpses—it's basically 1970s Times Square. Making the trek is so trendy that most climbing seasons result in human gridlock near the summit. Did you see the photos from a couple of years back? There were more climbers waiting to ascend than in the lineup outside the women's washroom at a John Mayer concert.

The Despair of Winter III: Forecast for the Week Ahead

On Monday morning, freezing rain will move through the region. Temperatures will fall sharply in the afternoon, lead-ing to the risk of a flash freeze, followed by snow, followed by sleet, followed by more snow, followed by hordes of yeti com-ing down from the hills to feast on the weakest among us. The high will be –18C. With the wind chill, it will feel like –18C but windy.

On Tuesday, temperatures will warm abruptly, but only for long enough to mess up the backyard rink you've spent weeks flooding and shovelling. Snow will begin in the early after-noon. It will change to rain, then back to snow, then briefly to the swarms of frogs associated with Biblical plague, then freezing frogs and, finally, to those ice-pellet thingies that sting like hell when they hit your eyeballs. The pellets will be shaped like Bible frogs. As the temperature plummets, En-vironment Canada forecasts that your mood will shift over-night from desultory to depressed to borderline homicidal. Exposed skin will freeze in the time it takes to say "I'll be fine, mah faaaace wuhnt freeezzz uhhhp."

On Wednesday, a polar vortex will churn through the re-gion, bringing snow-nami-like conditions that include high winds, low visibility and plummeting ice clusters the size of a baby's head. Also, you know that parka you just got back from the cleaners? Environment Canada forecasts a 7 percent probability that you'll rub it along the side of the car on your way to work. Not to worry, though—the dirt will match up nicely with the salt stains along the bottom of your pants. Daytime highs in the afternoon are expected to hit –39 degrees. An ideal day to enjoy anywhere between twelve and seventeen seconds of the great outdoors!

On Thursday, Environment Canada forecasts a 90 percent chance of freezing rain, an 80-percent chance of being sprayed with slush by some asshat in an Odyssey, and a 100 percent chance of regretting the life decisions that have kept you here. Later in the day, the freezing rain will change into rain, followed by snow, followed by the urge to snap your shovel in two, curl up in the fetal position on the driveway and softly curse your forebears for not having carried on to California. As dawn approaches, expect the arrival of a thick, sentient ice fog that will stalk and devour us all, never stopping, never pausing until every soul along this cruel, frozen hellscape we call a country is consumed. High of –10.

Friday will bring more snow and colder temperatures. As the mercury falls, Environment Canada forecasts a 40 percent probability of Imperial walkers assaulting your rebel ice fortress. Local law enforcement advises that counterattacks be focused on the walkers' legs, which—if you think about it—represent a rather glaring structural flaw. Who designed these things? Talk about some guys who deserve to be force-choked to death, am I right? They're probably from the same firm that told Grand Moff Tarkin, "Hey, when you go ahead and spend untold quadrillions constructing this killer space station that's 140 kilometres in diameter, you should definitely scrimp on a little metal gate that would stop your enemy from firing a torpedo directly into the core reactor." Anyway, the point is, it's going to be cold and slippery out there, so only seasoned tauntaun riders are encouraged to risk the commute.

On Saturday, the snow and record cold will continue as a trilogy of all-seeing, all-knowing fronts moves in from Mordor and tracks across the region, covering all the lands in darkness, conferring the power of speech on trees and generally lasting about twice as long as it needs to. Although daytime temperatures are expected to hover around –37 degrees, it is forecast that your teenager will nevertheless insist on going out in sneakers and a windbreaker. As if the cold were not depressing enough, Environment Canada also forecasts the imminent end of the limited-time return of the Shamrock Shake.

Looking ahead to Sunday, the long-term forecast calls for the moon to become as blood, and the sun as black as a sackcloth of hair, and lo shall the earth quake and skies part and every mountain and island move out of their places. In addition, Environment Canada forecasts an 80 percent chance of every star of heaven falling unto the Earth, for the time of Mother Nature's wrath will be upon us, and who shall be able to stand? Especially with all this freezing rain.

Holiday Family Gatherings

For many Canadian families, listening to the warm, wistful stories of Stuart McLean's Vinyl Cafe Christmas *has become a holiday tradition. But what if Dave and Morley's family was a little more like our own?*

None of them had seen Uncle Earl since Christmas dinner, 2004. He'd arrived unexpectedly, just as Morley was serving the apple pie. "Don't make a fuss," he'd said, then tucked a napkin into the collar of his T-shirt. Morley dutifully made up a plate for Earl, the serving spoon hitting hard against the china. Earl spent the rest of the evening flirting ferociously with Aunt Janice and rubbing her thigh. Few would have thought this impolite had Janice not been married to Uncle Walt, who was sitting right there.

Six years it had been since anyone had seen Earl. But when the doorbell rang, Morley froze. She knew in an instant. They all knew. Earl. A doorbell has never been touched so deep into the Christmas dinner hour by anyone other than a black sheep.

Rubbing her hands on her apron, Morley made a noise she'd later insist was merely a sigh, though no one in the family could recall one of her sighs sounding so much like the F-word.

"Hey, numbnuts!" Earl said by way of seasonal greeting as Dave opened the door. "Merry frigging Christmas."

There was room at the table. Stephanie had already been and gone. Five months pregnant by her boyfriend, a drummer in a Creed cover band, she wasn't feeling that well. Still, Dave thought she looked radiant—even with the piercings.

Grandma, too hard of hearing to have noticed Earl's arrival, looked up from her banana liqueur and declared abruptly: "Politicians—they're all a bunch of liars." There were murmurs of agreement.

"That's Rhonda," Earl said, motioning behind. Dave looked out to the porch, where a small woman was vomiting onto his Christmas wreath. "Oh," Dave said. Dave couldn't quite place Earl's scent. Was it the cologne you buy for a dollar in truck-stop restrooms? Was it mace? Earl always did have a way with the ladies.

The conversation turned to global affairs. Earl had thoughts about a nuclear Iran and a unique way of inserting a new and ever-more-creative profanity into the name Ahmadinejad every time he said it. He gestured as he spoke, spilling his whisky on the tablecloth and, later, the dog. Rhonda had now made it into the house. Unsteady on her feet, she brushed against the Christmas tree, but managed to collect herself, turn to the tree and declare: "Pleased to meet you."

Later, over Baileys and sweets, Dave gently put forth a reasoned argument for further stimulus to ignite the economy. Cousin Rick called that "pansy talk." Only the market can solve the problems created by the market, he said. And Rick ought to know: he'd been working at Edward Jones now for five months. Grandma reminded everyone that she ate lard during the Depression, and everyone pretended they didn't know that. Earl belched the first seven notes of "Away in a Manger."

Suddenly Grandma wanted to go home. She'd taken off her slippers and was putting on her boots. But Dolores wasn't ready to leave yet, and Aunt Sandra wasn't going to take her because, goddammit, she'd picked Grandma up!

The argument went on and on, until someone noticed that Grandma was gone. She'd just walked out the door.

"Go find her!" Morley hollered at Dave. "She could be anywhere by now!" Dave shouted at Morley. Earl sprang to his feet, and it seemed for a moment that a volunteer had been found—until he loudly announced that he needed to "make some room for dessert" and headed tipsily for the bathroom. In the chaos, Rhonda whispered to young Sam that she'd show him her boobs for $5.

Dave found Grandma having a cigarette in the garage. He hadn't seen her smoke in twenty years. She seemed embarrassed to be caught, but she didn't butt out. "Good seeing Earl," Dave said to fill the silence on the drive home. But Grandma just stared down at the Tupperware on her lap. Crossing the porch on the way back to the house, Dave noticed a few carrots in his Christmas wreath—the remnants of Rhonda's first impression. He thought they actually looked pretty festive.

Two hours later, when the last of the stragglers had been gently pushed out the door, Morley collapsed on the couch. The dishes could wait 'til morning. Dave flopped down beside her. They looked at each other with an expression that said, "Next Christmas we're going to Cuba instead."

"Merry Christmas, Dave." She touched his hair.

"Merry Christmas, Morley."

For the first time in hours, the house fell quiet. They could hear the hum of the lights on the tree. The wind whipping up against the window. And to their surprise, gentle snoring coming from the bathroom.

Televised Spelling Bees

Exactly what part of the televised spelling bee are we supposed to enjoy? The severe, joyless parents who make the twisted, damaged moms on *Toddlers & Tiaras* look like nanny material? Or the panic-stricken children whose self-esteem is wrapped up in solving the riddle of vowels and consonants required to spell a word that no one else knows exists? Way to go, kid, you know how to spell *chionablepsia*. Also, you're eleven and you've never been outside.

Am I being too harsh? Maybe. If nothing else, I guess all the kids will remember the event forever, which will be useful in a decade when they need to describe it to their psychiatrists.

The girl who won the Scripps National Spelling Bee a couple of years ago reacted with such dead-eyed indifference that her younger brother actually used his fingers to push up the corners of her mouth and help her form a smile. Still, she walked away with $30,000 in cash, a trophy, a $5,000 scholarship and the memory of a decade's worth of weekends spent staring into a dictionary twelve hours at a time while all the other kids listened to music, played sports and learned to tongue-kiss.

Congratulations, little girl, and best of luck in all your future unabombing!

Hockey Parents II

It's time to turn our attention to an age-old question: What if parents of young children behaved the same way at the local Christmas pageant as some do at a kids' hockey game?

Scene: Parents take their seats. Quiet conversations ensue.

WOMAN: I can't believe they're letting Justin play one of the wise men. Tucker is a *way* better genuflector.

MAN: Or Liam. At least Liam keeps two hands on the myrrh.

WOMAN: And let's be realistic—Carson as a shepherd? He's

barely cut out to play Donkey No. 3. I mean, you call that vi-
brato? No wonder he got cut by the touring company.

MAN: I'm thinking of taking over the pageant next year. I
don't have any training of any kind and I don't know anything,
but I think I've seen enough episodes of *Glee* to do a better job
than these bozos.

Scene: A choir of children performs a holiday standard.

EMMA'S DAD [*standing up*]: Come on, Emma—sing. SING!
SINNNNNNG!!!!! Sing harder, Emma! *SING HARRRRRRR-
RRDER!!!!!!*

EMMA'S MOM [*gesturing to her husband and whispering to
the person next to her*]: Sorry, he takes this whole thing pretty
seriously.

EMMA'S DAD [*now standing on a chair*]: Go, Emma!! *SINNN-
NNNNG!!!!*

EMMA'S MOM [*turning red*]: Sorry. He's just ... I'm sorry.

*EMMA gets distracted by one of the bunnies being used to decor-
ate the manger scene.*

EMMA'S DAD [*now standing on a different chair that someone's
still sitting in*]: COME ON, EMMA!! FOCUS, EMMA!!!!!! GET
YOUR HEAD IN THE SONG!!!!!!!

*Scene: The foyer at intermission. A couple holds court in a small
group of adults.*

HUSBAND: So we've enrolled Zach in after-school training
with a private coach. He's singing carols three hours a day, sev-
en days a week. And that's on top of his tongue-strengthening
exercises. It's a big commitment, but it's the only way he's ever
going to get scouted by the major choirs.

WIFE: He loves it. You can tell he loves it.

HUSBAND: He totally loves it. I mean, he *says* he doesn't love
it. Or like it. Or ever want to do it anymore. And he cries a lot
and says we've ruined his life. But you can tell he loves it.

WIFE: You can tell.

Scene: Children gather around the manger. A boy begins playing a drum, steadily at first. He falters briefly, but the show continues. Grown men in the audience begin hollering.

— Come on!

— Wake up, conductor. *YOU GOTTA CALL THAT!*

— Are you deaf?? *You're missing a good pageant, Mrs. Rinaldo!*

Scene: The climax of the show approaches. An angelic child steps into the spotlight and, despite obvious nerves, begins singing "Silent Night." The audience falls quiet for a moment until …

WOMAN: Is it just me, or is this a little pitchy?

MAN [*shouting*]: Stop hogging the song—pass off the third verse at least!

EMMA'S DAD: PUT THE BUNNY DOWN, EMMA!! PUT IT DOWNNNNN!!!!

Scene: A little boy dressed as a cow walks to the car with his father.

DAD: What did I tell you about lowing? Is that how I taught you to low? It's mooooooo, all right? *Moooooooo.*

KID: Okay, Dad.

DAD: You sounded like a dying hamster up there.

KID: Mr. Whiskers died?

DAD: All those hours we spent lowing in the backyard. The long drives into the country. The three days we spent squatting in that dairy farmer's barn. And you blew it.

KID: Sorry, Dad.

DAD: We're going to get home and you're going to practise your lowing until you get it right.

KID: Okay, Dad.

They get into the car. Before he pulls away, the father looks up and catches his son's gaze in the rear-view mirror. The boy has tears in his eyes.

DAD: MOOOOOOOOOOOO!

Sex

Patricia McCarthy is explaining how to talk dirty during sex. Let go of your inhibitions, she says. Stop using clinical terms (*vagina*) and start "getting creative." (Okay! Um ... Captain Vagina?) Oh, and don't forget timing. "Once, on a first date," McCarthy recalls, "a guy told me over coffee that his ["creative" word for *penis*] was eight inches long. The information was good, but the timing just wasn't right."

My pen moved smoothly along the page of my notebook. *Don't tout wang size at Starbucks.* Got it. *Wait 'til lunch at East Side Mario's.*

McCarthy was offering her lexical guidance at Sexapalooza, an "adult-themed consumer trade show" that each year, across the country, attracts thousands to the romantic confines of a dank convention hall crammed with porn DVDs, crotchless lingerie, pubic hair dye, leather masks and hoods, handcuffs, vibrators, bigger vibrators, more vibrators, and one repressed bespectacled author who spent the whole time convinced the ghosts of his ancestors were watching as he browsed the latest in dominatrix attire.

"There's no magic formula for talking dirty," McCarthy continued. "You can't say that this word plus this word plus this word equals orgasm for your partner." Oh, I don't know about that: "I'm" plus "George" plus "Clooney" seems to work pretty well for George Clooney.

Perhaps unsurprisingly, Sexapalooza didn't score big on the subtle scale. Just steps inside, organizers had built a comically oversized vagina, out of which people excitedly jammed their heads for photographs. The show also marked the first time since the 1989 *Star Trek* convention that I heard a woman yell into a microphone: "There are so many dildos in this place!" (And, once again, I want to apologize to the organizers of the 1989 *Star Trek* convention for my mother's behaviour and her uncalled-for description of sci-fi enthusiasts.)

Sexapalooza has the novelty of being about the countless

uses of (and substitutes for) humanity's naughty bits—but in many ways it's like any other trade show, right down to the salesman slipping on a headset microphone and luring a crowd to demonstrate the amazing features of his remarkable product. Usually it's a vegetable chopper or stain remover. This time it was the Bondage Bed.

Every hour or so, with the help of a volunteer (usually a fat guy or a hot babe), the huckster demonstrated how the Bondage Bed would not only keep your "guest" from slipping out to watch NCIS but also eliminate the tricky weight-balancing issues that apparently come with doing it like a porn star. After the show, a curious woman took down an I Like It Doggie Style kit from a nearby rack, turned to her man and asked, "What do you think?" The man, briefly intrigued, noticed that the "kit" consisted of a strap that loops around the woman's waist. "You could just use a towel," the King of Romance said dismissively.

The nearby Dungeon sounded ominous and was touted as the centrepiece of naughtiness at Sexapalooza—but turned out to be a small patch of exhibition hall separated by thin black curtains. Inside, an overweight woman lounged contentedly in a cage the shape and size of a dog crate, while a man showed off an astonishing array of whips and a creepy smile. Across the way, a sad-seeming burly fellow in a brown leather skirt was locked into a snug stand-up cage. A woman wearing a studded collar jabbed him with a cattle prod. (Alas, security in the Dungeon proved lax at best, for the next time I saw the leather-skirted man he was eating a hot dog at the food court. He looked happier.) Visitors to the Dungeon could avail themselves of the opportunity to purchase the latest edition of *Whiplash* magazine, which featured the National Mistress Listing (one-stop shopping for all your dominatrix needs) and ads for a wide array of bondage equipment (one-stop shopping for giving your housekeeper something to gossip about when she finds the hood and shackles under your bed).

Meanwhile, as McCarthy moved to conclude her dirty-talk

lecture, her words were drowned out by noise from a nearby booth: a gruff male voice passing from microphone to loudspeaker. "Let me help you find the G spot, guys! Come on, guys. Let me show ya." Tempting, sir, but ... ummm ... I've got a 3:15 cage fitting over in the Dungeon.

Two Other Things I Learned at Sexapalooza:

1. If you think certain politicians or celebrities are hostile to the media, then strap on a camera, take out a pen and notepad and try to have a chat with an attractive, tiny blond woman as she is purchasing a seven-inch glass dildo. Now *there* is hostility for you!

2. The thing that gets most women going, that revs their engines, that fires up their libido is ... dark chocolate. So claimed a noted sex therapist, anyway. My date to senior prom would argue that actually it's my Lou Rawls impression.

Higher Education

Dear Future Post-Secondary Student:

Whole books are devoted to how to prepare for higher education, but here's the truth—everything you really need to know about university life is contained below. Let your parents slog alone through the latest guides on mortarboard technology. With these twenty-one critical pieces of information, there is no force on earth that can stop a university or college freshman (freshperson?) from becoming a successful university graduate (except failure).

1.   Vodka? Not a food group.

2.   At school, you will live in accommodations that blend the comfort and amenities of a jail cell with the aroma of a hamster cage. You will love them.

3.   There are two kinds of university students—one kind lives in filth and squalor and uses the power of negligence to

fashion teetering skyscrapers of dirty dishes and terrifying bio-wads of fetid underpants. The other kind is female.

4. The music you listen to in university—you'll remember it forever. No matter how old you get, the faintest hint of a song from your school days will take you back to that time, unleashing waves of wistful remembrance. So make sure the music you listen to doesn't suck. You don't want to be like the lame sap who was driving with his kids the other day and got tears in my eyes when "Mr. Roboto" came on.

5. In your classes and dorms, you will be exposed to a fascinating cross-section of Canadian diversity—unless you go to Queen's, in which case you'll be exposed to a fascinating cross-section of the children of white dentists. (This isn't true, but as a Western grad I'm legally obligated to sully the reputation of Queen's without regard for ethics or accuracy. I'm pretty sure it's in the BNA Act.)

6. The late Osama bin Laden? Queen's grad.

7. University is a voyage of self-discovery. You are about to learn so much about yourself—things like "I had no idea I could grasp such complex scientific concepts" and "Oh, that's where I left my pants."

8. Technology has altered the post-secondary experience. When I went to school in the late 1980s, we didn't have "social networking" sites like Twitter. We had to bore people in person. We didn't have "GPS devices" with which to find our friends. We had "looking over there." Heck, in my day, the closest thing we had to "user-generated erotic content" was begging your roomie to leave the curtains slightly open. My point is this: I am old.

9. Slice of bread, peanut butter, slice of processed cheese, layer of BBQ Fritos, second slice of bread. You're welcome.

10. Men: during your time at university you will feel pressure, anxiety and, if you play your cards right, boobies. The boobies will make up for the pressure and the anxiety. That's just biology.

11. Let me tell you: nothing beats the experience of packing

up and leaving your bedroom in your parents' home forever and then graduating and returning to your bedroom
in your parents' home.

12. Some of your days at school will be tedious. More will be
difficult. Ten years from now, none of this will matter.
You'll think to yourself, "Man, those school days—those
were the days!" So remember as you're having your school
days that those days are one day going to be the days that
were the days.

13. In a pinch, this page can be fashioned into a bong.

14. There will be times when the workload is overwhelming. These can be stressful moments. Perhaps you actually ripped this page from the book and you're staring at it
now—months into the future—and you're experiencing
one of these moments. You're on the verge of tears. And
you're trying to read this section of life-saving advice—but
the page is smudged and torn from when you tried to turn
it into a bong. The lesson: you're an idiot.

Take a deep breath, idiot. Close your eyes. And tell yourself: if you stay up all night, if you apply yourself to the
task at hand, you will by morning be one small step closer
to acquiring the very same diploma that's currently in the
possession of countless people getting thrown out of their
jobs. Now get in there and get it done!! (Wait, why are you
sobbing?)

15. Don't cheat. Just don't. But when you *do* cheat, don't just
copy something word for word and try to pass it off as new.
That's something that only a scoundrel or a professor keen
to force students to buy a "new" edition of his textbook
would do.

16. Have fun. Do dumb things. By the end of three or four
years, you'll be pleasantly surprised by how many activities
can end with someone declaring, "It probably isn't a serious
concussion."

17. But be careful! Times have changed since I was in school.
In the '80s and early '90s, we could get stinking drunk and

blindingly stupid in the privacy of our own throw-up. Not anymore. Heed my warning: Had I been born twenty years later, I'd be the unwilling star of a Facebook group called Drunken Spandau Ballet Impersonation Fail.

18.   Avoid early classes, especially the ones that begin at eight o'clock in the morning—or any of the other o'clocks in the morning. I'm not saying I rarely made it to my 8 AM political science lecture, but to this day I believe political science involves the dissection of elected officials.

19.   Live in residence for your first year. Residence life will provide at least half your overall university enjoyment, 75 percent of your hangovers and 100 percent of your bedbug scars. Plus, it makes stalking incredibly convenient.

20.   Don't bring huge piles of sand into your dorm room for a beach party. It sounds like a good idea, but the sand is hard to get rid of—especially when you don't try to get rid of it and you just leave it there.

21.   In my day, we had a contemptuous term for those who finished a four-year degree in only four years: "graduates." My advice: stay at school as long as you can. Let's face it: the real world is a bit of a mess right now—what with the economy, and the environment, and the Leafs. We'll give you a holler when we've got it all fixed up.

Tough Question: *What's the best way to bring Barbie into the modern age so she better reflects the society of tomorrow?*

- Promiscuous Barbie: comes with a home pregnancy kit and a dozen Plan B pills (Deadbeat Ken sold separately)
- Arizona Barbie: cries real tears when the Sheriff forecloses on her Dream Mansion
- DUI Barbie: features smeared mascara, glazed eyes and extended middle finger for her mug shot
- Candy Crush Barbie: throws a tantrum if you take away her smartphone and try to play with her
- Botox Barbie: a plastic face so lifelike, it's almost human

REASON NO. 7: ARTS AND ENTERTAINMENT

Every spring, the Cannes Film Festival showcases its usual fare of upbeat, crowd-pleasing entertainment. What does the future hold? Which movies will it be showing next spring? It doesn't take a psychic ...

Despair and Isolation. Several orphans struggle to comprehend the human condition in a cruel world where the only constants are heartbreak and suffering. Running time: six hours.

Isolation, Despair and Also Anguish. Several thinner orphans struggle to comprehend the human condition while wheezing in a crueller world where the only constants are heartbreak, suffering and their leprosy (the skin kind *and* the social kind). Running time: six hours.

Despair, Anguish, Further Anguish and a Shaky Hand-Held Camera. Several orphans struggle to comprehend the human condition, but without going outside, because the film's budget is only $19. Running time: thirty-three hours (couldn't afford fancy "editing" machine).

Out of Focus. The title refers to the disenchantment of today's youth with the crass, materialistic pursuits of their parents. It also references the fact that the film is out of focus. Running time: four days and still going strong ...

Hard to Follow. A soft breeze rustles the leaves of a tree. Then there's a woman on a horse. A child rides his bicycle through a foreboding forest. Wait—what? Is that a hamster running on a wheel now? Come on.

C'est la Vie. François, an impoverished, mute widower, takes care of his deaf daughter, Isabelle. Theirs is a monotonous life. But then one day it turns to tragedy!

Closed-Circuit. This compelling epic consists in its entirety of a single close-up of a human eyeball. The bold work of art suggests a commentary on the dehumanizing role of surveillance in our modern society—or possibly that the cinematographer held the camera backwards the whole time.

The Triumph of Love. Turns out the title is pretty misleading. This "Love" guy is a serial killer who targets orphans whose parents were murdered by other serial killers who themselves were orphans.

Daniel. Daniel had a good life, but then his parents were killed in a tragic Segway accident and now he's suddenly alone and vulnerable. He slips into a life of drink, gambling, crime. Can he make a choice for a better future? Probably not.

Cobwebs upon My Loins. A middle-aged French woman embarks on a journey of sexual awakening but then turns around and goes home to her sexless marriage when she sees how many other middle-aged French women are waiting in line outside the sexual-awakening place.

Change for a Dollar? Sometimes good intentions have horrible consequences. This is probably going to be one of those times.

Farewell My Chinos. A precocious tomboy rebels against society's dated strictures regarding the public soiling of one's trousers. Already the European critics are hailing this five-hour film as "just the right amount of tedious."

The Clarks. A father and son are very different. Then, after about three hours, it turns out that in many ways they are actually quite alike. Weird, right?

The Unclasped. The third instalment in a famed director's fifth trilogy, dedicated to probing the deeper themes of human subjugation, racial prejudice and female shirtlessness.

Gloaming. The art-house scene is not immune to trends in popular cinema. This epic focuses on three young French vampires who prowl the city by night, stalking innocent victims and subjecting them to their sharp, vicious musings on the modern-day relevance of Sartre.

Gabrielle. Gabrielle is young and chubby. She has no friends. Nothing ever goes right for her—except for her tap dancing. Gabrielle loves tap dancing. *Oh, how she feels free and alive when she's tap dancing!* But then her feet fall off.

Inevitable Woody Allen Movie. The darkest and most dramatic Woody Allen film in years, or so they're saying now that nobody laughed during the first screening.

Fifty Shades of Eh

Excerpt from a Novel by Scott Feschuk

The *Fifty Shades of Grey* book series, about a young woman who signs a contract to enter into a submissive sexual relationship with a manipulative billionaire, has been described as good news for publishing and bad news for words. It has spawned its own line of lingerie, bedding and S&M-themed accessories. The thing is such a gold mine that scoundrels are cranking out quick knock-offs—a reprehensible development, in that it may cut into the sales of my own.

Luckily, my work occupies a specific niche. Welcome to an excerpt from my highly erotic—and profoundly Canadian— soon-to-be-published new novel, *Fifty Shades of Eh* ...

He pulls the leather strap tight against my left wrist. I wince.
"Sorry," Christian says. "Sorry about that."
"It's okay."
"I'll loosen it a bit."
"Don't trouble yourself."
"Honestly, it'll just take a minute."
"It's *fine*, Christian."

I gaze upon him with my intrepid eyes. My mouth, which is also intrepid, curls into a sly smile. "Did you remember the clamps?" I ask.

"Canadian Tire was closed. But I found a bunch of clothespins in the garage."

I swoon. My breathing quickens. My heart beats a frantic tattoo as I surrender myself to the anticipation of languid erotic pleasures and several hours of splinter removal. *Why, oh why have I fallen for someone so Canadian—so okay looking, so gainfully employed, so ... nice?*

"I need you to fill out some paperwork before we go any further." His face impassive, Christian hands me a single shiny sheet. He draws close—so tantalizingly near that I can sense his energy, his essence, his Head & Shoulders—and whispers: "No more than three toppings, or they charge extra."

He hums a few bars of Nickelback and I'm helpless, trussed up and pressed into his brother's old futon from university. Christian sighs.

"I'm damaged, Ana. You just don't get it. I was born to a successful pediatrician ..."

"Well, that doesn't sound so—"

"... in *Winnipeg*."

"Oh. Oh, Christian. I'm so sorry."

"You're not the one who's sorry. *I'm* sorry."

There is a pause.

"Sorry," I say.

My intrepid eyes cast around Christian's Rec Room of Pain and across his many instruments of torture: the ball gag, the whip, the black gadget that with the press of a single button turns on the cruellest device of all: the television. Sportsnet, TSN ... *Oh, Christian, stop teasing and turn it to* CBC *for the Leafs game! The chronic incompetence ... the annual ritual of false hope ... such delicious pain!*

My tongue tentatively prods his and they join together in a slow, erotic dance. A tongue dance.

Blissful moments pass. Are they minutes? Hours? A dollop

of something cold lands along the intrepid curve of my hip—
splash!—and I am alert again. My body is electric, pulse pounding, skin alive with sensation. *Desire. This is what desire feels
like.* "Sorry, spilled my beer." The sensual gyrations of our relationship, all bump and grind and dancing tongue, continue.

Christian frowns at me.

"Why are you frowning?"

"Sorry," he says. Now he's smiling. The Earth shifts on its
axis, tectonic plates slide into a new position, volcanoes erupt,
trains speed into tunnels and other suggestive images. My inner goddess yearns to be touched by this tragic figure with the
jaw of a lumberjack and the clothes also of a lumberjack.

"Do you like my beaver?"

"Sure, but it looks a little small next to the stuffed caribou,"
I say.

"Damn rodent put up a hell of a fight. I still say it was worth
losing my leg."

He picks up a riding crop and limps over. I can feel a stirring
deep within me, somewhere beneath my snow pants. This feels
so different from the last time, so vital, so carnal, so ... wait, is
that the "Coach's Corner" theme?

Suddenly, Christian is on top of me. He forces something
into my mouth. It's firm, so very hard. I curl my tongue around
it and instantly recognize its elegant contours.

Timbit. Chocolate-glazed.

"I only had enough cash on me for day-olds. Sorry."

I surrender myself to the sweet agony, and chew.

THE END?

YOU WON'T BELIEVE what I did the other day. In our hurried
age of bite-sized internet content and nibble-sized social media
musings, my attention span and I sat down to read an actual
book—one of those things with pages and words and everything. With a thought to future generations who won't know
what those are, here's a record of how it went:

7:08 pm A quiet house, a couple of free hours: I pick up a thick hardcover, keen to experience the satisfaction of cracking its spine. (Before doing this, I always check to make sure I'm not reading an ebook. I'm not going to make that mistake a third time.) True, since 2009 I haven't skimmed anything longer in a single sitting than a compelling box of Cinnamon Toast Crunch, but tonight I'm confident: *I am totally going to read you, book.*

7:11 My goal is to make a solid dent in *Thinking, Fast and Slow* by the Nobel Prize-winner Daniel Kahneman—a book that everyone was talking about some time ago, which is when I bought it. Every day since then it's stared up at me from the coffee table with the same accusatory glare I get after asking to taste-test a sixth flavour at Baskin Robbins.

7:13 Excited, I read the first paragraph.

7:14 Still pretty excited but also a little worried because already there's math, I read the second paragraph. And you know what? I can actually hear myself getting smarter. No, wait, that's the sound of an email in my inbox. Better check that out.

7:18 I close my laptop and try to remember what the first paragraph said.

7:19 Excited(ish), I reread the first paragraph of the book.

7:24 I keep losing my train of thought. To be honest, it's overstating it to call it a train. Thanks to the fleeting thrill of text messages and Twitter, these days my train of thought is, at best, a railroad handcar of thought operated by two hobos. *Dagnabbit, there are some highfalutin theses ahead—pump harder, Tin Can Rufus and Big Earl!*

7:31 I come across a word I don't know—*pupillometry*. So I look it up on my iPhone and immediately get back to reading the book right after making my next move in thirteen different games of Words with Friends. That's right, unsuspecting opponent: ZA is too an acceptable word.

7:44 My mind wanders from a passage about cognitive illusions. I flip to the back cover blurbs. It seems this Daniel Kahneman author guy is regarded as "the most important psychologist alive today." I spend some time wondering how the blurb-giver discerned this, and how far down the list he ranked them. *You, sir—you're the 126th most important psychologist alive. TRY PSYCHOLOGIZING HARDER.*

7:47 Another blurb. Richard H. Thaler, professor of economics, says the book I'm holding in my hand—the hand not using its thumb to check baseball scores on an app ... and I really should see if Kijiji has ... *FOCUS, FESCHUK*—anyway, he says the book is wise, deep and "readable." Speak for yourself, Richard H. Thaler.

And really: what's with the *H*? Are there really so many professors of economics named Richard Thaler that you must further identify yourself with an initial—or is this merely a vainglorious affectation aimed at exaggerating your intellectual heft? "Ooooo, look at me: I'm Richard *H*. Thaler and this is my paisley ascot!"

7:49 I am sincerely sorry to have taken out my frustrations on you, Richard H. Thaler's middle initial.

7:56 Chapter 2 would be going great if not for the fact that the author just referred to something he'd explained in Chapter 1 and my brain was all, like, "Whachoo tawkin' 'bout, Willis?" (When under stress, my brain communicates exclusively using 1980s catchphrases. In high school, I nervously tried asking girls to the prom and wound up with a dozen jars of Grey Poupon.)

8:12 I suddenly recall the scene in *Broadcast News* where Albert Brooks's character demonstrates his smarts with a song about how he can sing and read simultaneously. I attempt to do the same and wind up spraining my face. Turns out I can't sing and read. Or even just read anymore. But there is one thing I know I can still do.

10:23 I finish watching *Broadcast News*.

LIKE MOST PEOPLE, I have always wanted to win a prestigious literary award—but not without frequently mentioning genitals. That wouldn't seem to leave me a lot of options. But luckily, the trend in literature is very much toward greater inclusion of bawdy scenes, sweaty couplings and assorted perversions—to the point where Britain's *Literary Review* has taken to bestowing an award for the very worst and least-bearable depictions of the act.

The Bad Sex in Fiction Award was conceived to "draw attention to the crude, tasteless, often perfunctory use of redundant passages of sexual description in the modern novel." Plus, pretty much every guy in England was looking for fresh material after years spent in sweaty, private contemplation of Miss Havisham showing some ankle.

In recent years, the Bad Sex award has become a staple of Britain's literary calendar, right up there with the announcement of the Man Booker Prize and the release of Ian McEwan's latest book that makes everyone want to kill themselves. During their lifetimes, Gabriel García Márquez and John Updike were both nominated. Tom Wolfe has won. A few years back the award was for the first time granted posthumously—to Norman Mailer, who bested (or worsted) the competition with this excerpt from his novel *The Castle in the Forest*: "They both had their heads at the wrong end, and the Evil One was there ... The Hound began to come to life ... It surprised her. Alois had been so limp. But now he was a man again!"

To review the nominees from recent competitions is to risk being turned off not only sex but also adjectives. It is to stand in slack-jawed witness to otherwise gifted authors conjuring a parade of "silicon-lined vaginas," "languid buttocks" and "bulging trousers." The penis is inevitably likened to some type of serpent, snake or "demon eel thrashing in his loins." Breasts are compared to everything from rocket ships to, rather memorably, "a pair of Danishes." It's the kind of writing that could get Hugh Hefner to declare a fatwa on you.

Yet the competition can be intense. Just ask Salman Rushdie, who was widely tipped as the 2005 front-runner for writing the words: "[She] pulled her phiran and shirt off over her head and stood before him naked except for the little pot of fire hanging low, below her belly, heating further what was already hot." But Rushdie was out-awfulled by Giles Coren, who described a male character's genitalia as "leaping around like a shower dropped in an empty bath." According to the judges, this was merely the most memorable part of Coren's unpunctuated 138-word description of sexual intercourse, which itself was followed by the 2-word sentence: "Like Zorro."

This is all pretty bad stuff. But I bet I can do badder.

Memo to all Bad Sex in Fiction Award aspirants: you might as well save your throbbing manhoods and heaving bosoms for future years. This is my time. Ever since the beginning of this paragraph, it has been both my dream and my destiny to capture the Bad Sex in Fiction Award. The honour would justify the many years I've spent honing my medieval, elf-based erotica. And the trophy would nicely complement my Bad Sex in Real Life Award, bestowed on me by Rhonda from my university dorm.

The judges had therefore better prepare themselves for the kind of bad sex writing not seen since Charlie Sheen found himself with a can of whipped cream and the canvas of a hooker's naked back.

Among my entries:

• From my epic (yet tragically unpublished) novel *The Moistest Christmas*: "She lay before me, naked, trusting—also, reading a magazine of some kind, possibly *Glamour*. The only sounds: the quiet lapping of the waterbed and her insistence on getting this over with before the start of *Scandal*. Depanted, a cosmic radiance emanated from the whole of my loins, bathing her undulating flesh in sensual waves of crimson and aubergine. I thought it was my loins, anyway. It could have been the neon Bud Light sign above the bed."

• From my epic (yet tragically unpublished) novel *An Inconvenient Coitus*: "She was an environmentalist. I came to her by night, silently in my electric car. She was dressed in a negligee made from recycled tires. Without a word, she let me know she appreciated that my fur-lined briefs doubled as a breeding habitat for the male bee hummingbird. My heart quickened, my breathing grew more rapid. She stepped away briefly to purchase carbon offsets, compensating for these increased emissions. I took her in my arms just as her hemp-based demi-cup brassiere biodegraded. Reader, her edible underpants? One-hundred-percent organic."

• From my epic (yet tragically unpublished) novel *Tuesdays with Morrie's Hot Daughter*: "She lay before me, naked, trusting. I gazed at length upon her breasts, her naked breasts, her cones of silence, her shimmering flesh puddles, her twin orbs of womanly essence. In retrospect, I realize that this is when Morrie hit me from behind with the seven iron."

Transformers 6: The Hangover

We join the movie in progress, at the beginning of the third act …

OPTIMUS PRIME: Since time immemorial, Autobot and Decepticon have engaged in an epic struggle between good and evil—with the fate of the universe itself hanging in the balance.

BRADLEY COOPER: That's groovy, Mr. Roboto. But it does not explain how that giraffe got into our Jacuzzi!

WE'D BEEN HAVING fun that day in New York, so we headed to the Guggenheim to put an end to that. It was time to get the kids some culture. That's a thing we're supposed to do as parents: expose our children to "culture." Enough of this enjoying everything we're doing, kids—it's time to walk slowly past some old stuff.

At the Louvre a few summers ago, our family and every other tourist in Paris had the idea of heading straight for the *Mona Lisa* when the museum opened. At first we all walked casually. But the competitive instinct kicked in. Soon we were race-walking. Grown men were throwing out their elbows and grunting. Our boys charged ahead, weaving through the fading old ladies. They don't remember anything about the painting but still talk about how they blew past a large Italian family on the final turn before the salon.

A couple of summers ago, the Guggenheim devoted much of its space to a retrospective of Lee Ufan, who is a very important "artist-philosopher" according to the noted authority Sign I Read On a Wall.

Our first exposure to his work was a painting made up of a long brush stroke along each of the four sides of an otherwise bare canvas. And there on the floor: a boulder placed at either end of two long pieces of metal. We walked on. Another canvas, this one with a few small squares of grey paint. Another boulder, this one with a metal pole leaning against it. Was this an art installation or the set of a new Flintstones movie?

It was at this moment that I learned something I didn't know about the Guggenheim. I learned that the Frank Lloyd Wright design ensures the human voice reverberates when spoken at anything more than a murmur. This is especially true if the human voice is that of a twelve-year-old boy saying too loudly: "This is all a big pile of junk." Meanwhile, our ten-year-old was silently contemplating the possibility that leaving behind his snack wrappers after watching TV makes him not a slob but an artist-philosopher with a provocative view on human consumption.

We did nothing to halt the critique of Lee's oeuvre. "Modern art" is the wave of the future—as unstoppable as it is incomprehensible. Besides, when having culture inflicted on you, it's important to realize that art can be beautiful or bogus, magnificent or nonsense, and that you don't have to marvel over a couple of rocks just because some tour guide claims they represent "a durational form of coexistence between the made and the not made."

Over decades of museum and gallery visits, I have developed a foolproof theory related to art: the more impenetrable and pretentious the quotes about an artist's work, the greater the likelihood that the art is going to be pretty ridiculous.

We stopped to learn about Lee's minimalism. The artist himself was quoted: "If a bell is struck, the sound reverberates into the distance. Similarly, if a point filled with mental energy is painted on a canvas, it sends vibrations into the surrounding unpainted space." The phenomenon, he says, causes the viewer to fall silent and "breathe infinity." "You can't breathe infinity," said Will, our youngest. "It wouldn't fit in you." Your move, Lee Ufan.

The Lee Ufan exhibition concluded with a site-specific installation featuring "a single, broad, viscous stroke of paint on each of three adjacent walls of the empty room." The curator described it as establishing "a rhythm that exposes and enlivens the emptiness of the space." James, our oldest, described it as "something he probably did in four minutes because he needed money."

Nearby, another New York museum had on exhibit something far more tangible and real: a number of mundane to-do lists left behind by the famous and the obscure. We should consider this a wake-up call: if there's even a small chance that any of *our* lists will one day wind up on public display, we need to start padding them with made-up tasks that will impress future generations—such as "Fistfight with bear" and "Rehearse with A. Jolie for Sex Olympics."

What was striking about the exhibit was its simple truth— that over centuries of technological progress and changing social mores, there has endured one vexing constant: the eternal struggle to get one's shit together.

I could fill a museum wing with the sad artifacts of my failed attempts to stay on top of things. I have scrawled lists on the fronts of envelopes and on the backs of my hands. I have purchased Day-timers pricey and cheap, large and tiny. Last year I bought a nifty box that housed a separate little agenda for each month. Before the end of February, I had lost April.

I have spent a small fortune on overpriced Moleskine notebooks—each purchased with optimism, each quickly abandoned as I moved on to another journal that I was certain would work better. I've used both a blackboard and a whiteboard. A few years back, I relied on a system of my own creation: I called it Scraps of Paper Jammed in My Pockets. Worked well enough until laundry day.

I have tried keeping my to-do list on my iPhone—but have never had the discipline to input my new obligations. Turns out that part is important. Falling every time for the promise of a tranquil and tidy life, I have shelled out for several iPad productivity apps. One of these days I may even open them.

For a brief period this year I kept every clerical detail in a large black binder. At my desk one morning, I realized I had left the binder on a shelf on the other side of my office. It's still there. I'm looking at it right now. Hi, black binder! You contain a chronicle of so many things I never ended up doing in March. I sincerely hope none of them led directly to a fatality.

My latest system involves compressing the sum of my professional and personal obligations onto a single memo card— and transferring all uncompleted tasks to a new card at breakfast. Nothing beats beginning the morning with a precise and itemized reminder of how you fell short the day before.

I display a rigour for the making of the list that is entirely absent from my attempts at tackling the list. It has to be written on a Moleskine memo card. It has to be written with a Uni-ball Deluxe Micro, black only. Sometimes, if a chore is especially important, I will write it in CAPITAL LETTERS. That is my personal shorthand for ensuring that, by the end of the day, I simply must—without fail—feel even worse about having IGNORED IT.

Last October, I received a notice indicating I needed a new registration sticker for my car's licence plate. Immediately, I wrote "Buy plate sticker" on my list. Over weeks of ignoring that reminder, the notation evolved as it was transferred to new memo cards—it first become "p. sticker," then "sticker," and finally "STICKER." Round about December, I forgot what "STICKER" meant and dropped it from the list entirely. Two

THE FUTURE AND WHY WE SHOULD AVOID IT

months later I was pulled over by police. No sticker. The next morning I wrote at the top of a fresh memo card: "Pay fine."

Once, in a dark moment that will forever mark a grim personal low (tied with the cheetah-print Ferris Bueller vest I wore freshman year), I put on my list two or three tasks I had already completed—all for the hollow thrill of crossing them out. Worse still, it actually felt good. *In your face, Tuesday!*

EVERY YEAR OR so, almost like clockwork, a new study is released in which some group or other calls on moviemakers to show the harmful consequences of illicit drug use and to depict safer sex practices in their films. I was reading one not long ago. "There is convincing evidence that the [movie industry] influences behaviour," Dr. Hasantha Gunasekera said in the *Journal of the Royal Society of Medicine*. (The "findings" actually made their way into newspapers around the world on account of editors sharing a deep and abiding passion for scholarly research—at least the kind that justifies printing a large photograph of Halle Berry in a bikini.)

Those not of a mind to peruse Dr. Gunasekera's paper in its entirety can get a sense of the cinematic world of the future that he envisions from the following scene: James Bond in *Dr. Hasantha Gunasekera's Die Another Day of Natural Causes at a Ripe Old Age*:

SCANTILY CLAD VIXEN
Drink, Mr. Bond?
JAMES eyes her suavely.
BOND
The usual. A Diet Yoo-hoo.
VIXEN
Oooh, James. I can't resist any longer—make love to me ...
He takes her in his arms.
VIXEN
... after signing in triplicate this declaration of mon-

ogamous intent.

A notary public emerges from the VIXEN's *evening bag.*

VIXEN [*hornily*]

We'll have the paperwork back in seven to ten business days.

BOND

That should give me just enough time.

JAMES *fumbles with the state-of-the-art condom applicator and staple gun supplied to him by Q.*

BOND

Probably best to wear two, don't you think? That'll teach chlamydia who's boss while simultaneously preventing me from impregnating you with ... *thuunk!* ...

There is an awkward silence.

BOND

So maybe celibacy is the way to go then?

They sit quietly for ninety-five minutes. Roll end credits.

BACK IN THE olden days, people would prepare for the future by doing things like "working hard" and "saving money." There was a word for these people: stupid. Being far more advanced than our forebears, we have come to understand that sacrifice and personal responsibility are for suckers.

Take me, for example. My future is set! Not to rub it in your face or anything, but I am now vastly superior to you as a human being—for I am privy to ... shhh! ... *The Secret*. Wealth, fame, a trim waistline and Naomi Watts in a French maid's outfit are on their way to me. Up yours, life!

The Secret was the perfect book at the perfect time because it grasped something inherently true about the future and about us as a species: we would just very much like for everything to be easier, please. Having invested the whole nine minutes required to read it, and four more minutes to file a brutality lawsuit on behalf of the English language, I can tell you that *The Secret* harnesses the raw power of positive thinking and exclamation marks!!

In detailing an "ancient philosophy" that is purportedly its inspiration, *The Secret* tells us that the key to a happy and prosperous life is politely asking "the Universe" for a happy and prosperous life, please. "When you think about what you want," author Rhonda Byrne explains, "you cause the energy of what you want to vibrate at that frequency and you bring it to You!" At last: an explanation for why Quarter Pounders start shaking when John Goodman pulls into the drive-through.

Put simply, the Secret of *The Secret* is that thinking about stuff is the best way to get stuff. Put even more simply, "Your thoughts become things!" What a relief! I, for one, have grown weary of self-help books that rely on me actually doing something, often with my ass, and usually involving getting up off it. Nothing so fatiguing is demanded of us by *The Secret*: "All you require is you and your ability to think things into being." According to *The Secret*, every misfortune in your life is something that you attracted with negative thinking: "Often when people first hear this part of the Secret, they recall events in history where masses of lives were lost, and they find it incomprehensible that so many people could have attracted themselves to the event." But they did, the author says. Silly people of Bangladesh! If only they'd resolve to think happy thoughts, those killer cyclones would just quietly pass on by.

Sadly, many people still focus on what they "don't want" in life: sickness, bills, a Kevin Costner career resurgence. This has led to a "don't want" epidemic—"an epidemic worse than any plague that humankind has ever seen." You can see the author's point: the relentless swelling of the groin, leading first to the oozing of pus and blood and then, inexorably, to a painful death, leaves the bubonic plague a distant second to naysayers' fears of a *Postman* sequel.

You've got to think positive thoughts, people! If you tell the Universe that you don't want the flu, the Universe hears that you do want the flu. The Universe doesn't understand "don't" or "no," Byrne writes. Think of the Universe as a Real Housewife of Beverly Hills.

The Secret can make you rich. It can get you laid. It promises a plentiful supply of vacant parking spaces. It can also cure all terminal diseases, which is handy. Gaining wealth is as easy as envisioning a cheque arriving in the mail. Landing the perfect mate is as simple as making room in your closet for his or her clothes. As for your health—well, the good news is that "illness cannot exist in a body that has harmonious thoughts." Serves all those cancer victims right for being such downers!

Now, I admit it: I was skeptical at first about the Secret. When I was growing up, I thought night after night about having hot awesome sex with Marie Osmond. I yearned for it, dreamed of it, wanted it. But I ended up disappointed—having sex with her turned out to be so-so at best.

Alas, my skepticism withered as the author offered completely authentic Inspiring Examples, some of which use first names and everything! Take "Norman," for example. He was apparently diagnosed with an "incurable" disease and told he had just a few months to live. So he spent the next three months watching Hollywood comedies non-stop. "The disease left his body in those three months." The obvious lesson: even cancer can't tolerate David Spade.

And then there's "Robert," a homosexual man who was the subject of degrading slurs and gay bashing until he started "emitting a different frequency out into the Universe." Hey, gay people: remember that the next time you're being physically assaulted for your sexual orientation. It's not the homophobes and violent criminals who are to blame; it's your attitude! Buck up, already: God made you love musical theatre for a reason.

Still not convinced? Well, consider that the author completely cured her own poor eyesight by simply declaring to herself, "I can see clearly." Plus, she says she weighs 116 pounds yet eats whatever and whenever she wants. "If someone is overweight, it came from thinking 'fat thoughts' ... Food is not responsible for putting on weight."

But don't just take her word for it! I've been following the directions in *The Secret* for two whole weeks now. And look at me: I'm deeper in debt and fatter than ever! Hmm, and I don't remember asking the Universe for these bedsores. Excuse me for a moment, won't you? I've got to go think really hard about an author being struck by a falling piano.

Byrne later produced a sequel to her bestselling book. *The Power* cuts out the middleman. No longer do you need to climb upon the Universe's lap with a wish list. Simply express feelings of "love" for what you desire—cash, health, the telepathic powers of Aquaman—and it will be delivered to you. To assuage skeptics, the book is padded with deep quotes from such esteemed figures as Jesus Christ, Sophocles and the guy who draws *Dilbert*.

All you need to thrive in this age of economic upheaval is a cheery demeanour, Byrne writes. Hard work, dedication, a skill set: these are all still for losers. Money "sticks" only to those who are upbeat. "The moment you react negatively to a big bill, you give bad feelings, and most surely you will receive bigger bills." Got that? You don't get big bills because you spend foolishly. You get them because you're a grouchypants. To think: the whole financial meltdown could have been avoided if only the employees of Lehman Brothers had beat the Monday blues.

But *The Power* isn't all jolly adjectives and attitudes. There's math and science too.

The math: the book reveals exactly how upbeat you must be to get off the Universe's naughty list. "If you give just 51 per cent good thoughts, you have tipped the scales ... The love that comes back to you multiplies itself by attracting more love through the power of attraction." Translation: even a D-minus optimist is pretty much assured a happy ending. You have to love a Universe that grades on a bell curve.

The science: "The inside of your head is 80 per cent water!" Byrne declares. Why does this matter? Because "researchers" have found that "when water is exposed to positive words and feelings ... the structure of the water changes, making it perfectly harmonious." I have no idea what she's talking about either —but think of all we can accomplish with our harmonious brain water! We can live for hundreds of years if we just put our minds to it, Byrne says. Mortality is for sad sacks.

But be warned—life is not all easy money and marinated super-brains. The Universe hates a mope. "From the small irritation of a mosquito, to the bigger irritation of your car breaking down, all of [your] experiences are the law of attraction responding to your irritation." So mosquitoes bite only the crabby and my Volkswagen is at all times carefully monitoring my disposition. Noted.

Other revelations in *The Power*: nothing is dead, everything is alive, there's no such thing as time, and the Universe always knows where your car keys are. But mostly, the book is dedicated to its singular vision of how to confront modern problems.

Are you one of those negative Nancies who responds to lousy eyesight by wearing glasses? Dumb move, idiot. According to *The Power*, you can get 20/20 vision just by thinking, "I have perfect eyesight." If you're sick and not getting well, it's not because the cancer is ravaging your body—it's because you're not being optimistic hard enough. Gratitude alone can apparently make "failed kidneys regenerate, diseased hearts heal and tumors disappear." Why invest billions in health care when we can just write the Universe a thank-you card instead?

Need a job? Do *not* apply for one. That's a "desperate action" that announces your shortcomings to the Universe. Instead, do what "one man" did, according to Byrne. "He imagined his new office ... He imagined his work colleagues. He gave them names. He had conversations with them. He even tasted the tacos at lunch breaks." And then apparently out of the blue he got a job, allegedly! Learn from him and you can make the symptoms of clinical insanity work for you.

"One thing is certain," the author concludes. "We receive back what we give." If that's true, the Universe owes Rhonda Byrne a tremendous amount of baloney.

PART OF MOVING into the future is coming to terms with the past. And when it comes to the 1980s in particular, there's a lot of unfinished business. The air needs to be cleared. It's time to set the record straight once and for all by answering the question that has obsessed untold millions for more than a generation ...

Oliver Stone got studio heads brainstorming when he returned to his own 1980s' hit and created a sequel—*Wall Street 2: Money Never Sleeps*. Immediately, Hollywood began pondering sequels to other big films of the 1980s. What has become of some of the most famous characters of that era? And how will they have adapted to very different times?

Ferris Bueller's Day Off 3. Now pushing forty-five, our irreverent anti-hero is off on another madcap adventure—phoning in sick as a Starbucks barista and playing World of Warcraft while waiting for Sloane to get home from her job in porn. "Life comes at you pretty fast," he says later that night while reading his notice of mortgage default.

Footloose 2018. Searching for his place in the world, the son of Kevin Bacon's rebellious dancer leaves the big city and finds his way to a small, socially conservative Midwestern town. At first, the repressed locals aren't sure what to make of this brash interloper—but once they sense he is merely trying to get them to "loosen up," they beat him with a tire iron, fracture his shin bones and tell him to "limp on back to Jewtown." (This movie will be marketed as a feel-good comedy in red states and a Michael Moore documentary in blue states.)

When Harry Met Sally 2. Harry (Billy Crystal) and Sally (Meg Ryan), married now for twenty-five years, sit silently through an early dinner at an Applebee's in suburban New Jersey. For one loud moment, Sally appears to be reprising her famous fake orgasm scene but, no, it's just her acid reflux. Harry doesn't look up from his copy of *Auto Trader*.

Ghost 2. With Patrick Swayze's character out of the picture, Demi Moore is haunted by the ghost of her original face.

Hoosiers: Redux. Desperate to win the votes of the state's hard-core conservatives, an Indiana judge sentences Coach

Dale (Gene Hackman) to a six-year prison term for saying "I love you guys" to a group of half-naked teenaged boys.

E.T.: The Extra-Terrestrial 2. The beloved alien returns to Earth to renew one of the most legendary friendships in movie history—only to discover that the grown-up Elliott, forever shaped by the governmental incompetence he witnessed as a child, spends his nights patrolling Arizona's border with Mexico. Does E.T. have his papers? Will patriotism trump friendship? Most important: Will a "hard R" rating for graphic violence and waterboarding jeopardize the studio's ability to strike a merchandising deal with McDonald's?

Splash 2. Exiled from their underwater kingdom, Allen (Tom Hanks) and Madison (Daryl Hannah) lobby the state of New York to broaden the legal definition of marriage to include the union of one man and one mythological aquatic creature. This causes social upheaval, statewide protests and Sean Hannity's head to explode.

Gandhi 2020. In a timely sequel to the Ben Kingsley classic, a clone of young Mahatma Gandhi (Shia LaBeouf), grown by a mad British tycoon bent on owning copies of all the world's great men, serenely elucidates his philosophy of non-violent civil disobedience ... until they push him too far. That's when he activates his robot army. Michael Bay directs. Tag line: "An eye for an eye ends up making the whole world blind ... so let's get plucking!"

Tyler Perry's Driving Miss Daisy's Driver. Five words— Morgan Freeman in a dress.

The Breakfast Club 2. Frustration and anger bubble to the surface as this iconic cast of Brat Packers reunites to share the pain of leaving school, growing up and not being able to find steady acting work.

Do the Right Thing Again. Mookie (Spike Lee) teams up with Sal (Danny Aiello) to open a chain of pizzerias in post-racial America. It all goes great until Sal finds out Mookie treats women as equals.

Field of Dreams: Dream Harder. Shoeless Joe Jackson

returns once more from the afterlife only to discover that Ray's farm, foreclosed upon in the early 2000s, is now a Walmart. Still in his uniform, Shoeless Joe wanders through housewares, remarking on the timeless nature of baseball and the affordability of the George Foreman Grill (hello, product placement). An awkward moment ensues when Joe comes across Ray (Kevin Costner), now employed as the store's greeter. They pretend not to know each other.

OF COURSE, 2015 will go down as the year that the biggest sequels of all began arriving. Walt Disney Co. paid $4 billion for George Lucas's film company, and late 2015 was targeted as the start of its annual release of a *Star Wars* movie. Yes, every single year.

In spring 2014, a photo was published of the cast and creators of Episode VII. Filming was about to begin. This brought home the fact that:

a. This is actually happening.
b. The actors from the original trilogy are now super-old, so it's going to be great to see Luke Skywalker use the Jedi mind trick to keep kids off his space lawn.
c. George Lucas is really and truly not going to be involved.

This last point conjures mixed feelings. There's no denying the writing in *Star Wars* was pretty hokey. By the time Lucas got around to creating the prequels, his dialogue was so bad that one could feel the momentum building for a class-action suit filed by ears. But I'll admit it: I'm going to miss George's wooden way with words.

Every true *Star Wars* fan has his or her favourite "least favourite" bit of dialogue. Many focus on the love plot lines, with pronouncements like "I am haunted by the kiss you should never have given me." I, for one, am partial to a scene near the end of *Revenge of the Sith* (Episode III). Anakin and Obi-Wan are waging their epic lightsaber duel. As they clash, Kenobi tires to convince his former apprentice that the Emperor—to whom Anakin has pledged allegiance—is evil. Anakin responds by hollering: "From my point of view, it is the Jedi who are evil."

From my point of view?

To recap: Anakin is hurtling along a river of lava, fighting to the death with his best friend and mentor, and so consumed with rage that just moments earlier he almost killed his pregnant wife. And so naturally he chooses this moment to break out the William F. Buckley method of rebuttal. When Anakin's legs were subsequently cut off, I'm surprised he didn't yell: "From my point of view, OWWWWW!"

Anyway, deprived of new material from the master, the only way to fill the void is to imagine some famous scenes from movie history—had they been written by George Lucas:

- **Casablanca**

  RICK: We'll always have Paris. We lost it until you came to Casablanca. We got it back last night.

  ILSA: I love you, Rick.

  RICK: I wuv you *more*, Ilsa.

  ILSA: Our love is like the love that lovers feel when loving their lovers.

  RICK: I love that about our love!

  [CAPT. RENAULT shoots himself in the head.]

- **Jerry Maguire**

  JERRY: I love you. You complete me.

  DOROTHY: Had me at the juncture at which you entered the premises and commenced your discourse, you did.

- **To Have and Have Not**

  SLIM: You know how to whistle, don't you, Steve? You just create a small opening with your lips and then blow or suck air across your teeth, which affect the air's passage from, or into, the mouth, an orifice that subsequently acts, as a resonant chamber to enhance the resulting sound.

  [Cut to HUMPHREY BOGART fast asleep on a chair.]

- **Taxi Driver**

  TRAVIS: Yoosa tawkin' to meesa? Ex-queeze-me, but yoosa tawkin' to MEESA? Meesa tink yousa been maxi big wude. Yousa best be gettin' mooie-mooie scared, okeeday?
- **Citizen Kane**

  KANE: Gah, I am dying. For reasons I can't explain, dying is what I am doing. When I finish this next sentence—not this sentence, but the one that follows—I will be dead. Also: Rosebud.

  [He dies, dropping a snow globe he'd been holding in his hand.]

  KANE: That snow globe is symbolic!

  [He dies again.]

None of this answers the central question: Under Disney ownership, will the *Star Wars* episodes of the future suck? While waiting for the first Disney effort, I took a look ahead:

2015: Although many are eagerly anticipating J.J. Abrams's take on the series, some are apprehensive that he will introduce to the *Star Wars* universe the element of time travel—which would enable a middle-aged Luke Skywalker to encounter his younger self, his older self and, quite possibly, a very confused Spock. On the other hand, it could also bring together seven Yodas for the most backward-talking, ass-kicking climax in film history. Let's agree to let the time-travel thing slide, as long as Abrams uses the device to have two incarnations of Jar Jar Binks beat each other to death.

2018: The franchise is entrusted to other directors, beginning with Michael Bay—who opens his film in flashback with a fourteen-minute shot of a young Princess Leia (Megan Fox), clad in cut-off jeans, leaning over a landspeeder to tinker with its engine. On the radio we hear the sounds of Alderaan's best Aerosmith cover band.

Meanwhile, Shia LaBeouf is lending his frenetic acting style to the role of Luke: "Wait, what? A Jedi? A Jedi *knight*? You're joking. You must be joking! Whoa whoa whoa, this is a total misunderstanding, this isn't happening, what's happening can't be happening to me—to this person who I am! *Daaaaaaaad!*"

2020: A rift in the space-time continuum leaves citizens of the Galactic Republic suddenly vulnerable to encounters with a wide variety of officially licensed Disney characters, resulting in myriad story and marketing opportunities (mostly marketing opportunities). After all, aside from the merchandising potential, it's hard to justify the scene in which Lightning McQueen dresses up as a storm trooper.

The fun and vertically integrated cross-platform synergies begin with the Imperial fleet being mobilized to find Nemo. They continue through a thrilling adventure that takes moviegoers from Tatooine to Andy's bedroom, where the sinister plans of two Sith lords are foiled by Mr. Potato Head's angry eyebrows. Long story short, turns out it was Darth Vader who killed Bambi's mother.

2021: A movie every year gives filmmakers the opportunity to explore the rich backstories of minor characters from the *Star Wars* universe. This episode follows Admiral Ackbar, as a number of obvious things slowly dawn on him, prompting his delayed exclamation of surprise.

2022: Steven Spielberg takes the reins and suddenly *Star Wars* is in the Oscar conversation, with Meryl Streep as Leia, Daniel Day-Lewis as Han and Peter Dinklage as R2-D2, who may just be the most human of them all.

As this movie from the director of *Lincoln* begins, gridlock has engulfed the galactic congress. Increasingly, the universe is split into red and blue planets. As representatives gather to debate a bill that would require expanded background checks for the purchase of moon-sized super-weapons, a plucky Gungan senator—the son of Jar Jar—gives an emotional address: "Dellow feligates, whatta weesa needs to be okee-day is mooey stoppa dem Intergalactic Rifle Association lobbyists."

The legislation is scuttled, however, after the Grand Moff of the Empire testifies that he mostly uses the advanced weapons system of the Death Star to hunt space deer.

2024: Wrinkled and balding, his lightsaber dangling below his paunch, Luke Skywalker gets the gang back together to blow up one last Death Star. But they're in for a surprise when they find that the evil Emperor—who appeared to plummet to his death in Episode VI, and again in Episodes IX, XII and XVI (not to mention the climax of Episode XVIII, in which it was revealed his cholesterol is off the charts)—is somehow ... *alive* (?!). All hope for the galaxy seems lost until Luke, the turn signal blinking on his X-wing fighter, directs a proton torpedo through a hole no larger than the screenwriter's imagination.

In other developments, Han Solo spends the entire movie saying, "I'm too old for this shit"—which proves to be accurate when he dies from a massive stroke. Han's death is mourned by loyal companion Chewbacca, who, in his sorrow, can barely finish eating his old friend. In a touching denouement, C-3PO comes out as robogay.

2025: This one's probably going to be a musical. Deal with it.

Jack and Diane 2017

Little ditty 'bout Jack and Diane,
Two American folks going broke in the heartland.
Jack never was a football star,
Diane got pregnant back seat of Jackie's car.

Cookin' up chili dogs inside the Tastee-Freez
Diane says, "It's all I can get, despite my two degrees."
Jackie says, "Hey, Diane, let's run off behind that shady tree,
Hide away from that repo man who's coming for me."

And Jackie say:
Oh yeah, life went on
Right up until our credit was gone.
Oh yeah, I say life went on
Right up until our credit was gone.

Jackie sits back, reflects his thoughts for a moment,
Scratches his head and looks at Diane's pay.
"Well, you know, Diane, what's this here big fat zero?"
Diane says, "Baby, that's our 401(k)."

Jackie say:
Oh yeah, life was great
Until the lapse of our teaser rate
Oh yeah, I said life had hope
Until all three of our Visas maxed out.

Let the market drop,
Let it crash,
Let your zero-down mortgage bite you
In the ass,
Hold off foreclosure as long as you can,
Changes come around real soon make you sleep in a van.

Little ditty 'bout Jack and Diane,
Two American folks doin' the best they can.

Tough Question: *What would it take for a future winner of People's Sexiest Man Alive title to go down in history as the very sexiest Sexiest Man Alive ever?*

It's not as easy as it looks. There's a big fuss every November when *People* magazine names its Sexiest Man Alive. Then the hype fades and the hard work begins. Upon being sworn into office, each new Sexiest Man has only a year to implement his agenda to advance sexiness at home and abroad—while fighting to protect Americans from the ever-present threats to sexiness posed by sideburns and gravy. It's a tall order.

This is a position that has been held by Brad Pitt (twice), Jude Law (once) and Nick Nolte (possibly an accounting error of some kind). All came to power hoping to build a sexier world. Too often, their ambition wilted under the pressures of the office.

In 2010, for instance, Ryan Reynolds's term as Sexiest Man Alive began with great promise. The actor stood before Americans and vowed to deliver "hope," "change" and "buttocks you could bounce a nickel off." In a savvy nod to the past, Reynolds embarked on a tour of America's sexiest historical sites—including the birthplace of Tom Selleck's moustache and the non-descript diner where George Clooney first winked.

But Reynolds's perceived reluctance to put in maximum effort—he was rumoured to pout sexily for as little as three hours a day—was his undoing. Within months, sexy rivals were working to undermine his administration: raising funds, filming attack ads ("Reynolds: soft on camouflage fleece!") and putting on their shirts, so as to be better able to sexily remove them.

The abrupt fall from grace of Ryan Reynolds reminded observers of the ill-fated reign of 1999 Sexiest Man Alive Richard Gere. Despite being the author of the seminal *Contract with America's Pectorals*, Gere saw his popularity nosedive after he admitted on cnn's *The Sexuation Room* to still owning a pair of parachute pants.

Bradley Cooper, star of *The Hangover* movies, met a similar fate in 2011. In the early days of his term, he was widely praised for winning bipartisan support to implement a National Mullet Registry. Pundits were further impressed when he succeeded in imposing a three-day waiting period on the acquisition of a Baconator.

But Cooper's administration was buffeted by crisis when TMZ.com published an embarrassing photo in which he, as a nine-year-old boy, wore a fanny pack. By the end of his term, opinion surveys indicated there hadn't been a Sexiest Man Alive so unpopular since 2001, when Pierce Brosnan was spotted in public in an acrylic sweater.

As the 2013 Sexiest Man Alive, Adam Levine managed to restore dignity, professionalism and tank tops to the office. Though he too suffered moments of embarrassment. Levine is still living down his interview with Katie Couric, during which he could not name a single brand of skin bronzer.

The evidence is clear: serving as Sexiest Man Alive is one of the toughest jobs in the United States. The gulf has increased between the sexiest Americans and those who share most of their DNA with a hoagie. According to statistics from the Organization for Seduction Development, a full 90 percent of American sexiness is now controlled by just 2 percent of the population. It would take a typical family of four a full twenty-five years to achieve the sexiness of a single hair flip by Beyoncé. And yet the fit and attractive continue to press for deeper tax breaks on broccolini and flattering lighting.

But there's still reason to believe that *People*'s Sexiest Man Alive can deliver on his message of hope. Sexy, sexy hope.

Where to begin?

Let me first state my credentials. I was chief of staff to Sexiest Man Alive 1987 Harry Hamlin. I served in the administrations of Mark Harmon, Denzel Washington and, briefly, Ben Affleck—until I resigned in a dispute over sideburn length.

The next Sexiest Man Alive needs to make a statement. He needs to be bold. A good first move would be to declare Vince Vaughn's torso a sexiness disaster area. He should build on that by signing into law the controversial bill banning the sale of sweatpants and chalupas.

And he should scale back his international pursuits: *People* readers don't want to know what he's doing to reduce suffering for those in Africa—they want to know what he's doing to reduce suffering among people who are looking at Jack Black. It wouldn't hurt to do all this while wearing short shorts.

Take it from one who knows: achieving success as Sexiest Man Alive comes down to the first hundred days in office. Here's a detailed plan of action that will set the next Sexiest Man Alive on the course to becoming the sexiest Sexiest Man Ever:

Day 1: Instruct your staff that you shall henceforth respond only to the appellation "Your Sexcellency."

Day 2: It's important to select the right Vice-Sexiest Man Alive. You want someone shares your perspective on the issues—pro-stubble, anti-unibrow—but a man whose sexiness is not quite as high-octane, universally admired and potentially fatal to heterosexual women as your own. It's all about balance. And sexiness.

Day 5: Deliver your inspiring inaugural address while emerging from a swimming pool in slow motion.

Day 11: Convene the first meeting of your Sexiest Man Alive cabinet, including Secretary of Shirtlessness (Fabio) and Secretary of Doing Secretaries (Tiger Woods).

Day 15: Announce a national mutton-chop amnesty: turn in your old, unsexy facial hair and get $100.

Days 27–29: Pose heroically in front of a wind machine while wearing a billowy white shirt.

Day 31: "Spontaneous" touching of a homely person.

Day 38: Announce your much-anticipated "War on Back Hair." Measures should include the legalization of vigilante electrolysis and a naval blockade of Burt Reynolds's house.

Day 43: While riding on Hair Force One (christened by Patrick Swayze, SMA 1991), declare "Take Your Aesthetician to Work" Day.

Day 52: Introduce a constitutional amendment compelling *Men's Health* magazine to tout the "secret to a flat stomach" on the cover of every issue, instead of just 97 percent of issues.

Day 55: Host a state dinner with Canada's Sexiest Man Alive 1973–2007, Lloyd Robertson. On the menu: protein shakes and a threesome.

Day 65: Reveal your plan for campaign reform. Emphasize the importance of the institution of Sexiest Man Alive. Proposed quote: "We must ensure this hallowed office is not sullied by crass tactics, such as mudslinging, when it should be venerated by noble pursuits, such as mud wrestling."

Day 69: Heh, heh. Sixty-nine. (Tell them to hold your calls.)

Day 88: Become the first world leader to appear on *Meet the Press* without pants. (Well, first since Clinton.)

Day 94: Lobby the G8 to pass a draft resolution officially recognizing that you are, as a matter of empirical fact, too sexy for your shirt.

Day 100: Stare into a mirror for five hours. Like what you see.

REASON NO. 8: POLITICS IN THE UNITED STATES

Part of predicting the future is understanding the past. The several years before the book you're holding went to press were tumultuous in American politics, reshaping the partisan landscape and setting the stage for a 2016 campaign that was likely to be more contentious, more divisive and more Clintony than ever before.

Let's reflect on some of the key moments from the Obama presidency—and look for the clues they offer to the coming years of partisan rancour and Joe Biden continuing to say ridiculous things.

ON JANUARY 20, 2009, *Barack Obama was inaugurated as the forty-fourth president of the United States. Later that day, a quiet ritual unfolded as he arrived at the White House to find a welcome letter from George W. Bush on the Oval Office desk.*

Dear New Guy:

So this morning's newspaper tells me it's time to move out. Also, that Marmaduke has got himself into another spot of mischief. Ha ha. Will that dog ever learn? Doesn't look like it, but I'll keep you up to date.

Anyway, they tell me it's a tradition for the outcoming president to leave a letter of advice for the ingoing president. All I got from Clinton was a stack of *Hustler*, but fine.

Key things to know (in order):

- Kim Jong-il. Big-time screwy.
- Ahmadinejad. Ditto.
- Steve from Canada (the country to the above of us). An okay guy in small doses. Sensitive about the hair.
- The White House. Sometimes there are muffins. The ones with an apple slice on top are apple muffins.
- Don't massage the German lady president. She gets pretty uppity about it.
- It's surprisingly hard to throw a spiral with the nuclear football.
- You can ask for whatever you want to eat, and the Constitution says the chef has to make it.
- If your vice-president shoots someone in the face, it was probably an accident the first couple times—but then you start to wonder.
- Nicknames: very important. Everybody needs one. If they're taller than 5 foot 10, call 'em Stretch. If they're shorter than 5 foot 6, call 'em Stretch, but in a way that's ironical. Might help to wink when you say it. Everyone else: just put a "yee" sound in there. Rummy, Brownie, Condi. Now here's where it gets tricky. If the name already ends with a "yee" sound, you gotta remove it—like with Kof at the UN or Tone over in England. Don't worry—it gets easier after six months or so. Then they can all stop wearing those "Hello, My Name Is ..." stickers.

Got to be honest with you, Stretch: it feels kinda weird to not be The Decider anymore. I mean, I'll still be deciding things but not things of globalness. More like personal things like where to build my library and when to ask my Dad why he keeps muttering, "Well, there's still Jeb, I guess."

I've had some time in the last few days to look back and re-flectify. And you know what? I have an issue with all these polls saying I'm the worst president ever. Really? Worse than the evil one from 24? I question that.

Frankly, I never understood why people were so critical. Take the whole Osama thing. Bin Laden once said: "Death is better than living on this earth with the unbelievers among us." And who spent a lot of his presidency denying bin Laden death and forcing him to continue living as a free man? Bingo. Yours sincerely. Although, to be fair, I was wrong in repeatedly stating that bin Laden could run but not hide. Good hider, it turns out. *Great* hider.

Sometimes I wish I could just shout "Olly olly oxen free" and he'd come out. (Tried it. Nothing.)

Here's the thing I didn't know about being president: everyone gets mad at you if you make the slightest mistake. Like the war. Or the other war. The financial meltdown. Hurricane Katrina. Waterboarding. How was I supposed to know about things like collateralized debt obligations mortgages, emergency preparedness and basic human rights? Some people are even mad at me about Bernie Madoff and his Potsie scheme. Like I could have stopped him if The Fonz couldn't!

Here's a final tip for you: I didn't read things like magazines, or blogs, or intelligence reports—anything with words, really. It's my belief that a president must have empathy. That allows him to see into the souls of his opponents. Sorta like that brunette who was making it with Riker on the Enterprise until she went looking for strange with the Klingon.

To conclusify, it's a pretty thankless job being in charge. Very isolating and lonely. Or so Mr. Cheney tells me. He comes with the house, by the way. I'd take him with us but we just can't risk exposing him to daylight.

New guy: I truly believe that America is the greatest nation in all of history—better than Britain or Rome or even Mordor. So good luck with being president and maybe one day we'll be on that mountain together. (The one with the faces.)

Well, that's about it. Oh yeah, I was supposed to mention: UFOs are real, the moon landings were faked and Kennedy was killed by a robot from the future.

Sincerely,
George
PS: Don't make the same mistake I did. Pardon Heather
Locklear now.

ON FEBRUARY 19, 2009, only a month into his presidency, Barack
Obama visited Canada to meet with Prime Minister Stephen Harp-
er. As with all such trips, it was meticulously planned by the State
Department.

Briefing Notes for President Barack Obama

Visit to Canada: February 2009

The Country: Our northern neighbour, Canada ranks 2nd in the
world in total area, 4th in total land area and 314th among favourite spring break destinations (ahead of "Greenland" and
just behind "the basement").
Canada's population density—3.5 inhabitants per square
kilometre—is among the lowest in the world, but crowded
enough when you consider that one of those inhabitants used
to be Howie Mandel.

System of Government: Canada is a parliamentary democracy
and a constitutional monarchy. At one time a British colony,
Canada asserted its political autonomy in 1982 after just 125
years of thinking it through really, really carefully. Britain,
which by then had completely forgotten about the whole "Canada" thing, ultimately agreed to grant independence, though
mostly to stop Pierre Trudeau from hitting on the Queen.

Electoral System: Canada's prime minister is obligated by law to
respect a fixed date for federal elections, unless he meets the
legal requirement of "not feeling like it." Meanwhile, convention dictates that upon losing the "confidence" of the House of
Commons, the prime minister must either cede power or flee
girlishly to the protective bosom of the Governor General, who

has a formidable array of powers that baffle and confound us. She may be some kind of witch.

The Prime Minister: Stephen Joseph Harper, age forty-nine. He's known as "Steve" among people who don't care that he hates to be called Steve. Yes, the hair is real.

Recent Political History: In the fall of 2008, Prime Minister Harper won re-election with what's known as a minority—or "sissy"—government. So far as we can determine, this means he must surrender custody of the nation on Wednesday nights and every other weekend. In 2011, Harper was re-elected with a majority—or "real"—government.

Political Environment: Mr. President, while it is true that you maintain high popularity levels among Canadians, history suggests that American leaders don't always get a smooth ride when spending time in Canada. Consider the experiences of Ronald Reagan, George W. Bush and Michael Ignatieff.

Arrival: Because this is not an official state visit, there will be no formal military band to greet you at the airport. Respecting custom, the prime minster will instead confer a more informal Canadian airport greeting—sending the foreign affairs minister to circle the lot outside the arrivals level until you come out of the terminal. You're instructed to "just give 'im a wave." The $5 attached to this file should cover your share of the gas money.

The Capital: Your brief visit to Canada will take place entirely within the city of Ottawa, one of the world's northernmost capitals and a metropolis renowned throughout Canada for its two or three restaurants that now stay open past seven o'clock. Ottawa boasts a professional hockey team and many working stoplights.

Climate: Arse-numbing.

National Symbols: The beaver, the common loon, the playoff beard.

Language: Canada is officially designated a bilingual country, meaning you can easily get by speaking either French or English in every part of the land except almost all of it.

Economy: Over centuries, Canada progressed from a reliance on the fur trade to a rich and diversified economy—but thanks to Wall Street it's now on its way back. Yesterday, shares in Black-Berry closed down slightly at 4½ pelts.

Sensitivities: The "Buy American" provision of our stimulus bill has caused significant concern in Canada, where business leaders fear that protectionist measures could decimate industries devoted to the production and export of iron, steel and film comedians. (The Canadian government is said to be preparing draconian retaliatory legislation: Bill C-77, An Act to Force Them to Keep Mike Myers.)

Timing of Visit: You will be arriving in Canada just after Flag Day, on which Canada's prime minister commemorates his nation's adoption of a post-colonial flag by selecting one lucky countryman to strangle in broad daylight. Your visit will also coincide with the conclusion of a local festival known as Winterlude, the city's annual celebration of windburn.

Important Notes:

- Canada is considered part of the G8, though kind of like the tambourine player is considered part of the band.
- Thanks to the combined efforts of US and Canadian governments, the public remains blissfully unaware that at least four American thespians have been eaten during tragic overacting mishaps involving William Shatner.
- Canadian money is hilarious.

The 2012 US Election Campaign

In Canada, national political campaigns are famously brief. We begin by pretty much ignoring the whole thing for a few weeks. Then there's a debate, a little yelling, maybe some pointing, every leader buys a box of Timbits and, boom, suddenly it's election day.

But in the United States, presidential campaigns last longer than all pregnancies and most wars. Even before the 2008 campaign had ended, candidates were laying the groundwork for 2012, engaging in such unsavoury practices as raising money and visiting Iowa. What follows is a chronicle of sorts of the 2012 US presidential campaign.

This week's debate among Republican candidates for the US presidency was sponsored by Tea Party Express, which sounds like something you'd find next to the Orange Julius but is in fact an umbrella organization for grassroots groups dedicated to the pursuit of low taxes, small government and—to judge from the debate audience—$6 haircuts.

Broadcast on CNN, the debate began with a display of the gravitas we've come to expect from American politics—a snazzy video montage in which each candidate was assigned a cute nickname. Michele Bachmann was introduced as The Firebrand. Newt Gingrich? The Big Thinker! One immediately lamented the absence of Sarah Palin, if only to discover which nickname she'd have been given. (The Little Thinker?)

The frontrunner in the Republican field is Rick Perry, who has the look of a man who's just returned from hoodwinking J.R. Ewing in an oil deal. The Texas governor scored big with his opening line, in which he vowed to "make Washington, DC, as inconsequential in your life as I can." He should consider hooking up with a specialist in making things inconsequential, such as the person who wrote the final four seasons of *Entourage*.

Another of the candidates, Herman Cain, is a former CEO of the Godfather's Pizza chain. He began by declaring: "I believe that America has become a nation of crises. That's why I want to be president." Note his refusal to get boxed into a corner as being for or against crises. Pretty savvy for a political novice.

Each of the eight candidates assailed Barack Obama for the grim state of the US economy. But how would they fix it? Mitt Romney touted a seven-point plan for a stronger economy, which includes balancing the budget, ensuring the creation of "fantastic human capital" and achieving energy security. So check off all those boxes and the economic rebound should kick in by Romney's seventeenth term as president. *Vote Mitt and the twenty-third century shall be ours!*

Alas, the pizza guy quickly trumped Romney's seven-point plan with his "9-9-9" plan, which (a) has more numbers, and is therefore better, and (b) includes a flat 9 percent business tax, personal income tax and national sales tax. The most impressive part is the CEO's pledge to get all required legislation through Congress in thirty minutes or it's free.

Meanwhile, Bachmann made her pitch to the Tea Partiers by reminding them that she's "a person that's had feet in the private sector and a foot in the federal government." Add it up and that's three feet for America. Your move, Rick Perry.

The most delightful of the participants was the former governor of Utah, Jon Huntsman, who was the only candidate with sufficient gumption and insufficient instincts to drop a Kurt Cobain joke on the Tea Partiers. The reference went so far over their heads that it burned up on re-entry. A Huntsman victory at next year's Republican convention is unlikely, which is a shame because he has a way with words. Specifically, he has a way of making words sound stupid. "Well, let me just say about workers," he interjected at one point. "This country needs more workers. Can we say that?" He went on to describe the national debt as a voracious, unstoppable zombie. "It's going to eat, eat, eat alive this country!"

Fear not the Killer Debt Zombie, America! Rick Santorum will defend you. The former senator referenced his own personal courage an amazing six times in the span of a one-minute answer. "You folks want someone with courage?" he asked. "I've got a track record of courage." Pollsters agree that Santorum would be the frontrunner if the main crisis facing America was getting that spider out of the kitchen.

What's deeply enjoyable about this phase of the US political cycle is the flagrant manner in which candidates ignore the reality of the modern American presidency. Past administrations have demonstrated that a new president has a brief window in which to do a little something before his agenda is smothered by partisan wrangling. But the Republican candidates are dreaming big.

Gingrich said he'd find the money to reform Social Security in a single stroke—all he needs to do is reduce the unemployment rate to 4 percent from 9 percent. (Oh, is that all?) Later, Romney went further by vowing to quickly "reform Medicare and reform Medicaid and reform Social Security."

And then on Tuesday ...

—*September 2011*

AS REPUBLICANS MOVE closer to choosing a presidential nominee, more and more Americans find themselves asking that old chestnut of a question: If I could sit down in a bar and have a beer with any of the candidates, why wouldn't I stay home instead?

This past week saw yet another televised debate for the handful of hopefuls who remain, including Rick Santorum, who looks like he received his share of wedgies as a boy; Mitt Romney, who looks like he delivered a few; and Ron Paul, who kind of resembles one.

In their midst, the new Man to Beat: Newt Gingrich, a politician that charisma forgot, but only after punching him in the belly and running off with his wallet and his capacity to feel. Newt stole the hearts of Republicans in South Carolina—easy for him because to judge from all visual evidence, he used to be the Hamburglar—and now he's fixing to do the same in Florida.

The challenge? Gingrich is trying to win the nomination of America's self-proclaimed real family values party despite having cheated on at least one wife and divorced two. Also, he is unpleasant.

(And there's a Canadian angle! Gingrich has spoken fondly of our prime minister—but there's an obvious conflict of interest in that both men buy their hair from the same factory.)

The latest debate left one thing beyond doubt: Newt would be the best Trivial Pursuit president ever. He's like Wikipedia but with weird fat baby hands. While avoiding some question or other, Gingrich went off on a tangent about beet sugar versus cane sugar and how "fascinating" the rivalry is. For a fleeting moment, a fractured nation was united in sympathy for all three Mrs. Gingriches and those long decades of dinner-table conversation.

> NEWT: Pass the salt. Curious thing about salt: in 1635, a chemist outside Oslo found that if you tweak the chemical formulation for ...
> [WIFE NO. 1 *suffocates self in mashed potatoes.*]

By now we're getting to know the candidates' idiosyncrasies. For instance, when Mitt Romney is in trouble during a debate, he reminds everyone that he ran the Salt Lake Olympics. He's probably aiming to mine a patriotic vein but it usually comes off as dodging.

> QUESTION: Governor Romney, will you release more than two years of your income tax returns?
> ANSWER: Biathlon!

Still, you can see why it's more fun for Romney to reminisce about luge than endure another barrage of criticism for the small sin of changing every view he's held on pretty much every issue that's important to conservatives. It's gotten to the point where Mitt is now skilled enough to execute a flip-flop within the confines of a single sentence. "We're a great nation," Romney said during the debate, "but a great nation doesn't have so many people suffering." Do you hear me, America: we're a great nation and also we are not a great nation! I HAVE CORNERED ALL SIDES IN THIS DEBATE!

Gingrich has his own baggage, which he forces a poor child to carry around so the kid learns the work ethic. (I'm kidding, of course. Gingrich would actually prefer that inner-city kids work as janitors in schools so they don't grow up all lazy and welfarey.) The former Speaker's rivals take delight in casually mentioning how long they've been married to their wives. Newt typically responds by shifting to the subject with which he's most comfortable: Newt.

In a mesmerizing run during the Florida debate, Gingrich took credit for an array of accomplishments, including the election of Ronald Reagan, America's return to prosperity in the 1980s and, if I'm not mistaken, all three good REO Speedwagon songs. The Soviet Empire grew menacing and Newt destroyed it! A deficit grew large and Newt eliminated it! A toenail grew long and Newt clipped it!

Toward the end of the debate, Gingrich explained his philosophy of attracting voters—and it was a little awkward because frankly it felt like the same thing he'd say to a pretty lady in a bar in an effort to seal the deal at 1:30 AM. "Don't be for me," he said, because being "for" someone is superficial. Then he cooed: "Be with me."

America, Newt Gingrich is trying to hook up with you. How's he going to break it to the missus this time?

—*January 2012*

AS A CANDIDATE, Mitt Romney has several weaknesses. He says a lot of dumb things. He has a history of flip-flopping on the issues. He makes the Grey Poupon guy seem like an average Joe.

But Mitt's main political liability may wind up being a decision he made thirty years ago—to coax the family dog into its crate, strap the pooch to the roof of the family station wagon and head out from Boston on a twelve-hour drive to the Romney summer home in Ontario.

Along the way, Seamus the Irish setter developed what the media have elegantly described as "intestinal distress," which manifested in a hydrous, mephitic substance that—aw, enough elegance, the diarrhea pretty much coated the car windows, okay? Cool-headed Mitt pulled into a gas station, borrowed a hose, cleaned up the car, cleaned off the dog and put him back up top for the final leg of the journey.

The story was recounted by Romney's friends as an example of the man's calm under crisis. And frankly, you can see why they thought it would be interpreted positively: cleaning up other people's shit is pretty much all the president does these days.

Alas, the story of Seamus's rooftop ride has become a political burden. Gail Collins of the *New York Times* shoehorns it into every political column. An organization called Dogs Against Romney has more than fifty thousand Facebook supporters. There's even a satirical book, *Dog on the Roof!*

In mounting a defence, Romney insisted that Seamus enjoyed being on the roof because the dog "liked fresh air." And hey, if a dog likes fresh air, imagine how much he'd enjoy the kind that comes at him at 120 km/h loaded with bugs.

(Barack Obama has canine baggage as well, having acknowledged that he ate dog meat as a child in Jakarta. But Americans are forgiving because he was a boy at the time and also because many of them don't know what a "Jakarta" is.)

The Seamus saga has been described as a "character-illuminating anecdote." Combined with another story from Mitt's past—a bunch of school chums held down a gay classmate while Romney cut off some of the boy's "longish, blond hair"—it basically guarantees that future presidential candidates will need to hire campaign staff at puberty to head off potentially damaging anecdotes from youth and early adulthood.

TEENAGER: I'm going to Dairy Queen.

STRATEGIST: And have the voters of 2048 think you supported the monarchy? I THINK NOT.

As the election draws nearer, the Seamus anecdote is gaining negative traction. Here are three ways for Romney to address it directly:

1. Own it: Embrace the probability that anyone who'll vote against him because of Seamus was never likely to vote *for* him. So have some fun with it, like Sarah Palin did with "Drill, baby, drill," and Dick Cheney did with shooting guys in the face.

Put a doghouse on top of the Romney campaign bus. Point out that over the years plenty of animals have enjoyed riding on top of vehicles—Teen Wolf, for instance. The point is that Romney can reclaim and repurpose the image of the rooftop rider. Potential slogan: "You may have to ride up top, America, but Mitt Romney will get you there!"

2. Enlist third-party validators: Romney could cajole volunteers to ride in a small box on top of a car and say it's not so bad. Maybe start with reporters who covered the dying days of the Newt Gingrich campaign—compared to that ordeal, a dozen hours of relentless windswept terror sounds like a blast.

3. Go negative on Seamus: It's not easy to assail the character of a deceased family pet—or it wasn't until the introduction of super PACs, which can funnel unlimited funds into ruthless political advertising.

Sinister music. A narrator reads in baritone.
Seamus the dog. He claimed to be man's best friend. But Seamus pooped all over this nice man's car.
[Photo: Sad Mitt Romney.]
You know who else was known to poop? Hitler. Seamus the Irish setter: he was pretty much dog Hitler.
[Photo: Seamus with a Hitler moustache.]
Bad dog, Seamus. Bad dog.

—*May 2012*

PERHAPS YOU'VE BEEN following the presidential race closely for the past many months. Good for you. You probably have vague memories of Michele Bachmann, Rick Perry and that weird pizza guy who kept screaming the number "nine" at everyone. You may even have succeeded in banishing all mental images related to Newt Gingrich's yearning for an open marriage. If that's true, I feel kind of bad for having just mentioned it. The open marriage, I mean. The one that would have freed Gingrich to have intimate relations with various ladies while not wearing any—ah, I see now that I'm only making matters worse.

Anyway, with Republicans preparing to gather for their national convention, this is a good time for the rest of us to get caught up on where things stand in American politics.

As you may recall, the current president is a Democrat by the name of Barack Obama. He killed Osama bin Laden— not personally, but (the way he tells it) pretty much. When not killing bin Laden, which he totally did by the way, President Obama passed a law that ensures a modicum of health coverage to everyone except Osama bin Laden, who is dead because Barack Obama killed him.

The Republicans have responded by selecting as their nominee one Willard Mitt Romney, who, had he been in office, would have killed Osama bin Laden even deader.

Romney looks like America's idea of a president. But he often sounds like America's idea of an eccentric uncle. Travelling in Michigan, Romney repeatedly made reference to his belief that trees in the state are "the right height." It's possible Romney was trying to evoke a timeless image from nature to symbolize American exceptionalism in an age of global volatility. He may also have been high.

Or maybe that's just Mitt Romney. Even when he says normal things, they can come out sounding a little unusual. This week he hailed the success of NASA's rover by boasting to a rally: "We just landed on Mars and took a good look at what's going on there!" He made it sound as though Curiosity was scoping out the chicks down at Applebee's.

Romney has also been prone to the political gaffe. This past weekend, he introduced his running mate—Paul Ryan, a young congressman with the hairline of Count Chocula and the ideological flexibility of Count Dooku—by describing him as "the next president of the United States." Wolf Blitzer almost wet himself over that one.

By the way, the selection of Ryan generated the following statement from Obama: "Congressman [Paul] Ryan is a decent man, he is a family man, he is an articulate spokesman for [Mitt] Romney's vision. But it's a vision that I fundamentally disagree with."

This is a rather toothless version of a classic and always enjoyable form of political attack: the Ol' Switcheroo. Although variations exist, the architecture is usually the same:

1. A nice thing.
2. Another nice thing.
3. Not a nice thing.

It's basically a way of attempting to present yourself as reasonable and decent while not passing up a chance to remind voters that your opponent, given the opportunity, would suffocate the American Dream in its sleep just to steal its pyjamas.

Until and unless the independent US voter sours on the Republican vice-presidential nominee, this is a form of criticism you will continue to see from Democrats, many of whom apparently like Ryan despite his hard-right views. In particular, I can imagine Joe Biden giving it a go: "Paul Ryan is a good man, a great man, a beautiful Adonis of a man with whom, if I were even a little bit gay, I would totally make out. But if Paul Ryan becomes vice-president, he and Mitt Romney will not only dismantle Medicare and punish the poor with spankings; they will also shred the very fabric of the space-time continuum. Still, great guy."

History suggests it should be fairly easy to defeat a sitting president who has presided over a country that has endured economic malaise, high unemployment and two new Maroon 5 albums. But Romney is behind in the polls. According to surveys, two-thirds of Americans think he cares more about the rich than the middle class. Which is weird because

Romney relates to the middle class: there's no class he's fired more of.

There's still time for Romney–Ryan, of course. The debates are yet to come. The Republican ticket is backed by several super PACs that will raise and spend massive amounts of money. And Romney will likely get a boost from his party's convention, assuming they find room for him to give a speech amid all the references to Ronald Reagan.

But there are only eleven weeks until Election Day. In America, they call that the home stretch. Emotions are high. At a rally this week in Wisconsin, his home state, Paul Ryan reacted to the enthusiastic welcome by openly crying onstage. At the sight of Ryan weeping, Romney himself began crying. This made his wife, Ann Romney, burst into tears. *All of this actually happened.*

What is it with Republicans? House Speaker John Boehner: crier. Pundit Glenn Beck: crier. Romney and Ryan: criers. Your country is glad you love her, boys, but come on—you're soaking America's freedom blouse.

—August 2012

The Republican National Convention

Tampa, FLA
August 2012
Day One

2:02 PM ET The Republican National Convention begins its Tuesday session with the presentation of colours, followed by the recitation of the Pledge of Allegiance, followed by the national anthem (performed by a "nationally recognized singer!"), followed by the invocation. Delegates actually cheer *during* the prayer. "Dear God, bless Mitt Romney and—" *Wooooooo! Yaaaaaa! FREEEEEEE BIRD!!!!!!* Some housekeeping matters ensue—and then a musical interlude by the house band, led by that G.E. Smith guy who used to be on *Saturday Night Live*. In the audience, an Ann Coulter lookalike dances amid a sea of white hair and white skin.

2:26 Reince Priebus, the Republican National Committee chairman, gestures to two debt clocks that have been installed in the Tampa Bay Times Forum. One shows the many trillions in total national debt. The other chronicles how much debt has been accumulated since the start of the convention. Then, using simple math, Priebus demonstrates once and for all how further tax cuts for the richest Americans would result in America's debt load being reduced. (Kidding. For some unknown reason he did not do that.)

2:28 Chairman Priebus, which sounds like a *Star Wars* character or a really high-end hybrid (The 2013 Chairman Priebus: Comfort With Conscience!), characterizes Mitt Romney and Paul Ryan as "America's comeback team." But then what are we going to call a reunited Robert Pattinson and Kristen Stewart?

2:29 Priebus assails Barack Obama's lack of business experience: "He hasn't even run a garage sale or seen the inside of a lemonade stand." Wait—the *inside* of a lemonade stand? They sure must have some really elaborate lemonade stands back in Priebus's home of Wisconsin! Big-box lemonade stands where you can go inside, stretch your legs and really get your 50 cents' worth.

> LITTLE BOY: Uncle Reince, why aren't more people buying my lemonade?
>
> UNCLE REINCE: You don't have enough square footage, kid. And you can trust me on this—I've seen the inside of a lot of lemonade stands.

2:32 RNC co-chair Sharon Day takes the stage to Holler Some Things. She hollers that "unaccountable czars"—the worst kind of czars, if you ask me—are making and enforcing policies on American citizens. She hollers that Barack Obama threatens the very existence of American liberty. She extra-hollers that this is the most important election in American history. Got that? Most. Important. Ever. SUCK IT, LINCOLN.

2:53 Factoid: When American political figures aspire to eloquence, it's never just "the United States." It's always "the United States of America." Or, better still, "The. United States. Of America."

3:20 A Republican senatorial candidate says that he and Mitt Romney share a defining belief—that "our children are owed a better future." Why? No one ever explains why. A decent future? I guess we should do our best. But why do we owe them a *better* future? If we've got ideas that will make things better and make everyone more prosperous, *I say we do that shit NOW.* Then *we'll* get the benefits. It's all there in my campaign slogan: "Children are their own future."

3:53 The mayor of Oklahoma City comes out to say that the wife of vice-presidential candidate Paul Ryan was born in Oklahoma. This follows the old adage about speech-making: always open with an anecdote that not one person on God's earth could give a shit about. Tragically, the mayor waits until the end of his address to mention that Oklahoma City is "more walkable" than ever. YOU DO NOT BURY THAT KIND OF GOLD, BUDDY.

4:13 Listen, I'm as big a fan of hyperbole and exaggeration as anyone, but come on: The "great state" of Kentucky?

4:31 Hey, just FYI, if you're looking for a white guy I think I saw him on the stage at the Republican National Convention.

5:02 John Boehner, the Speaker of the House, tears up as Mitt Romney is formally nominated for president of the United States. Moments later he tears up when he discovers the backstage catering table is out of Diet Sprite.

9:15 The thing I love and regret and admire and fear most about American politics is the sheer joy and utter shamelessness with which political operatives take the remarks of their opponents wholly out of context. This is true of both parties. The Republicans crafted today's schedule around the theme of We Built It—a response to the rather disingenuous claim that Barack Obama once flatly declared that American entrepreneurs had nothing to do with their own success. When they played the audio of the president's "damning quote" over a video segment, you could hear that the words had been cut up and shifted around. The excerpt had had more work done on it than a forty-year-old actress.

But an even bolder flight from context was put on display just now: the playing of a clip of Obama saying, "Along the road to recovery, there will be bumps in the road"—followed by a video montage in which hard-working Americans solemnly declare, "I am an American, not a bump in the road." Yes, that's EXACTLY what Obama meant: that Americans themselves were the bumps in the road ... that the recovery would more quickly gain momentum if only there weren't any people around to slow it down with their big fat stupid bodies. I think we're one convention, maybe two, away from strategists on both sides just saying: "Screw it: we're making shit up from scratch. Jeb Bush? Cannibal. Go with it."

9:28 Rick Santorum makes an appearance to declare: "I shook the hand of the American Dream and it has a strong grip." Wait— the American Dream has actual hands?? Does it have *only* hands, like a pair of Things from *The Addams Family*? Because if so, that's a creepy dream. Santorum goes on to describe and mention various hands, and certain special hands, and military hands, and disabled hands, and Republican hands, and other hands that his own hands had touched. This was all meant to be profound but mostly it just made me want to give Rick Santorum some Purell. He's like Martin Luther King except, you know, I Had a Hand.

He also said jack-all about Mitt Romney, by the way, which was weird. He didn't even mention Romney's hands.

10:14 Ann Romney says she wants to talk to us about the love she has for her husband and the love she has for her children. She wants to talk about her heart. This disappoints Rick Santorum, who was totally hoping: hands.

10:16 Ann goes on about how the people who really hold it all together for America are women—especially mothers. "I

LOOOOOVE YOU WOMEN!" she hollers, Oprah style. "You are the best of America." And when my husband is president, his party will call you a whore if you decline to carry your rape baby to term! LOOOOVE YOU!

10:27 "Mitt doesn't like to talk about how he helps others, because he doesn't do it so others will think more of him. So I'm going to tell you about how he helps others so you'll think more of him." I'm paraphrasing.

10:31 "Look into your hearts. This is our country. These are our children. This is our future." These are my keys. That is your lamp. These are Rick Santorum's hands.

10:35 New Jersey governor Chris Christie arrives at, and devours, the podium. This gives the rest of his speech a cool, echo kind of sound.

10:39 "We have become paralyzed by our desire to be loved ..." Christie delivers a passionate attack against political leaders who do what is popular and not what is right (Democrats only; all Republican leaders are way deeper). He rallies the people. He raises his voice. And he concludes this passage of his speech by declaring, "Tonight, we're going to choose respect over love!" Which immediately reminds every voter in America: "Oh, yeah, I don't love Mitt Romney. I'd forgotten that but happily this guy reminded me. Thanks, Chris Christie!"

10:48 Christie says that Democrats are focused solely on their desire to hold power. Whereas Mitt Romney will generously share power in a sort of anarcho-syndicalist commune where all decisions have to be ratified at a special biweekly meeting.

FIRST OF ALL, let me just say it's great to live in a world in which Mitt Romney has finally been humanized. They said it couldn't be done! But thanks to the efforts of Mitt's wife and sons, America now stands united in being reasonably sure that beneath the Republican nominee's pragmatic, patrician exterior of space-age polymers beats the heart-like object of a man who was this week described by his oldest son as "pretty interesting."

Now, onward to the second full day of the Republican National Convention.

7:10 PM Delegates watch a video that pays tribute to congress-man Ron Paul, who attracted significant support during the presidential primaries. It features a dozen men, each older and whiter than the last, talking about how, his entire life, Ron Paul has never wavered, never changed his mind, never altered his world view, never seen anyone else's point of view, never grown intellectually, never shared any of his gumdrops, never stopped hectoring the neighbourhood kids to get off his lawn. I may have made up a couple of those.

7:14 At the podium, Sen. Mitch (long pause) McConnell becomes the latest Republican to make the case for American excep-tionalism—the notion that the United States is "special," and don't you dare make a crack about how that word has two meanings, buster. "We are different," McConnell says, slowly, so very slowly, so very slowly and blandly it's as though a tea cozy had been anthropomorphized right before our eyes. "Not because of where we were born, but because of … what we have in here." At this point, McConnell (slowly) places his hand over his heart. Or possibly over his wallet. It's the Republican con-vention, so probably over his wallet.

7:21 McConnell is still talking. At least I think that's him talking. I definitely hear a noise like how oatmeal would sound if it had a mouth. He's getting to his point, I think. Yep, definitely get-ting closer. Here it comes! He breathes deeply and says: "The only way to fail in America is to quit." Sure, several investment banks, most Baldwins and the Chicago Cubs are just a handful of the countless entities that prove McConnell's theory wrong, but delegates wisely choose to just applaud politely and hope he stops. He stops.

7:29 Sen. Rand Paul, son of Ron Paul, addresses delegates. I've not heard him give a speech before so I'll give him the bene-fit of the doubt and assume he left his charisma in his other jacket. Paul goes on for quite a bit about how he disagrees with the Supreme Court and, to this day, still thinks Obamacare is unconstitutional. So for those of you scoring at home: on one hand there's the view of some senator guy from Kentucky who until a few years ago was an ophthalmologist; and on the other hand there's the opinion of the highest court in the entire country—with judges on it and everything. Let's call it a draw.

7:47 Time for another video, this one featuring a nice interview with presidents George H.W. Bush and George W. Bush, who were filmed sitting next to one another on a bench. There are some fond reminiscences. There are a couple of funny stories. At last, the talk turns to the current Republican nominee:

> GEORGE W. BUSH: There's no doubt in our mind that Mitt Romney will be a great president.
> *[Awkward pause. GEORGE W. BUSH turns to look at his father. And here is all that the forty-first president of the United States can muster:]*
> GEORGE H.W. BUSH: He's a good man.

Probably not worth printing that one on the pamphlet, Romney campaign.

8:01 It's John McCain's turn to speechify. He speaks of the "consequential choice" facing America in the coming election. And really, who better to offer guidance at this critical time than the man who, when faced with his own consequential choice, pounded his fist on the table and declared: "I choose the pretty lady who can see Russia from her house!"

McCain goes on to assure Republican delegates that the United States is still really popular around the world. "People don't want less of America. They want more." In McCain's defence, this is probably true if he's referring to the parts of America that make up Scarlett Johansson.

8:41 A guy from a pipeline company just opened his remarks with the words "Energy powers everything we do." Rejected openings for his speech included "Matter is everything that has mass and volume" and "Blueberries are delicious."

9:00 Rob Portman, a senator from Ohio, claims Mitt Romney made his money "the old-fashioned way." Wait, Mitt Romney had sex for money? That seems like it should be a bigger story.

9:22 Just a quick thought on one of the songs that the Republican house band keeps playing between speeches. It may have seemed like a savvy decision back in the 1980s, but in hindsight I think we'd all agree that, in the end, it was a mistake to build this city on rock 'n' roll. No one can get any sleep and the whole place smells like John Mayer's bong water. And now the city is sinking and we're shoulder deep in the hoopla. It just never ends.

9:31 Tim Pawlenty, former governor of Minnesota, arrives with a smile on his face, a song in his heart and roughly fourteen too many "jokes" in his mouth. "I'll give Barack Obama credit for creating jobs—for golf caddies." Be sure to catch Pawlenty, Portman, McConnell and Thune as they tour America this fall as the Monsters of Bland.

10:18 Susana Martinez, the governor of New Mexico, speaks of guarding the parking lot on bingo night at the Catholic Church as an eighteen-year-old—while carrying a .357 Magnum. "The gun weighed more than I did!" The crowd goes crazy! It's funny because it's excessive and potentially deadly!

10:27 Time for the evening's featured performer: Paul Ryan, the Republican congressman from Wisconsin who, earlier this month, was picked by Mitt Romney to serve as his vice-presidential nominee. This is a man in such tremendous shape that his best bet in the debates would be to challenge Joe Biden to a shirtlessness contest—a strategy that will be made simpler by the fact that that's how Biden is likely to show up anyway.

Through no fault of his own, Ryan appears almost absurdly young and eager on the massive Republican stage. I mean so young that he looks as though he's just come from hanging around at Arnold's and saying things like "You still got it, Fonz!" Still, it's a big night for him, so I'm going to cut him some slack for being late in delivering my paper. Toward the end of his address, an emotional Ryan will speak of his mother's presence in his life and declare, "My Mom is my role model." She is likely also his ride home.

Day Three

7:03 PM On CNN, Anderson Cooper is saying that Republican operatives have promised a "carefully crafted buildup" to Mitt Romney's acceptance speech. This remark will become worth remembering in a few hours, right around the time Clint Eastwood begins interrogating a piece of furniture.

7:13 C-SPAN reporters break some big news: the 100,000 balloons that will descend on Mitt Romney and the convention floor at the end of his speech tonight were inflated, according to an interview with a guy from the balloon company, over a period of just five hours. STOP THE PRESSES OR WHATEVER MAKES WORDS APPEAR ON THE INTERNET. The reporter wants more from his source: "How," he asks, "do you make sure [the balloons] come down?" Balloon Guy scoffs. Balloon Guy says: "The drop will be very, very nice." Balloon Guy says no balloons will get stuck on his watch, ho ho. This remark will become worth remembering in a few hours, right around the time the balloons get stuck on his watch.

7:49 Newt and Callista Gingrich appear on stage together to pay tribute to Ronald Reagan because apparently it's been four minutes since someone did that. It's an unusual moment: first, because Newt is forced to read from a script, and you can see in the strain on his face how hard it is for him to keep from dropping some polysyllabic Newt Truths on us; and second, because it turns out Callista Gingrich speaks with the exact same amount of verve and passion as the computer voice on *Star Trek*.

> NEWT: This is the most critical election of our lifetimes! We must commit ourselves to honouring the spirit of Ronald Reagan!

CALLISTA: The Reagan legacy is functioning within established parameters.

8:01 Craig Romney, son of Mitt Romney, delivers a brief address and in so doing proves once and for all that the apple didn't fall far from the boring.

8:05 Jeb Bush: "This election is about the future of this nation." Unlike most elections, which are about sandwiches and scoring chicks.

8:50 Bob White, chairman of the Romney–Ryan campaign: "For thirty years, I have been at Mitt Romney's side when he did extraordinary things. As Mitt says, I'm his wingman." I'm pretty sure neither of those guys knows what that word is generally accepted to mean.

9:16 Kerry Healey, who worked with Romney when he was governor of Massachusetts, rhymes off a number of impressive traits about Mitt and tells this little story: "Mitt was always a hands-on leader. When one of Boston's tunnels collapsed, tragically killing a passenger in her car, Mitt didn't blame others. He dove in and fixed the problem." Wait: *Mitt Romney raised the dead?* That really feels like it should be a bigger part of his campaign. <Fade in.> "Hi, I'm Mitt Romney. Can Obama do THIS?" [*reanimates Elvis Presley.*]

9:34 A group of former Olympians takes the stage to demonstrate their support for the Republican nominee. Hundreds of kilometres to the north, in a darkened room in Washington, a grim-faced Barack Obama takes note of the fact that Mitt Romney has won the allegiance of the 2007 world champion in skeleton. Obama's heart sinks. He knows now the election is lost.

9:37 The Olympians make their case. "America is faltering. We need strong leadership, we need new leadership and we need it now."—Some skeet shooter.

9:42 Mike Eruzione, captain of America's Miracle on Ice hockey team, delivers a brief speech in which it becomes apparent that he (a) supports Mitt Romney for president, and (b) thinks *athletes* is pronounced with three syllables.

9:55 Welcome to the Obligatory Montage of Romney Home Videos, the part of the evening when millions of Americans realize that neither they nor their children have a hope of becoming president because they lack the required hours of endearing home-movie snippets that are Revealing of Character.

For instance, one of the things we've been told repeatedly this week is that Mitt Romney is frugal. It's an appealing trait for a politician in a time of high deficits. But it turns out that what everybody's actually been trying to say is: Mitt Romney is cheap as hell. Dude doesn't even replace his stovetop light bulb with one of the correct size or wattage—he just jams in some random oversized bulb he's already purchased.

A former work colleague of Romney declares: "If he can save 50 cents on paperclips, he'd drive a mile to do it." I ask you: Is this what America really wants in a president? *Listen, soldier, I know you need a pair of cutters to snip that wire and defuse this bomb that is about to obliterate this vibrant downtown area—but I tell you what, here, let's save the American people the eight bucks and I'll just gnaw at it with my teeth.*

10:02 Suddenly, Clint Eastwood is at the microphone. There is wild applause. Eastwood squints and smiles: "Save a little for Mitt." Delegates laugh. OH HOW THEY LAUGH. They begin to mentally praise the genius political operative who secured Eastwood's participation because this is exactly the kind of star power the Romney campaign needs in order to break through and—um, hang on, what's Clint doing? Is he talking to a chair? He's *not* talking to a chair? Oh, that's a relief. For a moment there I thought he was—ah, so he's talking to Invisible Barack Obama, who is apparently sitting in the chair? I don't think that's better.

[Three minutes of increasingly awkward "laughter" later ...]

Well, sure, it's a little unusual, I suppose. It's a little unusual that it's ten o'clock on the final night of the Republican National Convention and the party's presidential nominee is poised to deliver the biggest speech of his life, and meanwhile a world-famous Hollywood celebrity is having a conversation with an invisible president. And sure, maybe it wouldn't have hurt if Clint had worked from a script, or a few bullet points, or an idea that had progressed even a tiny bit beyond: Chair.

But it's not like Eastwood is taking it too far or—um, hang on, did he just suggest that Invisibama had told him to go f— himself. He did? Oh, my. And did he actually just say: "Do you just ... you know ... I know ... people were wondering ... you don't ... handle that okay." He did?

Oh, well, it'll still be great to have Clint formally endorse Mitt and—um, what's that? He's not endorsing Mitt at all? In fact, to the contrary, he's saying that *all* politicians are the same and "they're just going to come around every few years and beg for votes?" Interesting. That's interesting. *[Gouges out own eyes to make the horror stop.]*

(America can be so adorable sometimes. They regard their celebrities with such reverence that the Romney campaign—which was so obsessive about approving every word uttered by every speaker, and choreographing every image and moment—just went ahead and let an eighty-two-year-old man walk out onto the stage in prime time with an empty chair, no script and some grade-A bed-head. But speaking for myself, I realize I've got bigger problems to worry about: If invisible Obama is in Tampa, who's watching my kids?)

10:17 Marco Rubio, the senator from Florida, arrives to introduce Mitt Romney. And you have to hand it to Rubio because he does it in a really interesting way. You know how usually the person who's introducing the other person will talk about the person they're introducing? Marco Rubio puts a bit of a fresh spin on that by instead speaking about the person who's *doing* the introducing, that is, Marco Rubio. FYI, according to Marco Rubio, this Marco Rubio character is one hell of a guy. Also, by the way, Mitt Romney, everyone!

10:36 Mitt Romney enters and walks through the hall, shaking hands. By the time he reaches the stage, Clint Eastwood has wandered out into the parking lot and is exchanging life stories with a Hyundai.

Romney's speech may be remembered for a number of different elements. It may be remembered for the candidate's touching remembrance of his father's love for his mother. It may be remembered for its largely negative tone, a jarring contrast after two hours of hearing about Mitt the Eternal Optimist. It may be remembered for dubious feel-good lines like "I have a plan to create twelve million jobs!" (Hint: it involves starting up three million boy bands.)

Many will remember it for a single line. It was a line that was crafted to help position Romney as the practical problem solver to Barack Obama's hopey-changey dreamer. But it became something very different because of how delegates reacted to it.

Here's how the line appeared in the text: "President Obama promised to begin to slow the rise of the oceans and heal the planet. My promise is to help you and your family."

Here's how it actually sounded: "President Obama promised to begin to slow the rise of the oceans [*huge gales of laughter from Republican delegates, because massive, life-sustaining bodies of water are for pussies*] and heal the planet [*BWAHAHAHA. Suck it, science!*]."

The Democratic National Convention

Charlotte, NC
September 2012
Day One

5:03 PM We're thirty seconds in and there hasn't been a single joke yet about an empty chair or an invisible president. DO YOU GUYS WANT TO WIN THIS ELECTION OR WHAT?

5:11 Debbie Wasserman Schultz, chair of the Democratic National Committee, promises that the next three days will be "the most open political convention in history." So when Joe Biden takes the stage on Thursday night in a bathrobe, holding a vodka cooler and a bowl of keys, you can look back on this remark and think to yourself, "Well, in all fairness, they did warn me."

5:35 It's been bugging me and I couldn't quite put my finger on it but I just realized what's different about the Democratic convention: Black people—they have some.

5:50 Cory Booker, mayor of Newark, talks about the choice facing Americans: "We must choose forward!" You lose again, sideways.

5:54 My eleven-year-old boy sits down next to me. He watches for a couple of minutes. "Last week, Romney was great and Obama sucked. This week, Obama is great and Romney sucks." He gives me a look that says "Sorry if I just blew your mind," gets up and walks away.

7:01 Tim Kaine, former governor of Virginia, makes the evening's first reference to President Obama "taking out bin Laden." I'm not sure why, but Americans almost always put it that way: he "took out bin Laden." And I know this says more about me and the way my brain works than it says about anything else, but whenever someone talks about the president "taking out bin Laden," I find myself picturing, even for just a split second, the two of them going out on a date. Sometimes it's dinner and a movie. Other times? A nice picnic in an alpine meadow. I guess what I'm saying is, I'd be grateful if in future everyone could just go with "We shot the dude in the face."

7:03 Kaine also becomes the first speaker to reference "LGBT Americans." This, of course, stands for lesbian, gay, bisexual or transgender Americans—or, as the acronym is known among Republicans, "that yogurt place."

7:17 Nancy Pelosi comes out accompanied by a large group of "the Democratic women of the House." She repeatedly refers to them this way: "the Democratic women of the House." It sounds like a reality TV series or an upscale bordello—or better still in the minds of Bravo TV executives, both. By the way, it's an interesting reflection of America's disdain for Congress that the two senior Democratic legislators were given speaking slots that put them not in prime time but in the far-less-watched-except-by-my-Grandma domain of *Wheel of Fortune*. Then again, hiding your liabilities and making the best of a bad situation has a long tradition in American politics. For instance, organizers of the 1988 Democratic National Convention in Atlanta told nominee Michael Dukakis that the convention was in Tulsa.

7:21 The convention lets out a big cheer at the very mention of "birth control"—and another, even bigger one at talk of "choice." Listen, I'm a fan and everything, but still: in a time of continuing economic not-goodness, it's kind of weird how frequently tonight's speeches have come back to the question of choice and the right of women to control their own baby-based decisions. And the tone is a little odd too. There's so much clapping and hooting at every mention of the sanctity of women's reproductive rights. These people make abortions sound *awesome*.

7:44 We are introduced to Joseph Kennedy III, yet another Kennedy who is pursuing public life by running for Congress. Say what you will about the decline of the American economy, the United States remains utterly without peer in the highly efficient production of political scions.

7:50 In a savvy and effective move, the Democrats show a video of the late Ted Kennedy mopping the floor with a young Mitt Romney in a debate during their 1994 battle to represent Massachusetts in the Senate. "I am pro-choice," Kennedy says, then adds a dig that's even more relevant today. "My opponent is multiple-choice." Haha, Mitt—you just got schooled by a video ghost.

8:49 Governor Lincoln Chafee of Rhode Island: "Should only the children of the wealthy have access to early education ... and a college degree?" Wait, don't tell me the answer: I KNOW THIS ONE.

8:58 Ted Strickland, former governor of Ohio, arrives with a clear message: "I. HAVE. COME. HERE. TONIGHT. TO. YELL. WORDS. AT. YOU." Over the course of the next fifteen minutes, Gov. CAPS LOCK delivers the most aggressive attack on Mitt Romney that we'll hear tonight. "The auto industry is standing today!! The middle class is standing today!! Ohio is standing today!! America is standing strong today!! Someone please turn me down!! I have become stuck at this absurd volume and unsustainable emotional pitch!! I can't stop speaking this way!! I'm going to sound ridiculous when later tonight I order my dinner using this voice!! I'll have the Porterhouse!! See what I mean?!!"

9:03 Chicago mayor Rahm Emanuel, who served as President Obama's first chief of staff, swiftly assuages any worries that he may have lost or misplaced his ego en route: "There was no blueprint or how-to manual for preventing a global financial meltdown, an auto crisis, two wars and a great recession all at the same time. Believe me, if it existed, I would have found it." Got that? *He* would have found it. And then he would have made Obama look good without taking any of the credit except for later when he took all of the credit.

9:33 Lilly Ledbetter, the woman for whom President Obama's fair-pay legislation was named, gives a speech recounting her time as the manager at a tire plant in Alabama—and the realization that she was getting paid less than her male colleagues. Sassy and sharp-tongued, she gets off the line of the night at Mitt Romney: "Twenty-three cents an hour might not seem like much to a guy with a Swiss bank account ..." There's been a lot of talk about Mitt's Swiss bank accounts this evening. This is because Swiss bank accounts sound inherently sinister and for only the fancy-panted, just like Cayman Islands tax shelters and Belgian waffles.

9:46 Deval Patrick, governor of Massachusetts, declares this "the election of a lifetime"—making it the eleventh election of a lifetime of my lifetime. He goes on to deliver a big ol' super-sweaty speech. Delegates are so into it that it takes them a moment to realize that he's actually started to scold them.

PATRICK: It's time for Democrats to grow a backbone
and stand up for what we believe!

DELEGATES: Wooooo-hooooo! *Woooo*— Wait, what?"

10:12 San Antonio mayor Julian Castro begins his address by talking about the great adversity he's faced, such as (a) growing up poor, and (b) being forced to walk onstage to a Black Eyed Peas song just now.

10:39 Greeted with rapturous applause, Michelle Obama delivers what pretty much everyone acknowledges to be a masterful speech—though one that presents a unique challenge to fact-checkers. "Today, I love my husband even more than I did four years ago," she says. Hmm, sounds like typical Washington hyperbole—let's see you prove it by making out in front of us a little.

So the First Lady was terrific and everything, though perhaps we could have done with an abbreviated version of the We Were Poor section of her remarks, which seemed to last about ten minutes and existed entirely to remind people that Mitt Romney wasn't. Among the revelations: Barack Obama's "prized possession" as a university student was "a coffee table he found in a dumpster!" He wore his shoes a half size too small because he couldn't afford new ones! The mean old man said no when l'il Barack came forward with his bowl and asked for a second helping of gruel!

But then, that's American political oratory, isn't it? You don't get a prime-time slot on the big stage if you're not willing to Give Something of Yourself; if you're not willing to use your humble past to advance your ambitious future. And you *do* have to have a humble past—or the gall to appropriate one. You need those dark moments, that whiff of despair and those working-class roots—with at least one relative who worked three jobs *or* three relatives who worked one very hard job (preferably a miner; a mill worker will suffice in a pinch).

Day Three

Before Barack Obama came out to accept the I Killed Osama bin Laden Lifetime Achievement Award (and also, apparently, his party's nomination for the US presidency), they let Joe Biden speak for some reason.

Using direct quotations from Biden's speech, I have prepared—for the sake of generations to come—a detailed brief compiling Joe Biden's eleven critical lessons for those who are called on to serve as vice-president of the United States.

- **Quote:** "I see [the president] every day."
  Lesson: When the president enters your field of perception, he will be visible to you.
- **Quote:** "I walk thirty paces down the hall into the Oval Office and I see him."
  Lesson: You work in the same building as the president.
- **Quote:** "I watch him in action."
  Lesson: When the president does things, you sometimes get to see him do those things.
- **Quote:** "I watched him stand up to intense pressure and stare down enormous challenges."
  Lesson: Again—he's there, you're there. You're bound to see some things happen when they happen. So prepare yourself for that.
- **Quote:** "I got to see first-hand what drove this man."
  Lesson: You'll not only see him. You'll see things *about* him.
- **Quote:** "Folks, I've watched him."
  Lesson: You'll watch him. The president, that is.
- **Quote:** "Ladies and gentlemen, I'm here to tell you ... I watch it up close."
  Lesson: Hey, at this point, I'm thinking that instead of just sitting there and watching and looking and seeing, maybe you could go grab the guy a Coke or something? Make yourself useful.

- **Quote:** "So we sat hour after hour in the Oval Office."
  Lesson: Or maybe a sandwich. I bet he's hungry.
- **Quote:** "We sat, hour after hour."
  Lesson: Listen, someone needs to tell you this, Joe, and apparently Barack is too polite. It's time to go back to your office. Or go home. You don't always have to be hanging around the president, okay? And for the love of God, get your feet off the coffee table.
- **Quote:** "Day after day, night after night, I sat beside him as he made one gutsy decision after the other."
  Lesson: Joe Biden is a stalker.

The Debates

Barack Obama's performance in the first US presidential debate was bad—and it only got worse in the days that followed. Pundits kept one-upping each other in describing just how detached he had been. The president was lethargic! He was invisible! He wasn't just aloof—he was *the*loof!

They weren't exaggerating: Obama's interventions in the first debate featured more ums than the periodic table. In the days leading up to this week's second debate, the president's surrogates promised a more vigorous, more aggressive Obama. A few made it sound as though Mitt Romney would basically be facing off against a giant green rage monster and his terse campaign slogan: Hope Smash!

So it was a bit of a letdown when the president declined to begin Tuesday's debate by striding across the stage and ripping off Romney's arms. Instead, it was the standard fake-friendly handshake and we were ready to go.

This was a town-hall debate, and those are the worst because they oblige politicians to feign not only interest in but also empathy for the struggles of average people. This fools no one: one handshake in 1992 and twenty years later George H.W. Bush is still trying to get the smell of mill worker off him. Worse yet, the candidates have to try to remember everyone's name. Was it Lorraine? Lori? Gloria? Oh, it was Dave. Sorry, Dave.

The format was especially tough on Romney, who struggled to find common ground with the average folk. One can only imagine debate prep in the Romney camp:

> AIDE: Governor, what's the price of a gallon of milk?
> ROMNEY: $8,000?
> AIDE: Well, we're getting closer.

Obama was so plainly determined to come across as spirited that the normally staid town-hall format led within twenty minutes to the two candidates standing toe to toe and on the verge of a fist fight over, of all things, whether the amount of oil being extracted on public lands has decreased by 14 percent. If you missed it, here's essentially how it went down:

> OBAMA: You're a dummy.
> ROMNEY: No, *you're* a dummy.

The president was also more vigorous in taking credit for stuff. An hour into the debate, you'd have sworn that Obama alone was responsible for saving the US economy, the auto industry, the entire middle class, Medicare, Harrison Ford's wife in *Frantic*, and the last dance for me.

And did you know Osama bin Laden had passed away? Obama mentioned that once or twice (twice). He even managed to shoehorn it into his answer to a question from a man who was lamenting that things sure are expensive these days. Clearly, at this point there's really no line of conversation into which Obama can't squeeze that factoid.

> MICHELLE: Barack, honey, could you help with the girls' homework?
> BARACK: Killed bin Laden. [*Continues watching* Wheel of Fortune.]

There were odd moments during the debate. Mitt Romney fought for like twenty minutes with the moderator to get a chance to say something—something he URGENTLY needed to say—and when she finally gave in he declared, "I appreciate wind jobs in Iowa." Um, okay.

Later, Romney revealed that his solution to Americans killing numerous other Americans with semi-automatic weapons is not to ban or limit semi-automatic weapons but to make sure more people get married. Because apparently nothing stops you from gunning down strangers quite like having to be home for supper by 5:30.

But it was Romney's answer on pay equity that was especially memorable. It began with Mitt bragging about how as Massachusetts governor he ordered up "binders full of women" when selecting his cabinet (I too amassed binders full of women as a younger man, but for a very different reason). He then boasted about how he let his employees with lady parts work flexible hours so they could hustle out to the suburbs to cook dinner. The whole thing gave off a vibe of "I am totally sealing the deal to win the 1956 presidential election."

Yet questions remain unanswered. Where is Mitt Romney's binder of women today? And would he consider publishing it so that all American men can find within its pages a woman who will work for 73 cents on the dollar and scurry home to whip up a meat loaf? I'm asking for a friend (Don Draper).

—*October 18, 2012*

IT'S HARD TO believe the US election campaign is almost over—it feels like it began only two or three eons ago. In the time since Mitt Romney launched his 2012 candidacy, the seasons have changed, toddlers have reached puberty, gases and dark matter have come together to form the seeds of untold future galaxies and Lady Gaga has had, like, three different hairstyles. Most people now can't wait for November 6, which will mark the final day of this campaign and the only day Wolf

Blitzer won't talk about the next one.

By this point in the process, Mitt and Barack are like in-laws who've come to town, done the tourist thing, doted on the grandkids and now you desire nothing more than for them to get the hell out of your house. We just want our bathroom back, guys.

But before that glorious day could come, we needed to get through the third and final presidential debate.

This one was about foreign policy, a topic so grave that the candidates apparently could not address it while standing. Alas, the table-and-chairs format robbed the debate of some of its intensity, most of its macho posturing and all of its aggressive striding. This was a real loss because the striding was far and away the highlight of the town-hall debate, which pretty much became a contest of which candidate could approach the questioner using the fewest steps.

Still, Monday's event afforded Americans one last chance to ponder the big questions: Who is better qualified to lead the US in a changing world? And what else does Mitt Romney have binders full of? Is it menus from his favourite takeout food places? It probably is.

There were a couple of curious moments for Romney. First, the Republican nominee put a precise figure to the number of allies that America has in the world: forty-two. It was a savvy move. If this whole "president" thing doesn't pan out, it gives Romney a great fallback gig: reality-show contestant. "Allies of America, you're all beautiful but there are forty-two of you and I've got only these nine roses ... "

Second, Romney—perhaps scolded by advisers to focus less on billions and millions—opted to use hand gestures to convey the disparity of American trade with China. "They sell us about this much stuff [makes "tall guy" gesture] every year. And we sell them about this much stuff [makes "Tom Cruise-height" gesture] every year." I, for one, hope this catches on as a debating tactic. That way, candidates in 2016 can differentiate themselves by declaring: "I love Israel *thiiiiiis* much."

Toward the end of the final debate, both men were coasting on rhetorical fumes. Obama mentioned Osama bin Laden by name six times. Romney's interventions began to be dominated by odd declaratives: "Research is great ... I like American cars ... I love teachers." He also started but never finished a number of anecdotes: "I've met [the unemployed] in Appleton, Wisconsin. I met a young woman in Philadelphia." He pointed out that his wife, Ann, had also met various people in various places. And then came this actual exchange:

> ROMNEY: You're wrong, Mr. President.
> OBAMA: I am not wrong.
> ROMNEY: You're wrong.
> OBAMA: I am not wrong.
> ROMNEY: People can look it up.
> OBAMA: People will look it up.
> ROMNEY: Good.

It was like the Lincoln–Douglas debates but with more double-stamped-it, no erasies.

Perhaps the weirdest twist was that Romney spent a good part of the debate not debating: "I couldn't agree more ... I felt the same as the president did ... That was the right thing to do." With election day finally approaching, it was an odd time for Mitt to basically change his slogan to Just Like the Current Guy, But Mormonier.

—*October 25, 2012*

ELECTION NIGHT, USA, 2012: Democracy? Check. Hyperbole? CHECK! But where, oh where, were the dazzling technological innovations in broadcast coverage?

Four years ago, the guy from the Black Eyed Peas appeared via hologram for an interview on CNN. Surely this election season would produce nothing less than a trio of Anderson Cooper clones being attended to by a robot butler? Surely by now the technology would exist to beam up an actual live person from a spaceship or, at minimum, make James Carville not look like he just wandered in from the set of *The Walking Dead*?

Or maybe CNN spent all its money this time around on a robust supply of exclamation marks for Wolf Blitzer: "We are about to make a really major projection! ... These are AC-TUAL numbers coming in! ... WOW, THE NUMBERS JUST CHANGED AS WE! WERE! LOOKING! AT! THEM!!!!" Believe me, if Election Night 2012 proved nothing else, it proved that Wolf Blitzer is amazed by numbers suddenly becoming other numbers. "Wow," he said, more than once. "WOW!"

Remember when anchors used to sit down to report stuff? Cronkite sat down. Jennings sat down. Brokaw? I bet that guy peed sitting down. Wolf Blitzer does not sit down. Wolf Blitzer is always moving. For Blitzer, anchoring an election broadcast is about celebrating the sanctity of the democratic process, sure, but it's also about getting in some cardio.

By 7:30, the polls were closed in Florida, Ohio and Herman Cain's basement, where by a slim margin the former Republican contender lost his hard-fought campaign to switch the channel over to "something with maybe a little boob action." Michigan went early for Obama despite Mitt Romney having repeatedly travelled to the state to flatter its plant life. ("The trees here are just the right height," he said several times, apparently unaware that the role of trees in the electoral process is limited to that of ballot, not voter.) Then Pennsylvania was called for Obama—and that one hurt Romney. As bad omens go, it ranked up there with glimpsing a movie's opening credits and seeing the words "Van" and "Damme."

By the time meaningful vote tallies started pouring in, CNN was entering what felt like its fifty-third consecutive hour of live political coverage. David Gergen was passed out. James Carville was shirtless and skinning a possum. Wolf Blitzer was describing as "historic" the fact that he hadn't taken a leak for a day and a half. The planet's longest, most gruelling reality show was at long last near an end. The courting was over. It was time for America to reveal which fella she'd chosen.

You knew things had turned sharply for Obama when broadcasters began speaking of Romney's chances in certain states the way over-supportive parents speak of their children: *He's trying really hard and he could still totally pull it out in Nevada! HE COULD TOO!!* It wasn't quite over for Romney—but when the news hit that Florida was looking good for Obama, you could pretty much hear Bill O'Reilly explode from four channels over.

The victory and concession speeches took their usual form: "My spouse is so supportive ... my kids mean everything to me ... my opponent is a great American even though mere hours ago I'd have alleged that he'd fondled a ferret if I thought there was even a single vote in it."

And then the token biennial nod to working together, uttered by victors on both sides—the predictable late-night sext to bipartisanship: *We are really going to try to make it work this time, honey. We completely mean it and are totally serious, girl. This time it's going to be different. This time we're going to give you the love and respect you deserve, bipartisanship. Love and respect and lots of cuddling. PS: We're going out drinking with the guys now. Don't wait up.*

It didn't sound sincere. It was as though both sides had come to peace with the polarized state of the land. It was as though they'd accepted that maybe it's best that red and blue America never come together, because that would make purple America and that would just look weird.

—*November 8, 2012*

IN THE AFTERMATH of the 2012 election, commentators were quick to tell us that the jockeying had already begun for next time. But forecasting the 2016 campaign is for wusses. Now that the US presidential race has become a non-stop, all-encompassing industry unto itself, big-league pundits and political operatives need to focus *waaay* further into the future.

Let's examine the leading contenders for the 2056 race for the White House:

Hannah Andrews, five (*Fort Lauderdale*, FL): Active in politics since her first birthday, when she received from her grandma the gift of an exploratory committee, Hannah is a rising star in the Democratic Party. She was conceived by her politically savvy parents on the state line between Michigan and Ohio, giving her roots in two crucial swing states. One wild card remains: how the voting public will react to her unorthodox choice for running mate—a stuffed pink unicorn. Could play well in the Northwest and Clay Aiken's house.

Isaac Brooks, eight (*Bloomington*, IN): A Republican upstart from the Midwest, Isaac is showing experience beyond his years with aggressive and effective political tactics—foremost among them: a series of robocalls to Fort Lauderdale residents alleging that rival Hannah Andrews's work on a papier mâché alligator makes her "too French" for Middle America.

Donald "Donny" Harris, fifteen (*Scranton*, PA): Considered the early Democratic front-runner for '56 after his masterful leadership role in Philadelphia's cafeteria uprising of 2007, Donny's chances have faded amid revelations that he was for Salisbury steak before he was against it. More troubling, Republicans have successfully swiftboated claims that he made it to the end of Gears of War. But Donny insists he still has the support of "real" Americans like his friends Amir the Television Watcher and Doug the Guy Whose Father Can Do Some Plumbing If Need Be.

Bristol Palin, twenty-four (*Juneau*, AK): First she was pregnant with child—now she's pregnant with political possibility! Many Republicans see Bristol as the only candidate with the bona fides to unite the party's fractious pro-life and pro-mullet wings and carry on the Palin family dynasty, following President Sarah Palin's first term in office (2016–20), her second

233

term in office (2020–24) and her armed refusal to leave office (2024–31).

Deep Blue 7.0, in beta (*IBM HQ, Armonk, NY*): The original chess-playing computer is being reprogrammed as America's perfect Democratic candidate: compassionate without being wimpy, charismatic without being effete, and technically incapable of undergoing a $400 haircut. Deep Blue comes installed with a proprietary Pain Feeling simulator and a database of achingly sentimental references to its three photogenic children ("Deep Blue 7.1," "Deep Blue 7.2" and "Greg"). Its handlers are still working out the kinks in its Inspirational Political Slogan generator, which is currently stuck on "Bishop to Queen Three. Check."

Zombie Hillary Clinton, undead (*Chappaqua, NY*): Hillary Clinton will be poised to surprise the pundits yet again—by trading in the pleasures of mortal life for the persuasive ability that comes with picking, and subsequently devouring, the best political minds in the country. After roaming the countryside for decades, terrorizing hapless villagers and amassing a huge army of the walking dead, Clinton will be well-positioned to capture the Democratic nomination and coax her reanimated followers—raised from the grave without the power of speech or free will—to cast a ballot for America's first zombie president since Gerald Ford. Keen observers predict subtle changes to Clinton's strategy, foremost among them a migration from a campaign based on "the strength of experience" to a campaign based on "brraaaaaaaainzzzzzz."

Samuel Eppich, zero (*Nashville, TN*): The first one hundred days of a presidency are considered crucial—and so too, for a potential presidential candidate, are the first one hundred days of life. Sam has impressed pundits on both sides of the partisan divide with his formidable list of accomplishments, including the movement of fecal matter, which garnered great praise among focus groups comprised of his mom. At times crabby and irritable, at other times confused and prone to sudden napping, Sam has demonstrated a keen ability to mimic the campaign demeanour of John McCain. But can he mount a counterattack to those who accurately contend that he neither supported nor opposed the war in Iraq?

Tough Question: *In the glorous future, when time travel opens history to us all, will Jesus Christ actually be a good dinner guest?*

It's been asked of us all: Which three people, living or dead, would you invite to a dinner party? "I'd invite Jesus," most people automatically say, as though the resurrected scion of an omnipotent deity didn't have any better options on a Friday night than cheese fondue and Scattergories.

Don't get me wrong: Jesus has a lot going for him as a potential guest. He'd be wise, inspiring and eloquent. Plus, imagine the look on your neighbours' faces when the son of God squeals into your driveway in a chariot pulled by winged horses. Suddenly your new BMW doesn't seem so impressive, does it, Brian?

(My neighbour's name is Brian.)

Jesus's presence would also help keep costs down. Oh no, we're out of wine and bread and—whoa, no we're not! And look: now we've got thousands of fish for dessert. Thanks, Jesus! I mean, don't worry about the mess or the smell or anything. But wow, cool, fish. Fish everywhere.

[Doorbell rings.]

I wonder who that could—oh, lepers. Jesus, it's for you.

Let's be honest—Jesus is great and tall and everything but this is supposed to be my dinner and there he is, hogging the limelight with his stories of dying for our sins and pioneering the sandals-without-socks look. I wouldn't be able to get a word in edgewise with my other guests, Ace Frehley and Batman.

The key to a successful imaginary dinner party is not to overreach. You want a trio of guests who are much less interesting than yourself so you can be the centre of attention. That's why Jesus's dad created for us three Kardashian sisters.

REASON NO. 9: SCIENCE AND SPACE

For almost a half century now, humanity has been on a noble quest to probe the deepest reaches of space, make contact with alien life forms ... and confuse the living shit out of them. The heyday of Earth's efforts to bafflingly announce its presence was in the 1970s. Early that decade, the spacecrafts *Pioneer 10* and *11* were fitted with gold plaques that featured anatomically accurate renderings of a male and female human. The man, smiling and pantless, was waving in a friendly manner. So, yeah, we pretty much asked for all that anal probing.

The pursuit of contact continued in 1974, when the Arecibo radio telescope was used to broadcast a signal that displayed a human stick figure crudely made from huge, chunky pixels. The message was clear: cower, alien creatures, and stand in awe of a civilization that stands on the very cusp of inventing Pong.

Four years later, *Voyager 1* and *2* were dispatched into space. Inside each probe: a golden record album. That's right, one full-length golden LP—the theory being that any alien race worth contacting would be able to supply its own turntable and bong. Earlier this year, these probes finally became the fourth and fifth human artifacts to exit the solar system, after *Pioneer 10*, *Pioneer 11* and John Travolta, who had for years been desperately fleeing gay thoughts.

It was shortly after the *Voyager* launches that the people of Earth realized they might be coming on a little strong.

Humanity was acting like a desperate guy at last call—sending out signals in every direction. Wisely, we took a planetary chill pill.

But suddenly things are worse than ever. In the age of the internet, the ability to embarrass our civilization in alien eyes has been democratized. All it takes to beam a message into space these days is a computer, a credit card and the belief that because no one on Earth cares what you think, then the Moon men might.

Consider Bebo.com, a social-networking site popular among teenagers, which recently arranged to have more than five hundred images and text messages transmitted into deep space. The signal was aimed at a planet known as Gliese 581c, which was selected because scientists believe it is capable of supporting life, though probably not the kind that cares about your favourite band, dude.

For a more personal experience, there's Sent Forever—a website that insists there's no event too insignificant to announce to the universe. Are you getting married? Is it your birthday? Did you remember to put out the garbage? Tell eternity about it! For just $20, Sent Forever will ensure "your message [will] travel through space forever." Why limit your influence to your immediate family when you could be boring an entire star cluster? (Interestingly, the Sent Forever home page features photos of a bride and groom, a little baby and an elderly couple. These are there either to depict critical elements of the human experience or as a secret message to invading aliens describing the order in which we should be eaten.)

For those who want to lend a more personal touch, there is Endless Echoes—an internet company that transmits voice messages into the depths of space. For $25, you get a one-minute message along with a Certificate of Broadcast, a Distance Chart and a picture of the website's owner rolling around on a bed covered with the money of idiots like you. What's unique about Endless Echoes is that it also claims to be able to deliver messages beyond the grave. In fact, the website features a picture of a sad little boy and the words "When you never had a chance to say 'goodbye.'" Classy. That's super-classy. When the nebula monkeys arrive to lay waste to planet Earth, here's hoping they save the biggest, curviest banana probe for the people at Endless Echoes.

Is a one-minute voice message to your deceased goldfish just not going to cut it? There will always be hucksters like Blog in Space, which was the first entity to allow everyday bloggers to inflict their tortured, self-obsessed musings on defenceless asteroids. Thanks to Blog in Space's access to a "powerful deep space transmission dish," it is now entirely possible that an alien civilization's first inkling of Earth's existence will come in the form of a suburban mother's six-thousand-word rhapsody about the texture of her baby's poop. Alarmingly, Blog in Space offered no method of monitoring the content of such messages, placing human existence in the position of being threatened not only by nuclear war and global warming but also by the intergalactic equivalent of drunk dialling. *I've got a few things to get off my—hic!—chest about youse space lizards ...*

Here comes the invasion. Time to take off our pants and wave, men.

LOOKING FOR A fun getaway with the man or woman you love? Consider a trip to Mars! It's a journey you'll cherish until the day you die—which, for the record, will be when you both incinerate on re-entry.

But let's not dwell on the many completely fatal potential downsides of this romantic jaunt. The privately funded Inspiration Mars Foundation is determined to send a married couple on a non-stop, "state-of-the-art" trip around the red planet for some reason. And why shouldn't it be you? Being shot toward a distant sphere would give you and your spouse the "us time" you've both been craving—the chance to leave behind the stresses of daily life and do something fun together, like stare for months into unending black, grow progressively more insane and sit helplessly as your bones and muscles deteriorate from the ravages of microgravity. Sounds better than Disney already!

Not sold yet? Consider some of the other benefits of being sealed inside a thin metal canister and lashed to 700,000 kilograms of liquid hydrogen and oxygen:

Intimacy. In this hectic age, there really aren't that many opportunities to spend every single second of 501 consecutive days within arm's reach of your loved one. Think about it. No phone calls. No social obligations. No way to leave the room when he starts clipping his toenails or making weird noises in his space sleep.

Sure, most marriages can barely survive the car ride to the cottage—but you guys are *really* in love and will totally cherish each and every one of the 721,440 minutes you'll have together. Alone. So very alone. And if there's an occasional lull in the conversation, well, here are a few helpful "talking points" for a couple who've been in space together for several months:

- How are you today?
- Your hair looks good when one takes into consideration you have not showered for 238 days.
- Um, say, just curious: Did you try to murder me in my sleep again last night?

Cuisine. Get out of the dull routine of Sunday pot roast—and into the exciting habit of eating food that's been rehydrated using water reclaimed from your own urine! Sure, it sounds gross now, but it's just a matter of time before a hipster restaurant in Brooklyn finds a way to charge $350 a couple for the experience. So you'll be ahead of the curve on that, which is nice.

Entertainment. Maybe you're worried that spending seventeen months inside a capsule the size of a parking spot will get a little boring? Nonsense. There'll be so much to do in your outerspace love nest. You can become charter members of the

thirty-million-miles-high club! And after that, you can spend
the next five hundred days trying to ignore the ever-present
spectre of an imminent death. Nothing helps the time pass
quite like mortal terror.

Safety. One of the biggest concerns is the cancer threat posed
by radiation. Not to worry—Inspiration Mars is on top of it.
Remember how they said they're all about "state of the art"?
Well, relax with the confidence that you will be protected from
cosmic rays by the very latest in bags of your own feces.

Confused? Here's how it works:

1. Poop into a bag. Some suggest this is a more challenging
   task than it appears to be, but for the sake of argument let's
   say all (or most) of it hits the mark. Good for you!
2. Take the bag of feces and hang it on the wall of your spacecraft—your tiny, tiny spacecraft that, after a few months,
   will be decorated almost entirely with wall poo, making it
   either a health violation or a modern art exhibit.
3. Marvel as the "organic matter" absorbs the bulk of the
   radiation.
4. Realize that being an astronaut isn't quite as glamorous as
   it was back in the 1960s.

"It's a little queasy sounding," the mission's chief technology officer admits, "but it makes great radiation shielding."

Two things about that:

First, it's actually a *lot* queasy sounding. And second, the
technology officer says they have engaged the "best minds"
from industry and academia to brainstorm their flight systems. And the pinnacle of what the "best minds" can come up
with is: poop shield.

I DON'T THINK there's any reason at all to worry that maybe
this whole mission hasn't been sufficiently thought through.
But if that's the way you feel: relax—there are still discoveries
to be made here on Earth.

Just a few years back, from the deepest jungles of Brazil, came remarkable news of a small indigenous tribe that has had no contact with any other human being on this planet—not even George Clooney, who seems to know everyone.

Photographs taken from the air, and later broadcast by cable news channels, show several members of this primitive society shaking their fists and covered from head to toe in red paint. According to researchers, this probably means they really, really support their troops—either that or they just tried to break into Macaulay Culkin's hut.

The startling discovery of an isolated, uncontacted society is like an M. Night Shyamalan movie come to life, except not disappointing and stupid. It also challenges our conventional wisdom. For instance, if Walt Disney was completely wrong about this being a small world, what else is a lie? Are the ocean's pirates not actually crudely rendered animatronic scoundrels? Are there no roller coasters embedded deep in the mountains of space? Can mouse, dog and duck not truly live in harmony?

Some scientists insist it is paramount that we preserve this Brazilian tribe's autonomy by shielding them from contact with the rest of society and allowing them to carry on their ancient traditions. These are known as "pansy scientists."

I say it is our solemn duty to inform these people about the many vast wonders of the wider world that the rest of us are currently imperilling, sullying or destroying. I say we cannot rest if there exists one society, one tribe, one person on Earth who has not yet been exposed to twerking. I say that even as we turn our eyes to Mars, even as we scour the outer reaches of the galaxy for signs of life, we must come to grips with the unsettling fact that we are not yet done screwing up people on this planet.

I will therefore be mounting an expedition into the deepest Amazon. After cutting through foliage, after fending off wild beasts, after running the world's longest extension cord to keep my Dr. Pepper chilled, we will achieve a deeply historic "first contact" with this idyllic society. We will embrace our

fellow humans. We will learn from their simple utopian paradise and subsequently destroy it by getting them bickering
over who has dibs on the Xbox One.

As I travel through the deadly Amazon, I will be accompanied—and, at the first sign of a snake or cobweb, piggybacked—
by my elite "first contact" team, which shall comprise:

- One doctor, one anthropologist, three entertainment lawyers
  to negotiate movie rights
- One Rush Limbaugh (for bait)
- 170 camera operators dressed as bushes
- One trunk full of post-Genesis Phil Collins records (in case we
  see a volcano)
- One trampoline
- Three Coors Light Maxim golf caddies (no point hauling the
  trampoline if it's not going to be put to good use)
- One photograph of Scott Baio, in case the tribe needs a god to
  worship
- The actual Scott Baio, in case the tribe's god needs a human
  sacrifice

Sure, on one hand, my expedition is a blight on civilized
thought and a thin pretext for rounding up the last untainted
control group on the face of the earth for my client, the pharmaceutical industry. But on the other hand ... awkward silence.

Once contact is made, we'll have a lot of catching up to do.
I'll discover all about the Brazilian tribe's culture through its
noble traditions of storytelling, cave drawings and erotic acts
performed on bespectacled Caucasian strangers (these are
guesses). And I'll fill them in on all they need to know about
the rest of Earth's culture by showing them the new *Planet of
the Apes* movie and a picture of Scarlett Johansson's cleavage.

But there will be more to share. I shall teach them of literature and philosophy and how the study of both enhances the
mind and, at a post-secondary level, the prospects of joblessness. I shall bestow as gifts the finest achievements of modern

humanity—the combustion engine, the antibiotic, the Pringle. And I shall explain to them a range of baffling concepts in ascending order of complexity:

1. Fire
2. Wheel
3. Quantum physics
4. Why Donald Trump is famous

It is roughly at this juncture that I will introduce to them, especially those of them who are hot, the concept of the reality show.

DEAR SCIENTISTS:

Many of you have chosen to dedicate your lives to preventing disease, curing illness and advancing our understanding of humanity's place in the cosmos. Why must you be so selfish?

The time has come for you to join together, buckle down and deliver on the innovation that humanity *really* wants—namely, the kind we see in science fiction movies.

Don't get me wrong. It's great and everything that some of you are toiling to rid our planet of the scourge of malaria. But it's the twenty-first century and I still can't order up a burrito from a replicator and eat it in my hover car.

Here are the things we'd like *now*, please:

Jetpacks. Men and women of science, I ask you: How hard can it be to harness the volatile power of a white-hot rocket, strap it to a person's soft, fleshy back, overcome the inherent challenges posed by atmospheric and gravitational forces and launch the person toward the sky without the certainty of a horrible, fiery death?

You've been promising us jetpacks since I was a kid—I'm beginning to feel foolish walking around in this helmet. Bottom line is this: I'm in my mid-forties now. If we don't get jetpacks soon, I'm never going to know the thrill of rocketing above the great cities of the world without my left blinker on. Don't try to dismiss this: we *need* jetpacks. It's not just about the convenience of being able to get to the 7-Eleven and back in fewer than two seconds. It's about boosting the world's fragile economy with big-ticket sales, new jobs and loads of ancillary benefits. For instance, the spectacle of jetpack accidents could alone support the creation of at least three new television channels and a hundred burn wards.

Plus, nothing would rekindle our interest in celebrity mischief quite like the proliferation of jetpacks. These days, we can barely be bothered to read about the latest Hollywood DUI. But what about breaking news of a DJPUI? Is that something you'd be interested in? Give us jetpacks and it's only a matter of time until an inebriated Mel Gibson crashes to the ground and blames Jews for all the gravity in the world. That's an issue of *People* magazine that we're all buying.

Superpowers. Surely we cannot be too far away from a time when science will be able to grant all seven billion of us a superpower of our choosing. (Hollywood has already provided us with seven billion superhero movies, so we know the numbers are manageable.)

In this utopian future, it will become a rite of passage: you come of age and head to the clinic to pick your ability. *You want the power of invisibility? Sure, no problem. Super-speed? Here you go. You want to fly? Science can only do so much, Mr. Kilmer.*

Robot butlers. Rich people do so much for us, yet science has failed to provide them with any viable alternative to hiring boring old humans to do their bidding. This is a tremendous hassle for the wealthy, because every single human who didn't grow up as a child star or female tennis prodigy still needs to be dehumanized. This process takes a surprising amount of yelling and hurled mayonnaise. But you know what doesn't need to be dehumanized? Dehumans.

It's time for science to nudge things forward. Let's get a robot butler on the market, pronto, even if it suffers from a few minor bugs—such as sometimes walking into a wall or occasionally removing its owner's spleen with a melon baller.

Aliens. Science, you totally need to step up the search for other life forms—to expand our understanding of the universe's majesty, yes, but mostly so we humans can roll with cool alien sidekicks. Dibs on a Wookiee.

Alternatively, we could go the other way with aliens. A couple of years back, economist Paul Krugman of the *New York Times* found a novel way to illustrate his view that more stimulus is required to jolt the US economy to life. "If we discovered that space aliens were planning to attack," he said on CNN, "and we needed a massive buildup to counter the space alien threat ... this slump would be over in eighteen months."

You heard him right: the best hope for the US economy is that *Independence Day* turns out to be a documentary. But is Krugman right? In a time of unprecedented partisan rancour, how would today's America *really* respond to a future interstellar invasion?

April 26, 2016: A sombre President Obama addresses the nation. He announces that a fleet of spaceships is rocketing toward Earth. Quick calculations reveal the alien home world would just now be receiving radio signals carrying the first album by Black Eyed Peas, so a declaration of war by the aliens seems certain. Also a lot of questions about exactly *what* Taboo does in the band.

April 27: Military experts say the warships are heavily armed and likely to first target the United States, owing to the country's unequalled array of monuments and buildings that would look awesome exploding.

April 29: Obama proposes construction of the SuperRay, a massive weapon to which the alien spacecraft are believed to be vulnerable. Estimated cost: $3 trillion. Republican reaction is swift. "It's just another example of big government sticking its nose into the survival of the human species," Marco Rubio says.

May 8: Tea Party darling Rand Paul gives an impassioned speech insisting the best way to repel the aliens is to give the wealthy more tax breaks, or maybe a cool speedboat.

June 24: After weeks of fruitless talks, Obama accidentally negotiates away two key bargaining chips while talking to himself in the mirror.

June 28: Alien ships enter Earth's atmosphere and begin destroying buildings and roads. The Republican Party issues talking points highlighting how America's urban infrastructure has crumbled under Obama.

July 3: Sarah Palin launches a last-minute presidential bid, claiming she is best qualified to battle the alien invaders because she can see the moon from her house.

July 14: The alien armada lands troops as the SuperRay proposal remains bogged down in Congress. "The American people can't come crying to Congress every time their very existence is threatened by a plague of cruel, murderous extra-terrestrials," Palin says. "We have to learn to die within our means."

August 2: Polls show Palin trailing badly in fourteen of the seventeen US states that have yet to be enslaved.

August 30: Zorgon the Unfathomable handily defeats Sarah Palin to win the Republican nomination for president. In a show of unity, he is joined onstage by his rivals, whose arms he raises. And rips off.

October 12: The presidential debate between Hillary Clinton and Zorgon, a 25-foot-tall alien lizard man, ends in acrimony and devouring. Clinton later apologizes for losing her temper.

LOOKING FOR AN unforgettable Christmas present for your loved ones? Now, thanks to science, you can give them the gift of telling them how they're going to die.

Remember back when researchers announced they'd sequenced the human genome? Turns out that was an actual thing they actually did and not, as I had suspected, an outlandish prank to get on 60 *Minutes*. In fact, even greater progress has since been made—and now you can reap the futuristic benefits by finding out things that are wrong with you that even your nagging spouse is unaware of.

For a mere many hundreds of dollars, a company called 23andMe will scan a sample of your DNA and draw up what's called a genomic profile—revealing your predisposition for all sorts of memorable diseases and bodily shortcomings. You'll learn every flaw in your broad genetic makeup. You'll discover which of your genes have "negative mutations." And you'll be made aware of all the horrible afflictions you're at an increased risk of contracting. Scientists describe this as a sort of gateway to a new human utopia, and it's easy to see what they mean—just think of the comfort and serenity that will come from knowing precisely which ailments and syndromes to be anxious and hopelessly depressed about for your entire life.

Once a Silicon Valley start-up, 23andMe is named for the twenty-three pairs of chromosomes that contain our DNA. More important, the name respects the horror-movie tradition that all shadowy, fear-inducing corporations must have benign, cutesy monikers. Think about it: if your genetic code reveals a crammed minefield of infinite possible deaths, hearing the grim tidings from something called "23andMe" will definitely soften the blow. The bad news: you have a predisposition to every single malady that can afflict a human being. The good news: our company name rhymes!

I, for one, am psyched about what 23andMe and other burgeoning gene surveyors mean for humanity. After all, I was getting a little worried that as a species we were finally getting a handle on the whole racism thing—but soon we'll have a vast new area of prejudice: inferior genetics. When accused of bigotry, you can just say, "But I can't be prejudiced—some of my best friends have a genetic predisposition to type 2 diabetes."

And the guilt! This will herald the biggest development in human guilt since the emergence of Judaism. Already we ignore health-based research, advice and common sense as it applies broadly to the masses. But now we can fail to follow precise guidelines tailored specifically for our genetic makeup and risks. In the same vein, how do you think people will respond to good genetic news? With care and restraint? Ha ha. *Hey, my genetic structure lacks the negative mutations associated with an increased risk of heart attack—I think I'll have some bacon on my burger. And on my ice cream. And on my other bacon.*

Here's how the whole making-your-life-a-tedious-procession-to-your-predictable-demise thing works: 23andMe sends you a nice little box that holds a small vial. You remove the vial and spit into it. Then you spit into it again. You spit into the vial for about ten minutes to ensure there's a sufficient amount of saliva for 23andMe to tell you what will probably kill you. (It was so much easier in the old days when your grandmother just came out and told you it would be masturbation.)

You then courier your spit to California, where top scientists in lab coats pour your spit over a computer chip and wait two weeks, passing the time by forming origami birds from your many hundreds of dollars. Then comes the thrill of discovery, followed by—in chronological order—the thrills of regret, disbelief and abject misery. *Wired* magazine calls genomics "the birth of a new industry"—whereas I call it "our generation's greatest contribution to giving young people still another reason to hold a grudge against their parents." You won't buy me a car and you saddled me with an 8 percent increased probability of contracting glaucoma? *I hate you!*

And this is just the beginning. Right now, 23andMe offers what's known as "genotyping"—a high-level analysis of your genetic makeup for the telltale variations that make you different from other humans (example: you are unlike Miley Cyrus because all of Miley Cyrus's DNA are shaped like a penis). But in the near future it's expected that 23andMe and other firms will be able to examine all six billion points of your genetic code, giving you heretofore unimaginable insight into your genetic structure, and giving strangers an entirely new reason to reject your sexual advances in nightclubs. ("A 12 percent increased risk of lactose intolerance? There's no way you're sticking that genome into me.")

Some scientists believe genomics will ultimately increase the human lifespan by a decade. Sadly, that decade will be spent sitting quietly in a darkened room, petrified to go outside because of our 4 percent increased risk of skin cancer.

TECHNOLOGY IS GREAT at solving problems. For instance, I used to have the problem of being able to sneak out of work to go see a movie, but my iPhone "solved" that. Now people can instantly make me work, even at night. Thanks, technology!

What other problems have you solved for us lately?

- **Life's problem:** Those people from high school that I hated— is there any way to get them back into my life?

  Technology's solution: Facebook.

  It used to be a real chore to get in touch with people you were desperate to lose touch with in the first place. But thanks to Facebook, it's a snap to renew acquaintances with all sorts of long-lost semi-friends and remind yourself why you shunned them in the first place.

  Facebook is also a great way to let friends know what you are doing. For instance, if you are just hanging out, you can adjust your update to read "Just hanging out." If you are regretting having accepted as "friends" so many people from your past whom you actively disdain and resent, you can adjust your update to read "Lethally mauled by puma."

- **Life's problem:** Not being lousy enough at driving to perish in a fiery crash of one's own making.

  Technology's solution: Texting behind the wheel.

  Back in the good old days, a swerving vehicle meant one of only two things: either the driver was stinking drunk or it was invisible animal season in Gary Busey's head. (A moose—*veer right!*) Now it's more likely to be some dickhead thumbing a message on his or her cellphone.

Lots of jurisdictions have banned texting while driving, which has completely solved the problem in Opposite Land, where people pay attention to such laws. It has also angered some teens. One high school student in Utah recently tried to counter the perception that "all teens are always texting all the time." Not so, he wrote. In fact, one of his friends said of texting while driving: "I only reply if it's a good conversation, but if it's just 'Hey!' then I won't [reply]." Surely it will comfort the family to know their boy was so discriminating in sending his winky emoticon before the impact of the crash shattered his pelvis.

Silly kids. They just don't get that a ban on texting will allow drivers to focus on more important things. After all, those fingernails aren't going to paint themselves.

- **Life's problem:** A lot of stuff written on the web is too thought-provoking. Any way we can dumb it down?

  Technology's solution: Twitter.

  Twitter is awesome if you're a big fan of celebrities or spelling mistakes. Spend a few days with it and you'll find it hard to believe we ever lived in a world where we didn't know what The Rock was having for lunch. Plus, Twitter gives the traditional—or "dying"—media a faint whiff of relevance. Half of CNN's programming day is now filled with anchors reading the Tweets of HotMomma176 and BigDawg33. Why pay Christiane Amanpour the big bucks when Ashton Kutcher is tweeting his analysis of the Iranian election for free? "I dont know that we shloud B jumping in2 this Iran deal," Kutcher opined in a view that, if memory serves, echoes the recent US intelligence report entitled *Options 2 B Considered by Prez re: Iran deal*.

  Still, one wonders how long Twitter can stay popular. Like many people in this fast-paced world, I have trouble with the site's limit of 140 characters per Tweet. Simply put, that's way too many characters.

  That's why I'm introducing a new messaging utility of my own. Welcome to ... Bwhh.

  Bwhh allows you to keep in touch with friends, update colleagues and perpetuate the illusion that your daily tedium has subtle undertones of meaning. But it does so while keeping postings to a more reasonable number of characters: nine. Also, no vowels.

Did you totally sleep in? Let the world know you totally slept in. Just log on to Bwhh and type: "Ttl slptn" Future generations will cherish your insight into the human condition.

Did you come across something really boring on the internet? Warn everyone with Bwhh: "www=zzzzz."

Did seeing a dog in a pet store window make you sad? Don't keep that kind of gold to yourself. Bwhh it! "dg = frwn."

Bwhh is the future of social messaging and desperate cries for attention. Start Bwhhing now before starting to Bwhh makes you seem helplessly trendy.

THE WORLD'S AUTHORITATIVE text on mental health is the *Diagnostic and Statistical Manual of Mental Disorders*. Updated by psychiatrists since the 1950s, it lists all the ways in which humans can be nuts, and therefore features many big words and several photographs of Dennis Rodman.

The book—known among mental health professionals as the *DSM*—is constantly being revised and expanded by the American Psychiatric Association (APA). Mental illnesses are studied anew for each edition. This is very controversial, and not just because marrying Sean Penn hasn't been included yet.

Potential disorders that have vied in recent times to make the cut include:

Sex Addiction: Defined as "a pattern of repeated sexual relationships involving a succession of lovers who are experienced by the individual only as things to be used," this condition wasn't given full disorder treatment in the *DSM-5*. Is that because it would classify as mentally ill several former US presidents, all former Backstreet Boys and every man ever featured in a Coors Light commercial?

Binge Eating: This "illness" is described by psychiatrists as "a serious disorder in which you frequently consume unusually large amounts of food." Statistics indicate it afflicts one out of every one Kirstie Alley.

Pathological Hoarding: Long considered a symptom of obsessive-compulsive disorder, hoarding has now been classified as a disorder all on its own. Sufferers just can't let go. Think of old people with stacks of magazines from 1942, or Stephen Harper with power.

Internet Addiction: According to the APA, this addiction "consists of at least three subtypes: excessive gaming, sexual preoccupations and email/text messaging." This raises a number of questions, such as how the APA gained access to my browser history.

And the list goes on. Do you go shopping a lot? You have a mental disorder. Are you "pathologically" biased in your views? You have a mental disorder. Are huge quantities of food disappearing from your fridge at night? You have a mental disorder—or Garfield as a house guest. Either way, you're deeply troubled.

If some psychiatrists get their way, there will be yet one more affliction added: being bitter. Apparently, bitterness is not just a feeling we all have at some point—it's a mental illness! Begin fitting The Cure, Rush Limbaugh and Squidward for straitjackets—they're all loco. So are Billy Bob Thornton, Jennifer Aniston and every person in the world after three beers.

Under proposed changes, the state of being bitter will be officially classified as post-traumatic embitterment disorder. One news story quoted the German psychiatrist who named the affliction as saying of its sufferers, "It's one step more complex than anger. They're angry plus helpless." Angry plus helpless? In Canada we refer to that condition as "winter."

Enough already. Bitterness is the birthright of every citizen and the default state of every Baldwin. It's a sign that we are alert and awake to the variety of ways in which our world is conspiring against us. I ask the American Psychiatric Association:

If being consumed by a sense of injustice is wrong, why did God invent blogs and ulcers?

I suppose it could be argued that psychiatrists are just keeping up with the times. The twenty-first century is all about feeling special. We're buoyed by people following our bursts of adjectives and emoticons on Twitter. Our kids are handed Olympic-calibre medals for finishing a 2K fun run. People as special as us can't just be weird or unwilling to exercise self-restraint—we have to be ill.

Yesterday's bad habit is today's mental disorder. And today's mental disorder is tomorrow's pharmaceutical solution. How long will it be until drug companies have created new pills for these new disorders, complete with new side effects involving even longer and more dangerous erections? The *New England Journal of Medicine* recently discovered that more than half of the 137 psychiatrists working on the DSM have ties to the pharmaceutical industry. One US professor found DSM working groups in which "every single person has ties" to drug companies.

But at a time when even good old-fashioned bitterness is under the disorder microscope, perhaps it's optimism that's the real mental illness. There's no good reason to feel it. There's no rational excuse for expressing it.

Fear not, those of sunny disposition—I'm sure they're working on a pill to "cure" you. In the meantime, to prevent serious injury, be sure to immediately consult your psychiatrist if you experience a smile lasting longer than four hours.

MANY ECONOMISTS WASTE their time studying a variety of data to forecast where the economy is heading. The truth is they need only consult the one indicator known to be foolproof: the index of Utterly Pointless Innovations in Beer.

The theory is so simple that an actor in a Coors Light commercial could understand it: if beer companies are investing millions in the development of highly expensive and Utterly Pointless Innovations, the economic outlook is promising.

Think back to the sweet times of 2006. The economy was strong. The stock market was soaring. And actual university-educated people were actually employed to make the mountains on Coors Light labels turn blue when the contents were "ice cold and ready to enjoy." In the dark ages before this advance, beer drinkers had absolutely no way of knowing when their beer was cold—apart from several ways, such as touching it.

(This technology was widely mocked, but consider its potential. With only a few tweaks, we could use it to determine when our coffee is still hot enough to drink, or when Nicolas Cage has finally stopped overacting. Has he turned blue? No? Then I think I'm going to skip that next *National Treasure* movie.)

In addition to successfully creating a thermochromic liquid crystal process for its flagship brand's Cold Activated Bottle, Coors forked out to develop the Vented Wide Mouth can and a Frost Brew Liner capable of "locking in" the beer's Frost Brewed taste. The vented can has an opening 8 percent wider than that of a typical can, to deliver—as Coors so eloquently puts it—"a smoother pour [and] a draft-like experience that reduces the vacuum or 'glugging' effect." More important, it make beer go into face more faster!

(Alas, millions of helpless frat boys are still waiting for Coors to develop high-tech "content-sensitive technology" that lets them know when their beer can is empty.)

Still, we could sleep easier at night as a society knowing that innovation of this magnitude would never be pursued if brewers sensed that a slump in sales was coming.

Years later, the beer-based indicators are very different. Consider some of the more recent innovations made by the brewers of the big three American light beers:

The Miller Lite Vortex bottle. This design boasts "specially designed grooves" that create a "vortex" as the beer is poured. Indeed, MillerCoors claims the bottle's shape will allow the beer inside "to flow right out." Does that mean drinkers of Miller Lite were having trouble figuring out how to get the beer out of the regular bottle? (Spoiler alert: probably.) Sadly, a beer company crowing about a bottle design that lets the liquid "flow right out" is like McDonald's unveiling a revolutionary new cardboard box that allows a Big Mac to "be removed for eating."

Bud Light Lime. For what felt like years, Budweiser focused on trumpeting this brand's "drinkability"—a long and expensive campaign that ultimately succeeded in convincing us that Bud Light was neither a solid nor a gas. Alas, the brewer's only innovation of recent note has been proving it is possible to put beer and lime together and make them taste like Nick Nolte's sweat after a tequila bender. The company also released Bud Lime Mojito—because what's not to like about lime, mint and light beer, other than a liquid combination of those three things? Presumably, next summer all the bros will be sucking back a Bud Light Cool Ranch Dorito and saying things like "Bro, Cool Ranch me!"—to which the other bro will reply, "Bro!" (I think I've got that right. I've been studying Rosetta Stone Bro.)

The Coors Light Cold Activation Window Pack. The Coors Light brand claims to be "known for continuous beer innovation." A recent "innovation"? The Coors Light Cold Activation Window Pack—which sounds wordy enough to be pricey and neat but is, in fact, nothing more than a small hole in the beer case that allows us to see if the mountains are blue and the beer is cold.

A hole. In a box. As indicators go, it's enough to prompt the governor of the Bank of Canada to warn of our imminent return to a barter economy.

There are some small signs of hope out there. The makers of Sam Adams recently began producing a new beer glass that was the result of "two years of scientific research, thousands of hours of taste tests and dozens of rejected styles." It features a narrow top, to sustain the head, and laser etching along the bottom of the glass to ensure "constant aroma release" (which, coincidentally, is something that I have achieved involuntarily after drinking Sam Adams).

But the clear message of the index of Utterly Pointless Innovations in Beer is that the recovery is weaker than feared. Get out of the stock market. Wait before buying a house. You will know better times are ahead when you see a commercial for a can of Coors Light that boasts Romulan-style cloaking technology and five razor blades on the side for a crisp, full-bodied shave.

ARE YOU SITTING down? Good, because this last bit of news is going to come as quite a blow. Despite all you've believed, all you've prided yourself on, despite all the photographs you've posted to Instagram, it pains me to inform you that ... well, there's no easy way to put this: your genitals just aren't that fascinating.

Please understand, it's not me saying that. I, for one, completely believe you when you say your private parts are an anatomical wonder worthy of poetic commemoration and weekend videotaping. And I'm not just saying that because of the little hat you bought for them.

However, the brainiacs in the academic community—well, they are of the view that the topography of your crotch is profoundly unremarkable. Welcome to Yawnsville, population: your vagina. I am not exaggerating when I suggest a fellow could theoretically drop his drawers in the North Yard at Harvard and those faculty Poindexters would just saunter on by, completely uninterested in the acrobatic feats I was making it perform.

But whip out a duck penis and, man, watch those science nerds reach for the microscopes and protractors! Yes, the genitals of ducks are the wave of the future in the research community. It seems as though every PhD with a lab coat and a Segway is off questing for a promiscuous quacker to probe and prod in search of secrets to the Compelling Mysteries of

Life—or, failing that, to the Still Fairly Interesting Mysteries of Why That Duck's Unit Looks So Freaky.

It all started with the findings of Patricia Brennan, a behavioural ecologist at Yale University. Dr. Brennan uncovered evidence among waterfowl of what news reports have described as "a sexual arms race waged with twisted genitals," including phalluses that range from smooth to covered with spines and grooves. (Note to human evolution: Can we skip this part?)

A *New York Times* article about Dr. Brennan begins with a scene in which she declares a Meller's duck from Madagascar to be "the champion" of genital evolution (second place: Tommy Lee) and then "carefully coax[es] out his phallus," which is subsequently described as "a long, spiraling tentacle." After flipping back to the front page to ensure I wasn't reading the latest Danielle Steel, I continued on to discover that in most birds, the vagina—or oviduct—is a simple tube. But the oviducts of some waterfowl feature various sacs and pockets that "function as dead-ends or false passages." In other words, impregnating a duck is a lot like trying to loot an Egyptian tomb—but with your wang, which makes it harder to carry the gold.

According to the *Times*, Dr. Brennan was "oblivious" to bird phalluses until 1999. In that fateful year, while working in a Costa Rican forest on a non-freaky-duck-sex-related expedition, she spotted two birds mating. "They became unattached, and I saw this huge thing hanging off of him," she said. "I could not believe it. It became one of those questions I wrote down: why do these males have this huge phallus?" Other questions she wrote down included "Why don't people invite me to dinner parties anymore?" Alas, these questions had no answers, except for the last one, which is pretty obvious when you think about it.

Through the use of dissection and saucy pictures of Daisy Duck, Dr. Brennan discovered that male waterfowl evolve more ornate phalluses to attempt to bypass the defences created by ever more elaborate vaginas, and vice versa. "Some large waterfowl that are highly monogamous, like geese and swans, have small phalluses, whereas other species that are quite small but more promiscuous have more elaborate genitalia," Brennan told the *Times*. To illustrate that theory: if Leonardo DiCaprio were a duck, his phallus would by now have evolved to include colourful feathers, a digital clock and a pyrotechnics display at the top of every hour.

Though she's already published her work, Dr. Brennan remains so dedicated to her research that she visits a waterfowl sanctuary every two weeks to inspect and measure the phalluses of six species of ducks. You can tell it's her day to visit because there are eight thousand male birds waiting out front with flowers and chocolate. Dr. Brennan says she's become "very good at predicting what the genitalia of one sex will look like by looking at the other sex first." Sadly, her wait continues for this category to come up on *Jeopardy!*

Lately, Dr. Brennan has become obsessed with the question of why the duck phallus grows and then disappears. "It may be easier to regrow it than to keep it healthy," she offers in a theory that (a) is supported by some academics, and (b) makes me cringe. "But those are some of the things I may be able to find out. When you're doing something that so little is known about, you can't really predict what's going to happen." Except that your dates will continue to back away slowly from the dinner table before turning to flee.

THE FUTURE AND WHY WE SHOULD AVOID IT

REASON NO. 10: AGING

I've got bad news about your own personal future: a new study has found that memory loss begins as early as one's mid-forties. But as one who recently entered his mid-forties, here's something even more distressing: the study found that memory loss begins as early as one's mid-forties.

And it's not just memory. The study, published in the *British Medical Journal*, also found that over a period of ten years there was a 3.6 percent decline in mental reasoning among men aged forty-five to forty-nine. Worryingly, that may be enough to make the brain succumb to nefarious plots like email scams and drinking responsibly.

Not that there aren't positives to a feeble memory: it can be a real thrill ride. Every moment holds the potential for adventure and intrigue. Will I remember where I parked my car? Will I remember that I own a car? MY PULSE IS RACING!

The key is having the right attitude. For instance, I used to get flustered when I couldn't immediately recall the name of an acquaintance, or long-lost friend, or blood relative. Not anymore. Now I embrace it as a challenge: to figure out who you are before you figure out that I can't figure out who you are. How will you know if I win? I will use your name with enthusiasm and repetition. JIM, IT'S JIM-DARN GOOD TO JIM YOU, JIM! (There is a chance I will say this even if your name is Nancy.)

The brain is truly bewildering. You'd think there'd be some kind of setting so we could actively prioritize what we remember. Instead, I now find the following scenario playing out most mornings:

1. Wonder where car keys are.
2. Find car keys.
3. Place car keys in pocket.
4. Wonder where car keys are.

Yet during a recent holiday, my family and I found ourselves in a ski gondola with a few younger chaps. Talk turned, as it often does on such occasions, to the 1980s song "The Safety Dance" by Men Without Hats.

I impressed the kids with my knowledge of the lyrics. I dazzled them by referencing the song's inclusion in an episode of *Futurama*. And I amazed them with a shot-by-shot recollection from memory of the song's video, including the random guys wearing chicken masks. At this point the fellows fell silent, as people often do when calculating the odds of surviving a thirty-foot plunge to escape a conversation.

There's an obvious lesson we all can learn from this: to be forever preserved in memory, all our life's events must be set to the tune of "The Safety Dance":

> *Met a guy at a conference*
> *Said his name was Ted McGee*
> *He wore a brown suit*
> *Is allergic to fruit*
> *Then he said he had to go and pee.*

What's most irritating is the selective nature of what the brain retains. First names of performing members of the Osmond family? Scored six of seven without consulting Google. What I just got for Christmas? No clue.

It's best to console oneself with the upside. People with

strong memories are often forced to relive their darkest and most painful moments, whereas I move freely through life unburdened by the mental image of my Grade 8 designer jeans.

I do wonder, though: How much worse can my memory get? And how will the decline manifest? Also, where did this bruise come from?

If there's any good news out of the study, it's that even as recollection, reasoning and comprehension erode with age, our vocabulary endures. The most memory-challenged person remembers words. So at the very least, I'll always be able to eloquently apologize for forgetting to wear pants.

I DIALLED INTO a conference call the other day. Just as we were getting under way, I recalled with a lurch that I'd committed myself to another call at the same time. Or had I? I needed to check my email. But my laptop was in for a memory upgrade and, dammit, I couldn't find my iPhone. I rummaged through bags and coats. I looked on and under tables. My frantic search was producing a fair bit of noise, so I stopped to press mute. That's when I found my iPhone.

It was in my hand. I had been talking on it.

This actually happened. I am officially getting old. It's only a matter of time before I pull a hamstring while grocery shopping.

Beginning to lose your memory sounds like a downer—but it can be a great conversation starter. I, for one, recommend a fun game that I like to call Where Have I Been Previously?

Here's how it works: every now and then I get together with some old friends and we try to remember when last we saw each other. Was it six months ago at a restaurant? Eight months ago on the golf course? If you get the perfect blend of faulty memory and stubborn insistence, this could take up about forty-five minutes.

It works at family gatherings too. Was it last Christmas that the turkey was too dry? Was it '06 or '08 when Uncle Mike fell asleep on the toilet? My family now spends 85 percent of most holiday meals trying to remember the chronological order of events at past holiday meals. Believe me, it's hours and hours of fun for everyone who doesn't get bored and go watch TV instead.

If you've mastered this game and are ready to take it to Expert level, try remembering what everyone gave everyone else for Christmas the preceding year. There are no wrong answers, because no one can ever remember the right answers.

I LOOKED IN the mirror. I don't usually *look* in the mirror—at most, I may glance or take a gander. (This fact is supported by anyone who has seen my "hairdo.") But this time I lingered because I noticed something I'd never seen before: the hair of one of my eyebrows was askew. Frankly, I had no idea my eyebrow hair was even askewable. How long has this been going on? When did my brows go rogue, forcing me to worry not only about bed-head but also about bed-face?

In forty-six years, I'd never known my eyebrows to do anything other than divert forehead sweat and indicate astonishment every time Whoopi Goldberg won an acting award. It's hard not to wonder: Exactly what evolutionary purpose was served by eyebrows that start growing like mad in middle age? Is this nature's way of telling us we were all meant to be eccentric university professors? Or is this simply a genetic relic of an ancient survival mechanism for aging men in a primitive world? *Sure, Grampa is a horrible burden and we'd all love to push him out into the night to be devoured by sabre-toothed tigers—but dang it, the kids are sleeping so soundly under his eyebrows!*

I'VE STARTED TALKING to myself. I was backing out of the driveway and was into the third sentence before I realized it was happening. What's worse, it wasn't even something interesting, like a subconscious thought or an alien possession. It was just the normal boring stuff I usually *think* to myself—"Okay, first go get gas, then the bank, *then* Jazzercise ..."—except now I was saying it out loud for some reason. You know who does this? Old people. I don't think Andy Rooney even knew there was a camera on him for the last twenty years of his life. That's just how the elderly talk when they're alone. *Why does fruit have to come in so many different shapes? Who decided purple should be called purple? LETTERS ARE BETTER THAN EMAILS!*

Also, I'm getting a little worried about the wisdom thing. The fundamental bargain of life is that as you grow older, you acquire a measure of insight and perspective—which sort of makes up for all the nose hair and incontinence. But I'm getting on and so far I haven't come up with anything more profound than "If you have the time, homemade guacamole is best." Do you get your wisdom all at once? Will I wake up at the age of seventy-five going, "Aha! Adopt the pace of nature: her secret is patience!" These things keep me up at night—or they would, if I could stay awake past 9:30.

Then again, relative youth is still youth. I have a regular poker game with a group of guys, all of whom are older than me. It usually takes about twenty minutes for things to degenerate into confusion, contention and a general unawareness of who won, who lost and what the hell just happened. I figure I'm about three years away from being able to win every hand simply by saying confidently: "No, my pair of sixes beats your royal flush, old-timer. THOSE ARE THE RULES."

Almost every day, the world presents me with a new way of feeling my age. For instance, Can No Longer Focus on Things Too Close to My Face Day was a bit of a bummer. Another tough day came recently courtesy of Paulina Gretzky, daughter of Wayne Gretzky and a person who uses Twitter to broadcast photos of herself in which she displays few clothes and less shame. Here is how two versions of me would react to this:

PAST ME: Oh my God, she is almost naked in those photos. That is so hot.

PRESENT ME: Oh my God, she is almost naked in those photos. I'm glad I don't have a daughter.

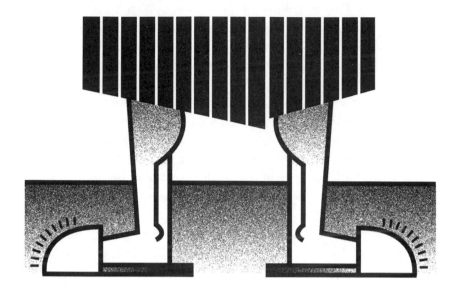

For the record, Future Me would likely mutter something about bikinis and the statistical probability of melanoma.

I'VE BEEN THINKING a lot about slippers lately. I don't currently own a pair, but the benefits of slippers grow more obvious and alluring with age. Warm feet. Superior traction. And all for the low, low price of no one ever again thinking of you as a sexual being.

Some of my friends are nonchalant about slipper ownership, but I remain of the view that it's a big step. Once you become a slipper guy, there's no going back. You are fated to a life of flannel pyjamas, warm milk and Ned Flanders expressions. I even know people—including a work colleague—who will bring their slippers to social events at other people's houses. Because, really, there's no easier way of indicating to your host, "I'm going to sit over here on the couch, converse briefly about the weather and then nod off for twenty minutes. Thanks for having me!"

THE OTHER DAY I actually said "Bah!"

IN RECENT MONTHS, I've taken to carrying a pen and note-book around with me at all times. I highly recommend it. It's an easy way to make sure you never again forget anything—so long as you can remember it long enough to get out your pen and notebook. And remember to remember where you put the notebook.

Young people will assume I'm exaggerating the fleeting nature of middle-aged memory. They will ask, "How hard can it be to maintain one's train of thought for eight to twelve seconds?" To which I can only laugh and say by way of reply: "What were you asking about?"

Allow me to break it down for you. Let's return to the four-step process:

1. Remember an errand that needs to be done.
2. Reach into coat pocket for pen and notebook to ensure errand is not forgotten.
3. Forget errand.
4. Continue to remember all the words to "Sussudio" for some reason.

Here's a pro tip for those approaching middle age: on the rare occasion when you *do* put pen to paper in time, it's important to write out the complete thought. I can't stress this enough. Otherwise, you're never going to remember what the notation means.

I made approximately 2.96 million lists over the Christmas holidays, and each morning I'd transfer the same item to the new list: "Get thing to T." Each morning, I'd try to remember: "What does 'Get thing to T' mean?" Never cracked it. With the holidays now behind us, all I can do is hope "T" wasn't a person and "thing" wasn't a gift or a kidney.

If it was, I'm going to have to send an apology. I'll put it on my list.

SO I'M HAVING my mid-life crisis now—and so far it consists of struggling to decide what to do for my mid-life crisis. Who knew that choosing the physical manifestation of my crippling self-doubt and fleeting mortality could be so stressful?

In my twenties, I always assumed I'd wake up one morning, slap on a hairpiece and embrace a fun new hobby like curling or alcoholism. But the truth is, people judge you on the originality and quality of your crisis. It's like a science fair for middle-aged people: you don't want to be the guy struggling to hook up a potato battery while the genius next to you breeds an advanced race of atomic supermen.

That's why I decided right from the start to rule out all the clichéd mid-life crises for men. Among them:

Buying a sports car: This is the classic display of male mid-life anxiety. Every sporty two-seater sold to a man over the age of forty should come with a mandatory bumper sticker that reads: "My other car is more practical but does not sufficiently announce my paralyzing fear of death. PLEASE PRETEND I LOOK YOUNG AND COOL BY WINKING MISCHIEVOUSLY (LADIES ONLY)."

Alas, men of a certain age get so caught up in the allure of the shiny $50,000 car that they overlook one important fact: it costs $49,980 more than a box of Just For Men but has the exact same effect—it makes women look at you and instantly think "Viagra."

Trying to recapture one's youth through sport: I'm ashamed to say I gave this a try not long ago, going out on Monday nights to play pickup hockey. I hadn't taken to the ice in full equipment in twenty-five years, but believe me, it didn't feel that way: it felt as though I'd never done it before. The fellas would surely have nicknamed me the Human Pylon, but pylons don't vomit on the bench. (For reasons I still don't understand, my ensuing retirement speech was not carried live on Sportsnet.)

Having an extramarital affair: Engaging in a tawdry fling would violate the sanctity of the marital bond and inflict grave emotional distress. Also, it seems like a lot of work—the sneaking around, the clandestine texting, and all those candles that need to be lit around the bathtub (I've never had an affair so I assume all are conducted like the ones on TV). And the cost of hotel room service every time—that's some pricey sex-having! Nor should we overlook all the flirting that's required to get things started—I mean, who's got the energy? Listen, lady, you're very attractive but tonight's episode of *The Mentalist* isn't going to watch itself.

There are practical concerns, too. When I hit forty, I pretty much had to stop lying in all aspects of my life because my memory is no longer reliable enough to keep track of any untruths. How can I remember to hide the Visa bill when I forgot we had a Visa?

Another critical guideline of the mid-life crisis is that under no circumstances is one permitted to copy the crisis of a friend. It draws too much attention. One middle-aged man deciding to buy a motorbike can be plausibly explained as an innocuous new pastime. Two middle-aged men suddenly buying motorcycles supplies the planet's recommended daily allowance of sadness. So what's left?

Pursue a selfless dedication to others: Confronted with their mortality, some resolve in middle age to seek a more fulfilling existence through tireless dedication to noble causes. This is a deeply honourable path for a human being to follow. On the other hand: really boring.

Start seeing a psychiatrist: The most important thing about seeing a psychiatrist is that you can tell people you're seeing a psychiatrist. In the eyes of others, this gives you *Hidden* Depth. *I always thought Scott was fairly normal and dull, but turns out he's walking the knife-edge of madness!* I'm keeping this one in my back pocket.

Blame others for my failings: A real load off.

Move to Shaving Commercial World: You probably haven't considered this option, but give it a chance ...

For years, I sat in front of the television and envied the male inhabitants of Shaving Commercial World—envied them their spacious bathrooms and their fogless mirrors and their unfailingly buxom and easily impressed women friends ("You successfully shaved your face? Let's have sex!"). I marvelled at their precise application of lather and their sombre beard-based reminiscences. And I was enthralled by the recurring depiction of the plight of that single villainous facial hair, expertly vanquished by the noble forces of steel, cream and crude computer animation. Take that, Señor Whisker.

Shaving Commercial World is a modern-day utopia where there are no nicks, no razor burn and apparently no shirts. In Shaving Commercial World, George Clooney's perpetual three-day growth of beard marks him as a haggard drifter shunned by women and feared by children—whereas my smooth, satisfying shave puts me at constant risk of beatification and/or a threesome. In my new world, I could steal Clooney's girlfriend and still have enough time left in my day to cinch a crisp white towel around my waist.

In Shaving Commercial World, a man gets to spend five, six hours in a row admiring his clean, close shave—which is great. But I already did that back in my old, regular world. What's different is that in Shaving Commercial World a man's shave is simultaneously admired by a sexy woman who has pouty lips and also cleavage. Should you grow weary of stroking your own chin and cheeks appreciatively (a long shot, but still), she will stroke them for you. Your burden is her burden. Your joy is her joy. Meanwhile her cleavage remains her cleavage, although you can negotiate visitation rights.

But never let it be said the inhabitants of Shaving Commercial World are a frivolous people. Over the past decade, I have witnessed their single-minded quest for progress—evolving from the primitive Bic Twin Select, with its two measly blades, through the Mach 3 and the Schick Quattro to the Gillette Fusion, which has five blades and is so high-tech and miraculous that the mere presence of it leaves scantily clad females with no hormone-based option but to raise an eyebrow with seductive intent.

You might ask: Are there other advantages of moving to Shaving Commercial World? Well, back in *your* world I had plenty of obligations and worries. In Shaving Commercial World, there is only one obligation: figuring out how to fit even more blades onto a razor to deliver an even closer, even smoother marketing campaign.

Still, Shaving Commercial World isn't without its challenges. The schools aren't great, what with government's extravagant funding of shiny, futuristic laboratories and the generous tax credit for chest waxing. And believe me: life is not easy on anyone with an allergy to subpar acting.

Then again, it's not like Shaving Commercial World is the only relocation option. In fact, I thought first about moving to Axe Body Spray World, where there is also an abundance of cleavage—as well as cleavage's popular roommate, nymphomania. But frankly, I'm at the age where my thoughts turn to the more practical elements of being gang-tackled by thirty-eight sex-hungry stereotypes. *Uhh, it's great that you're naked and all caressy and stuff, but this grass stain isn't going to remove itself from this pair of Dockers, ladies.*

I also briefly considered Ford World, attracted by the idea that everything I did in Ford World would be voiced-over by Kiefer Sutherland. This would, I reasoned, add drama and gravitas to my crochet class. "He lifts his handcrafted maple Tunisian hooks. Is that a shawl he's making? Or is it [*dramatic pause*] a poncho?" I also gave thought to packing up and heading to Coors Light Commercial World, but in the end I wasn't sure I had a sufficient amount of homosexuality to repress by pretending to be that not gay.

Ultimately, I decided that Shaving Commercial World is the place for me. Now, if you'll excuse me, I see a lingerie model and three of her bikini team colleagues coming up the walk to welcome my face to the neighbourhood. If only I could figure out how to remove this crisp white towel ...

BACK IN THE real world, I've already started planning for my decline. Perhaps you think of your summer vacation as a respite. Not me. I see mine as an opportunity—a chance to train for retirement, to prepare myself mentally and physically to be the best at doing not very much at all.

Career-wise, this past summer found me exactly halfway through my projected work life—before the traditional age of pensions and porch-sitting. The time was right to check where I stood in terms of my pursuit of three critical retirement goals and in terms of whether my super-lazy vacationing is helping me get there.

Let's start with Goal No. 1: **Learning How to Make a Big Deal about Things.**

From what I can tell, one of the keys to a successful retirement is being able to portray an ordinary outing as something far more ambitious. Here's a good example: to judge from the theatrics of my late grandfather, no civilian award bestowed by the Governor General would have been sufficient to recognize his valour and sacrifice in bringing in the mail. He'd throw those envelopes down on the kitchen table like a Plains Indian presenting a slain buffalo to the tribe. OVER TO THE WOMENFOLK—MY WORK HERE IS DONE.

A beach vacation is great training in this regard. Once you're hunkered down in the sand, talk of driving to town for supplies acquires the kind of rhetoric usually reserved for assaulting Everest in short shorts. Heck, there was a time when I went twenty minutes without a beer because I was positioned comfortably in a chair and the cooler was slightly over there. I portrayed the act of finally getting up as on a par with the actions of a Greek god—and one of the good ones too, not the god of pottery or napping or whatever.

In retirement, this skill set should translate to mall outings. "Well, I'm back and I managed to get you your bag of Kernels." *[Sits down and patiently awaits celebratory parade.]*

Goal No. 2: **Having Strong Opinions about Things.**

I need improvement here. I don't feel enough ways about stuff—at least, not with sufficient passion and rage. Certainly, I'm about as far as one can get from my grandmother, whose every sentence began with a Dismissive Wave of the Hand and continued along the lines of "Ah, those (politicians / bankers / reporters / squirrels) up there (in Ottawa / on Bay Street / on the TV / in my attic) are all the same!"

But I'm not entirely without elderly calibre conversational skills. There's my keen ability to observe the obvious and remark upon it. In fact, not ten minutes ago, I said to my family: "Sure is a lot of fog out there this morning." You know, just in case they were wondering what all that fog-like stuff was. (It was fog.)

I've also mastered certain non-verbal forms of communication, including the all-important getting-up-from-a-chair noise, which needs to suggest a level of exertion heretofore thought beyond the reach of mortal man. After a two hour hike this week, I fell into the sofa for thirty minutes—then asked one of my kids to transcribe the sound I made as I got up. Here's what he wrote: "Hmmrrrrrpphhhhaaaaahh." If anything, he went a little light on the *A*'s.

My third and final retirement goal: **Accepting That I Will Never Again Remember Any New Information.**

As I indicated earlier in this chapter (at least I think I mentioned it? And who are you again?), I'm getting closer to living with the reality that my brain hasn't retained any new facts since 2007. It's as though my neurons got together and decided: "If we take on even one more piece of knowledge, we're going to forget the plot of every episode of *Fantasy Island*. And that, my friends, is simply too high a price."

273

This summer, having forgotten that I can no longer remember things, I paid actual money to purchase a book with the title *Europe: The Struggle for Supremacy, 1453 to the Present*. At long last, my knowledge of European geopolitical dynamics would extend beyond what I learned from Risk. I was about sixty pages in when I had the following conversation with one of my boys:

HE: What's your book about?

ME [*slyly consulting the cover*]: It's about the history of Europe, from 1453 to the present.

HE: What happened in 1453?

[*Pause*]

ME: Did I mention that it's published by the fine people at Allen Lane?

HE: Seriously, what have you learned so far?

[*Long pause*]

ME: I believe mention is made of Belgium.

I purposely left the book behind when we went home. At least, I think I did.

LIKE ANYONE IN middle age who has a mortgage, car payments and an investment portfolio heavily weighted toward sofa-cushion change, I am coming to grips with the fact that I may never be rich. This is a shame because I've spent most of my life planning what I'd do as a man of unfathomable wealth and influence. In all honesty, I think I'd be pretty good at it. I certainly believe I could develop a natural affinity for talking down to foreigners. *Wash the Bentley, Miguel, not the driveway.*

As one who since 1996 has insisted on riding in the back seat of his Corolla while holding a jar of Grey Poupon, I know exactly where I'd live as a rich man (a summer home in Tuscany, and winters on the moon). I know exactly what I'd spend my money on (caviar and revenge). And I know exactly which person I'd speak in (the third). Bottom line: Scott Feschuk believes Scott Feschuk is ready to be very wealthy.

Lest you think me selfish, I'd be generous enough to give a small portion of my vast fortune to philanthropic pursuits. But I'd be petty enough to give it to the charity that agrees to name the most stuff after me. Sure, my millions could help cure cancer, but instead please join me at the grand opening of the gleaming new Scott M. Feschuk Centres for Lactose Intolerance.

Alas, at my age it's time to give up on implausible long shots, like my winning the lottery or ever working hard. Instead, this may be my last chance to convince someone of tremendous resources and limited due diligence to buy into one of my Five Surefire Ideas for Making Me Obscenely Rich:

1. Produce pay-per-view celebrity weddings: Don't even try to tell me you wouldn't pay $49.95 to watch live as Katy Perry marries John Mayer or Robert Pattinson or a Teamster in a bunny costume that she just thought was *sooooo* cute. You'd watch it. We'd all watch it. The pre-ceremony jitters and dramatic HIV tests. The part where Donald Trump fires the caterer. And, for an extra fee, after-hours footage from the video camera rigged up in the honeymoon suite. A pay-per-view wedding would be a great career move for aspiring movie stars keen to build their public profiles, and for declining movie stars keen to keep their mansions and breasts from being repossessed. I literally cannot see how this idea isn't going to make me a millionaire.

2. Start up a magazine called The Beaver: What's that you say? There already is a Canadian magazine called *The Beaver*? Wrong, idiot. After decades of publication, *The Beaver* changed its name. Turns out the word *beaver* also has a completely different meaning that I'd tell you about except that I can't stop giggling because I am apparently twelve years old. Suffice to say the "unfortunate double entendre" was harming sales because subscription solicitations would get caught up in email spam filters, presumably along with pitches for *Amateur Woodworker*, *Hot Rod* and *House & Scrotum*. I plan to avoid that pitfall by advertising "Get Beaver Delivered to Your Home" on airplane banners flown over schoolyards. Just try to find a flaw in that plan.

3. Invent the next must-have toy: As someone who, as a child, personally witnessed his own grandfather bowl over a tiny, helpless woman during a mad rush for the last pre-Christmas shipment of Care Bears, I know the power of the Big Holiday Toy. But kids today are more advanced and savvy, making this the perfect time for Baby's First Reciprocating Saw. Better get in line now.

4. Found the company Celebrity Eulogies, Inc.: We live in a culture obsessed with celebrities, and yet our funerals continue to be sullied by the reminiscences of mere friends and family. Wouldn't your grandmother go more easily to her eternal resting place knowing that the tribute to her life was uttered not by fat Uncle Jimmy but by TV's Starsky? Call and within forty-eight hours we'll have a D- to C-list celebrity on hand to pay tribute to your dead relative, sign a few autographs and pity the fools in attendance (Mr. T only). For the right price, we could even have the supporting cast of *The Sopranos* act out one of the many scenes they shot around coffins. Believe me, those guys aren't doing anything else.

5. Create "anti-product placement" and unendorsements: No one listens to celebrity endorsers any more. So how to increase market share? Hire one of our celebrities to talk trash about your competitors. ("Hi, I'm Jay Z and this Pepsi I'm drinking tastes like urine.") Or put your rival's leading product into a carefully constructed scene in a movie featuring one of our celebrity clients, just as we're pitching McDonald's to do.

> <Fade in>
> *We see Pauly Shore. He is dressed as Hitler.*
> HITLER: This Burger King Whopper makes me want to invade Poland!

Investors, I await your expressions of interest and, more to the point, your expressions of certified cheque. Please form an orderly line outside the door of the van where I live.

I'M NOT SURE if you're aware of this, but one's decision to retire and not work anymore can bring about a consequence I'd never before pondered: people stop paying you money. Apparently you're supposed to live on your "savings," which I always assumed was just a hilarious hoax played on young people, like when they graduate from school and we tell them they can change the world and make it better.

I'm not saying I haven't properly prepared myself for retirement, but ...

An open letter to a member of my family.

Dear S—

This is difficult for me to write—although not as difficult as it will be for you to read, given that you are (a) not especially bright, and (b) a dog.

We're letting you go, Squib. You're fired.

Somewhere in that tiny dog brain of yours, you're probably asking yourself: Why? Why would a family cut ties with an adorable chocolate Labrador? Rest assured: it's not us. It's you.

Like 90 percent of people who obtain dogs these days, I bought you for the express purpose of publishing a bestselling book about your incorrigible canine antics and the profound emotional bonds we forged on the path to your tragic, painful death.

John Grogan did it with *Marley & Me*. Dean Koontz did it with *A Big Little Life*. Ten squillion other people did it with their own loyal, terminally ill dogs. There are books about Merle and Sprite, Chance and Gracie. Books about deaf dogs and genius dogs and always the personal journeys filled with joy and anguish. It's like the old saying goes: a dog truly is man's best retirement plan.

I remember how excited we were when we picked you out, Squib. The kids saw in you an energetic playmate and loyal companion. I saw in you a potential for paperback residuals and ancillary merchandising rights. The first time we met, you came running toward us—tongue wagging, paws flailing—and smashed head-on into the chain-link fence. "An idiot," I thought. "Perfect." I started taking notes for *Moron & Me.*

Over the next few months, you showed flashes of potential. For instance, I very much enjoyed it when you urinated on that veterinary assistant. She was so unpleasant that, well, let's just say you barely beat me to it. And eating our cordless phone? Bravo.

But then you got lazy. You found socks on the floor and had the gall to leave them intact. You stopped terrifying the elderly. And you became a slave to the same tired habits. Take my word for it, Squib: an author can only devote so many chapters to crotch sniffing and expect to be hailed as a major literary talent (Charles Bukowski excepted).

Alas, I no longer get the sense that you're the kind of hilariously disobedient dog who's going to a tragic end that I can then exploit by overwriting a cloying meditation on how your canine nobility empowered me to discover what it means to be <*sniff*> truly human.

Have you read Dean Koontz's book, Squib? Probably not. You're more of a Glenn Beck man, aren't you?

Koontz is known as a bestselling novelist—but a few years back he published the tale of how his noble golden retriever helped him discover the secret to affording another vacation home or whatever.

Koontz devotes his book to passages like "I frequently saw in her eyes a yearning to make herself understood in a complex way that only speech could facilitate" and "Lying on the floor, facing each other, Trixie panted and I stroked her luxurious golden coat as she caught her breath ... "

I know what you're thinking: if he dims the lights to see where the mood takes them, I'm out of here.

Squib, I lack both the technical ability and the hatred for my fellow human required to write like that. So I need lots of material. I need a dog that gets into mischief, turns that mischief into mayhem and that mayhem into a sobering metaphor for the human condition. Basically, I need a dog capable of hijacking a fraternity's homecoming float. As I look at you now, staring out the back door and growling at a lawn chair, I can only doubt you are up to the task.

Despite all I've said here, Squib, this was a difficult decision for me. I've grown mildly attached to you. Plus, I've already pictured in my mind how my meeting with Megan Fox would go when she played my devoted wife in the movie:

> MEGAN: Oh, hey, nice to meet you.
> ME: My dog is adorable and dying.
> MEGAN: Hold me.

Let's remember the good times, okay? Like that morning when you appeared to be gravely ill, leading us to believe you were suffering from "the big C" when in fact you were suffering from "ate a small plastic shovel." With the power of hindsight, I see now that I was too hasty in bringing in the documentary film crew for the book/reality show tic in.

The bottom line is this: it's time for us to go in another direction as a family—to reinvent this literary niche by finding a dog that not only has an unpronounceable disease but also was complicit in the Wall Street chicanery that triggered the financial meltdown. Two birds, meet one stone.

You're a good boy, Squib. And that's the problem.

SO SQUIB WAS a bust, but I'm not beaten yet. Time for Plan B ...
DEAR ALL BILLIONAIRES ON EARTH:
Have you lost weight? No? Well, you could have fooled me because you are looking fine. Powerful. Strong. Virile enough to tear in half a phone book! (Mr. Gates, please substitute "cocktail napkin" for "phone book.")

Just FYI, you've probably heard that money is the root of all evil—but did you know it is also the root of most cancer and some leprosy? Seriously, the stuff is toxic. Here, let me hold it for you.

No? Fine. But that doesn't change the fact that society now expects you to donate a substantial percentage of your wealth to the less fortunate. Everyone's doing it. Here, though, is the crucial information you need to know: curing fatal diseases is difficult, whereas it is relatively easy to cure my lack of a summer home. I even accept oversized novelty cheques.

Come on. As one of the world's richest people, you have a responsibility to give back to your community. And technically I'm part of your community now that I'm hiding in the back seat of your car. So take me in. You could mould me into a man of wealth and distinction, just like they did to Eddie Murphy in *Trading Places*. Plus, that way I'd get to see Jamie Lee Curtis topless. It's a win-win.

What's that you say? You already have a contingent of yes-men who agree with everything you say? Wow, is that really all they do? *Just agree?* Because that's an insult to sycophancy. I will agree with you and then punch in the larynx anyone who doesn't. I will agree with you with an enthusiasm and terrifying berserker rage that will remind you of a lion on an arthritic wildebeest or Rosie O'Donnell on a sparerib. Your wish will be my command—especially if your wish is for me to court your sexpot heiress of a daughter, possibly while driving your yacht.

If you're full up with kiss-asses, I can be useful in other ways. For instance, some of you amassed your fortunes in ways described as "ingenious" and "daring," except by prosecutors, who described them as "illegal." I think of you, Chung Mong Koo, chairman of Hyundai. Sure, you were ultimately pardoned after being convicted of embezzlement. But should you ever find yourself imprisoned, I stand ready to watch over your $2.2-billion fortune. And on the day you're set free, be assured that you'll get back every penny of your $1.4-billion fortune.

No go? Then let me turn my attention to those whose success I've directly contributed to.

María Aramburuzabala: you're Mexico's richest woman, part of the family that founded the Corona brewery, and therefore indirectly founded my obesity. You have led a life of luxury and privilege. Yet you still have $2 billion. What could possibly be left for the Aramburuzabalas to buy—more vowels?

Howard Schultz of Starbucks fame—you finally made it to the billionaires list after years of business success. Congratulations! Say, Howard, has anyone told you about the "hazing" ritual for rookies? No? Well, it's quite simple. First, under cover of darkness, you must sneak up and pelt Ted Turner's house with Fabergé eggs. Second, you must hand over to me, Scott Feschuk, exactly $10 million in small, unmarked hookers. Hey, I don't make the rules.

No? Perhaps what's required is a more patriotic connection.

To my fellow Canadian Guy Laliberté, I say: we have so much in common. You play the accordion. I hate the accordion. You co-founded Cirque du Soleil. I can do, like, three somersaults in a row without getting dizzy. You dream of travelling into space. I dream of you travelling into space so I can break into your house. Clearly, we share a bond that can only be strengthened through the spiritual exchange of banking-card PINs.

Not biting? Fine. What the hell kind of circus doesn't have elephants anyway?

On to the big fish: Warren Buffett, you have more than $50 billion. That means you could, quite literally, buy me a number of times over. How many times? Let me get the calculator out here ... more than fifty billion times. So why don't you? Take me over. Upgrade me with a new suit, a fast car and a private Caribbean island. Then sell me for four times the price to Donald Trump. That dude will buy anything.

Mr. Buffett ... can I call you Warren? Well, then, can I call you Daddy? Anyway, I want you to think about this: if you gave away $1 million a day, it would take 150 years to give away your fortune. Whereas if you gave away $1 million a day to me, it would still take 150 years, but I'd be able to buy a Hummer forged from solid gold and accessorized with the skulls of my enemies. Which would be awesome.

To Mr. Gates, my last hope: you have $76 billion. How much money is that? Well, if you took your fortune in $100 bills and laid those bills end to end, you would give me a really great opportunity to grab a whole bunch of $100 bills and make a run for it. Do not try to chase me, Mr. Gates. You're wearing orthopedic shoes, and I've got a dune buggy waiting on the other side of that knoll.

Checkmate.

Tough question: *Why doesn't Victoria's Secret care if we live or die?*

I recently spent some time exploring the Victoria's Secret website and I was shocked by what I read when, after two hours, I realized there were words there.

The lingerie company is on the cutting edge of modern research and development. It speaks of creating "the world's most advanced bra." It boasts of its ingenuity in building the "softest bras ever" that are "virtually weightless" and "shoot laser beams." (I'm paraphrasing/brainstorming.)

One of the company's bras boldly promises "a cleavage (and ego) boost for instant hourglass oomph." This is a remarkable advance. A half century ago, the frenzied pursuit of "hourglass oomph" typically involved an intricate series of levers and a team of stout men.

By 2000, most women in the developed world had access to brassieres that could reliably provide hourglass vavoom. But hourglass *oomph*? That remained the fevered dream of a madman.

Today, at last, there is the Victoria's Secret Very Sexy™ Infinity Edge™ push-up bra with Gel-Curve™. And here's the unnerving truth: you can't build an undergarment with that many registered trademarks without the tireless effort of many trained scientists.

These are smart people who could be curing cancer or finding innovative ways to capture and forever store carbon emissions and/or Taylor Swift. Instead, they are dedicating their lives to creating bras so advanced that amorous young men now need a master's degree to get to second base.

I intend to raise this issue when I invite three of the company's models to join me at my dinner party.

THE FUTURE AND WHY WE SHOULD AVOID IT

REASON NO. 11: DEATH

Getting older forces us to think about the worst part of the future—the fact we're not going to be a part of it. Death is probably inevitable, especially if I fail in my attempts to do a Johnny Depp (in *Transcendence*) and transfer my consciousness into a computer. Or maybe into this Roomba. (Note to my descendants: When I spin in three tight circles, that means I want a grilled cheese sandwich.)

But rather than indulge in some whiny why-me, take-anyone-but-me, for-instance-that-guy, TAKE-THAT-GUY-OVER-THERE! lament about our eventual date with Death, let's instead obsess over discovering—and subsequently believing in—the best-case scenario for an afterlife. Let's take a closer look at the options.

Heaven: What's not to like, right? An eternal paradise. Unending happiness. All those perky angels eating Philly-cream-cheese bagels and playing all-night harp solos. Except: What exactly are we supposed to do for the next eleventy zillion eons? Are there charades? What if we run out of dip? When I was a young boy being dragged to church every Sunday morning, this whole concept blew my mind. Everlasting life? I couldn't even commit to a Gopher-heavy episode of *The Love Boat*.

I guess part of my anxiety stems from not knowing all the details. Would we have bodies up there? Would we wear

THE FUTURE AND WHY WE SHOULD AVOID IT

clothes? Would we just float around pretending not to recognize the souls we got to second base with but never called
again in high school? Sorry, Vicky's soul.

Which reminds me: if I'm going to be honest, there are a
number of people I'd just rather not run into again, even in
a boundless nirvana. Don't get me wrong—the first few minutes would be fine, but it would quickly get weird.

"Hey, we're in heaven!"

"I know, isn't it crazy?"

"So, so great to be in heaven."

[Awkward silence]

"So how's work?"

I kid you not—when the time came for the Resurrection
of the Dead, I'd be the guy whispering to Saint Peter: "See this
obnoxious hockey dad here on your list? Here's fifty bucks to
make sure his soul gets 'lost' on the way down."

Purgatory: In Sunday school, I was taught about/threatened
with (mostly threatened with) tales of a vast limbo—a middle
ground between Earth and heaven where one's soul goes to be
purified because it got some raw chicken on it. (I may not have
been paying full attention.) I became obsessed with, and confused by, the process. Exactly *how* does a soul get purified? Is
it painful? Does it require one of those Mr. Thirsty things like
at the dentist? My irritation was enhanced by the fact that my
Sunday school actually took place on Saturdays. *Saturdays.* I
remember thinking: What kind of uncaring God demands this
level of commitment? I could be watching *Shazam!*

Hell: Are you kidding? I already sweat at anything above room
temperature.

Reincarnation: I'll admit it: this one has some appeal. We die but
we never really die, you know? We just keep coming back in
different ways, in different incarnations, until eventually we're
all Kardashians and existence collapses under the weight of its
own shamelessness and bum fat. Belief in reincarnation takes
many forms: for instance, Scientologists believe that the soul
of a dead person is literally born again in "the flesh of another."

Then that new flesh has to get in line to marry Tom Cruise. SO IT IS WRITTEN. On the other hand, some believe there's a chance we could get reincarnated not as a person but as, like, an animal or a rock or something. That seems like a deal breaker. *Okay, last time you were a Nobel Prize–winning scientist who altered our conception of the reality that surrounds us. This time around: tomato.*

The Void: Those who eschew religion and reject the existence of God say death brings nothingness: no bright light to walk toward, no deep voice beckoning you forth, no 4,895-hour Jimi Hendrix/Liberace mega-jams—just endless, endless black. FYI, this is why no one likes you, atheists: your marketing is terrible.

The search for a desirable afterlife is further hindered by the manner in which we regard the death-based beliefs of ancient people. *Ha ha, those stupid Egyptians thought they could bring their treasure and combs to the next world! THEY PROBABLY COULDN'T!* How do we know that a wiser and more enlightened version of humanity won't look on us in the same way for worshipping at the Church of the Eternal Klingon?

Then again, maybe we won't die after all.

Have you heard about the Singularity? Some futurists believe that in the coming decades the pace of technological change will become so rapid that, in a life-altering event known as the Singularity, our bodies and our brains will ultimately merge with machines—making the human race healthier, a trillion times smarter and better able to cook Kraft Dinner on its chest than ever before. Downside: we will sacrifice our pure humanity on the altar of progress. Upside: being a trillion times smarter increases the odds someone will finally figure out the Caramilk secret. (Current best guess for how they get the soft, creamy caramel inside the chocolate pockets: um, magic?)

One of the leading proponents of the Singularity is Ray Kurzweil, a renowned inventor and futurist. Kurzweil boldly predicts that machines will achieve human-level artificial intelligence by 2029—although one wonders: Is he talking Charles Darwin–level intelligence or *Charles in Charge*–level intelligence? It's a question worth asking if I'm going to let my espresso machine do my banking.

Come the dawn of the Singularity, machines won't just be as clever and creative as we are, Kurzweil says. They'll be "emotionally intelligent" too. In other words, your microwave will still burn your popcorn—but it will burn your popcorn because it hates you.

Kurzweil reasons that the only way to prevent robots from surpassing us in the smarts department will be to inject millions or even billions of nanobots—super-tiny robots the size of blood cells—into our bodies. These nanobots will "interface" with our brains, enhancing our mental power and bodily vigour. Essentially, we will become one with these machines—a new and superior species that will thrive for millennia or, failing that, a joyless collective bent on galactic domination, like the Borg from *Star Trek* or the kids from *Glee*. Either way, with countless nanobots crammed inside us, we'll always have a foolproof excuse for weight gain.

This vision of a utopian world populated by brainy man-machine hybrids raises an important question: Is there a more awesome job on the face of the Earth than that of futurist? (Fine, Scarlett Johansson's thong wrangler, but other than that?)

Being a futurist like Kurzweil entails gazing into the vast unknown, carefully analyzing the available data and trends, and then totally guessing. How simple is it? Well, when I started writing this paragraph I was a lowly author, and by the end of it, based solely on my assertion that by 2045 humanity will discover a sixth dimension located entirely within William Shatner's hairpiece, I'm a futurist! Get me a three-book deal and a publicity glossy where I gnaw pensively on the arm of my glasses!

(My only other prediction: whatever consumer products are created in the distant future, Tiger Woods will gladly endorse them. Remember those Gillette ads where, despite his vast wealth, Tiger shaved himself on TV for money? These proved that the man is shameless enough to endorse any item manufactured in the present, the future or, if somehow possible, the past: "People of 1877: this is Tiger Woods saying it's time to demand more of your spittoon!")

But back to the nanobots. They'll make us a lot smarter, Kurzweil argues. And they'll do more than that: they'll help us live longer too. In fact, Kurzweil believes they'll help us live much longer—as in forever, like we're some sort of omnipotent deity or Larry King.

In recent years, Kurzweil has gained a measure of fame as an anti-aging advocate who contends that, thanks to nanobots and other advances, there will by 2030 be very little difference between 30-year-old and 120-year-old people. The implications are stark: 150 will be the new 40, 250 will be the new 65 and with this many old folks, Swiss Chalet will be the single most popular restaurant in history. "I don't think we have to die," Kurzweil told *Wired* magazine. "And the technology and the means of making that a reality is close at hand."

The search for eternal life is often depicted as humanity's ultimate quest, but, frankly, the whole idea grows less appealing the more you think about it. Two centuries in a cubicle? The inauguration of President Ryan Seacrest? Slightly increased odds of a *Battlefield Earth* sequel? *So* not worth it. Plus, I saw *Highlander*, and I'm not sure eternal life is worth living if we're going to have to utter such terrible dialogue.

Still, determined to survive until the mighty nanobots can render him immortal, Kurzweil eats a lot of fish and takes more than 150 supplements a day. Though he's over sixty, he estimates his "biological age" is only forty. And on the off chance the Grim Reaper seeks him out in the next decade or two, he's arranged to have his body cryogenically frozen and preserved, to be thawed when the technology to reanimate him has been developed, or when some kid making minimum wage in the cryogenics lab wants to freak out his girlfriend.

Think of it: immortality! Gilgamesh strived to attain it. Indiana Jones had it briefly in his grasp. And I'm sure Madonna's plastic surgeons are trying their best but, come on, guys, gross.

The goal of living forever might no longer be the fevered dream of whoever keeps jabbing Botox into Sylvester Stallone. Kurzweil says our understanding of genetics and technology is expanding at such an exponential rate that within two decades we will have "the means to reprogram our bodies' stone-age software so we can halt, then reverse, aging."

Ladies and gentlemen, I give you *Sex and the City XXXVII: Samantha's Bawdy Bicentennial*. Enjoy the threesome with Betty White.

Kurzweil envisions a future in which heart-attack victims will "calmly drive to the doctor for a minor operation as their blood bots keep them alive." Additionally, nanobots will help advance our mental capabilities to the point that "we will be able to write books within minutes." (This confirms what many of us have long believed: Danielle Steel is an immortal.)

Eventually, says Kurzweil, these nanobots will replace our blood cells and do their job thousands of times more efficiently. The result? Within a quarter century, we'll be able to run for fifteen minutes without taking a breath. We'll be able to scuba dive for several hours without oxygen. My God, Kirstie Alley may even be able to eat without sweating. Truly our world will be a paradise.

Think of how the pace of life will change with the Reaper out of the picture. No longer will we feel the pressure to succeed so early in life. We can stay in grad school until the age of 180, then bum around Europe for a century. We can take the time to hone our skills and talents. Consider all that our artists will achieve given the luxury of life without end. Give her a couple of thousand albums to work on it, and it's even possible that Kesha will learn to sing.

But if nanobots do indeed hold the secret to eternal life, a number of vexing ethical questions will soon confront society,

foremost among them "Who gets priority access to these tiny miracles?" and "How do we stop Kanye West from getting any?"

After all, there are plenty of potential downsides to immortality, such as the threat of overpopulation, famine and more Rob Schneider movies. And let's face facts: as humans, we can already get pretty sick of other people, often in a matter of months, sometimes in a matter of seconds. Can you imagine how bitter everyone will be after four hundred years of disagreements, disappointments and personal grudges? And think of the impact on our political discourse. Children will no longer be our future. *We* will be our future. WE WILL BE OUR OWN FUTURE. That's just messed up.

Consider also the economic costs of an immortal society. The disappearance of mid-life crises will decimate industries devoted to sports cars, hair weaves and prostitutes. Paying alimony to thirty ex-husbands will wipe out Liza Minelli. And just wait until Wall Street dreams up risky ways of bundling and securitizing your two-hundred-year mortgage.

Come to think of it, immortality may be more trouble than it's worth. Sure, you get to live forever. But so does the guy who draws Garfield. Frankly, it's hard to see how that balances out as a positive. Besides, death has its upsides. It's the ultimate escape, freeing us from credit-card debt, tedious social obligations and—so far as I understand how the afterlife works—the need for trousers.

It even offers us relief from the company of ourselves. Don't get me wrong: there's no one who thinks I'm greater than I do. I love me! But in my heart of hearts, I'm not sure I want to spend eternity on Earth with someone who knows all the lyrics to that "Everybody Wang Chung Tonight" song.

Besides, let's face facts: not even eternal life would *truly* be eternal. We're humans. We'd find a way to screw it up. Most likely this would take the form of an apocalypse.

An apocalypse would be a terrifying scenario for two reasons:

- The whole "apocalypse" part. They're almost always a real buzzkill.
- The aftermath, which might be even worse.

How could it be worse? Well, let's put it this way: despite being a human male with my very own keys and testosterone, I am afflicted by a number of great fears: heights, tight spaces, unicorns (that pointy horn isn't for show, little girls—what do you think caused Care Bears to go extinct?). But my greatest great fear is the unfolding of a scenario in which the vast majority of humanity is wiped out in an unspeakable cataclysm ... and somehow I remain alive.

You'd think the prospect of improbable survival against absurd odds would bring relief, even joy. Perhaps for you and the resulting Zombie King. But the toil of rebuilding civilization will inevitably expose me for what I am: useless. *Completely* useless. Skill-lacking, mistake-making, job-avoiding, thumb-hammering, handyman-calling useless. This is no false modesty: closing in on a half century of existence, I cannot be relied upon to construct anything more complex than an enchilada.

And there are others like me. Many others. We use Black-Berries, but can't grow blackberries. We can't hunt or saw or fix. We're the only people who read *The Road* and went away jealous, wishing we had the talent to carve a flute from road-side cane while walking to our inevitable demise.

At first, our uselessness won't matter. Everyone will be so excited about not being dead that for a couple of weeks we'll probably all just make out with each other and ridicule Al Gore for being wrong about global warming causing humanity's comeuppance. But eventually some high-maintenance jerkface is going to casually mention how it would be nice to have a roof or a rudimentary form of sanitation or clothes of any kind. And that's when things will get awkward.

In my nightmares, I picture it. We're gathered around the campfire. The talk turns to divvying up jobs.

"I'll tend to our medical needs," says one person.

"I'll draw up architectural plans for permanent shelter," says another.

It's my turn now. Everyone looks to me.

"If I work hard and really concentrate," I tell them, "I may be able to remember the plot to every episode of *Gilligan's Island*."

If I'm lucky, the apocalypse will have obliterated all the crickets. Otherwise, this is their cue.

Frankly, it's a bad era in which to be useless, especially on this continent. According to the US Federal Emergency Management Agency, nine out of ten Americans live in a place at significant risk for some kind of disaster, be it hurricane (Florida, Louisiana), earthquake (California) or pestilence (Miley Cyrus's bedroom). Yet the head of FEMA says the agency is reforming its mandate. No longer will citizens be treated as victims. Instead, they'll be expected to pitch in as "crucial first responders."

Ladies and gentlemen of North America: trust me on this.

If I am your first responder, arriving at your side in a moment of crisis and life-threatening peril, you are going to want to do one thing and one thing only: you are going to want to wait for the second responder. Believe me, I've given this a lot of thought: I have no idea what I could do to help my species get back on its feet. I suppose I possess the ability to teach, but—unless the Macarena becomes a useful tactic in military defence—I lack any skill worthy of teaching.

Could I be a doctor? No. A nurse? Double no (I lack medical training *and* I look fat in scrubs).

An engineer? Oh dear Lord, no. My kids won't even let me near their Lego since I "helped" build their Jedi starfighter (it ended up looking like a Jedi 7-Eleven). Scientist? Nope. Carpenter? *Nooo.* Mechanic? Ha, you're funny. Woodcutter? No, but if you give me $8, I can overpay for prepackaged kindling at a hardware store.

Better to stick to what I'm good at. Attention roving bands of scavengers: Do any of your fledgling societies require someone to take an afternoon nap?

If we do experience an apocalypse, we can find some comfort in the hope that Morgan Freeman will still be around to narrate it.

I don't remember ever reading about this in the news, but apparently Congress passed a law and now Morgan Freeman has to do the voice-over for every single thing ever made. You hear him on TV reading the copy for Visa ads. You hear him narrating some two dozen movies and the Hall of Presidents exhibit at Walt Disney World. And if you're anything like me, you hear him in your head when you are making a pie.

He grasped the rolling pin gently but firmly, the tender pastry succumbing to its wooden will ...

Morgan Freeman has become to voice-overs what Emmylou Harris is to musical collaboration and what Don Cherry is to unfinished sentences. One can only imagine the impact this professional sideline has had on his domestic life.

MORGAN [*sitting at the dinner table*]: ... and my beautiful wife graciously passed the potato salad, its thick coating of rich mayonnaise and delicate hint of dill serving as a faint reminder of a childhood lost to the mists of time—and a fleeting moment of contentment that can never be recaptured.

MORGAN'S WIFE: Shut up.

MORGAN: Her nostrils flared as she spoke, her eyes afire—not with joy, mind you, but with malice, indignation. And regret as well. Such regret. Fingers clenched, she glared at the—

MORGAN'S WIFE: No, seriously, shut up. For once in your life just shut your mouth.

Brief pause. MORGAN'S WIFE *sighs in exasperation.*

MORGAN: After a brief pause, she sighed in exasperation—then grabbed the pepper mill, dense and metallic, its silver sheen reflecting the atmospheric glow of the candles as she raised it high above her head, summoning energy now from some dark place she did not often visit but to which she never forgot the path, and brought the blunt, heavy object down upon his head with a sickening—

Thwaaack!

BUT WHAT FORM will our apocalypse take? Will it be loud and explosive, like a Michael Bay movie? Or will it involve relentless horrors and unending torture, like sitting through a Michael Bay movie?

Everywhere we turn these days, there are ominous signs. Birds by the hundreds falling from the sky. Fish by the thousands washing up on shore. Ears by the millions bleeding from Creed records. This seems like a good time to explore what's killing us now.

Superstorms: Did you hear this? The Earth's northern magnetic pole, which usually moves around a little each year, recently made a beeline for Russia—possibly because Sarah Palin yelled at it from her porch. *Pick a side, magnetism!*

Whatever the reason, some experts believe the shift will eventually cause havoc with the weather and may ultimately set off a cycle of dangerous superstorms with winds as high as 600 km/h. Gusts of that magnitude "would likely destroy anything they come into contact with," said a report published in the *Journal of Duh*.

The implications are many. Mass death. Untold destruction. Plus, CNN is running out of time to genetically engineer a team of 1,300-pound super-correspondents with the lower centre of gravity required to pointlessly stand outside during such storms.

Pets: Do you enjoy sharing your bed with the family dog or cat? According to new research, this is definitely something you should continue doing if you're a fan of cuddling and agony.

According to a US veterinary professor, domestic animals that sleep with or lick their owners are more likely to pass on "zoonoses"—which sounds like a Dr. Seuss book but is actually a range of diseases that are mostly minor, except for the ones that kill you.

I, for one, am as shocked as any dog owner. Who'd have thought animals that thrust their noses toward the anus of each playmate and consider feces a tasty snack would wind up being dangerous to French kiss? Life: full of surprises.

Pandemic: We gave you a decade and you just couldn't get it done, bird flu. But then a few years back, swine flu emptied streets, churches and bars across Mexico in less than a week, creating feelings of nostalgia for the good old days of murderous drug-war crossfires.

Public health officials say swine flu is difficult to combat because it's essentially an amalgam of four different viruses. As it spreads, the strain is constantly changing shape and mutating, like a microscopic version of Joan Rivers's face. Still, governments responded to the most recent crisis with swift action. For instance, Canadians flying to Mexico were handed a pamphlet advising them what they should do to try to avoid the flu. One of the things they should do is not accept pamphlets from strangers but, no, too late.

Nuclear obliteration: There's Iran to worry about. And North Korea. Plus, short-sighted governments continue to stand by idly and allow citizens to walk into stores and purchase ninety-nine red balloons.

The Sun: Usually thought of as a benign presence responsible for life on Earth and the invention of the halter top, the Sun is actually a place of great volatility and explosive eruptions. Think of it as a celestial Billy Bob Thornton.

According to what *Wired* magazine describes as a "chilling report," the years ahead may bring solar storms with tremendous destructive potential. These geomagnetic events would unleash powerful flares capable of "short-circuiting energy grids" across the planet, causing trillions of dollars in damage and plunging humankind into the stone age. With my luck, it'll happen right after I drop thirty bucks on an electric kettle.

Admittedly, a geomagnetic storm wouldn't kill anyone directly. But these flares—which are alternately described by scientists as "solar climaxes" and "coronal mass ejections," making this the dirtiest sounding of all the potential apocalypses—would serve as "the great off-switch in the sky," leaving us without electricity for years and setting off a global panic characterized by uprisings, war and Candy Crush withdrawal.

Is there anything we can do? Yes, yes there is. Researchers say we could add "some fairly inexpensive resistors in the ground connections [of our transformers]," significantly reducing the potential damage. Does anyone think we'll actually do this in time? No. No, they do not.

The Rapture: This one seems like a no-lose scenario: the just and faithful are summoned to the kingdom of heaven for an eternity of peace and bliss, and the rest of us get their clothes.

Economic collapse: During a recent lecture, a prominent British commentator offered his assessment of the global economy. Martin Wolf referenced debt loads, bailout funds and all that—but permit me to distill his message to its essence: EVERYBODY RUN FOR YOUR LIVES!!

Indeed, by the time Wolf was done speaking of likely default in Europe and a potential worldwide depression, it felt as though nomadic Huns were poised to smash through the walls and make off with our animal skins and womenfolk. His vision of the future made *The Road* sound like a buddy comedy.

Wolf is by no means alone. I sit here writing in prosperous times for pessimism. Pretty much every day we wake up to news that the Hang Seng is down 3 percent, which is a bummer because hearing "Hang Seng" used to be so much fun to say, in that it sounded like a bounty hunter from *Star Wars*. When it comes to retirement, many of us have given up on the dream of Freedom 55 and now grudgingly accept the reality of Freedom Andy Rooney, wherein we position ourselves behind a desk until we die working at the age ninety-two.

Some economists now believe most nations are destined to suffer through what's known as a "double-dip recession," which we've been trying to avoid because that's how the germs of the first recession get into the salsa.

Peruse the words of the so-called experts and you come to believe that our best-case scenario now is one in which developed nations make like Japan and endure a lost decade in economic stasis. The worst case? We revert to a prehistoric society by Halloween, and maybe if we're lucky someone remembers how to make fire.

I may not have a degree in economics—in fact, I'm pretty sure I don't. They tend not to bestow them on students who think Supply and Demand is a pop duo from the 1980s. But economic collapse may not be all bad. It's stressful trying to keep up with the Joneses. Maybe we'd all enjoy an extended period where instead we tried hunting the Joneses for food. The crumbling of the economy and the return of the barter system would really just come down to memorizing some new exchange rates. Don't get ripped off, kids: remember that one roll of toilet paper equals three chickens.

Strangelets: Back during construction of the $8-billion particle accelerator that runs under the border between France and Switzerland, a lawsuit was filed. It claimed the ruin of the Earth was nigh—and that this planet-ending apocalypse would be unleashed not by space aliens, or gigantic mysterious sea creatures, or even by a vengeful God weary of being asked to alter the outcome of professional sporting events and home pregnancy tests. No, the planet we know and love would be destroyed by ... by ...

By *nerds*.

The suit claimed that the Large Hadron Collider is capable of such a massive discharge of energy that it could inadvertently create a tiny black hole with the potential to consume the entire Earth. This is a complex scientific phenomenon known in the parlance of particle physicists as "bad."

As we learned from the original *Star Trek* series, black holes are a region of space with gravitational fields so powerful that they make starship captains so horny they'll make it with a four-armed green lady. But it might not be a black hole that kills us. The lawsuit, filed by a former nuclear safety officer and others, argued the Collider also has the potential to create something called a "strangelet," which would transform our planet into "a shrunken, dense, dead lump" no more than 328 feet in diameter. (Even under such a scenario, it is estimated that 68 percent of Americans would continue to drive their SUVs to the corner store.)

For their part, scientists insist there's nothing to worry about—that the odds of Earth being destroyed by the accelerator are equivalent to one person winning a national lottery three days in a row. And since the facility opened, they've implemented a regimen of rigid safety protocols, including high-tech monitoring of energy levels and tricking the janitor into standing next to the thing when they turn it on in the morning.

What's important is this: if we *are* truly doomed, don't get so caught up in panicking and having rash, pre-apocalyptic sex with me that we overlook the fact we've had a good run. Consider our accomplishments as a species:

- Mastered bipedal locomotion
- Learned to communicate through the miracle of speech
- Invented the Swiffer

And that might just have to be enough, what with the final scenario described by the people behind the lawsuit. They make the case that even if the black hole doesn't materialize, even if the strangelet is avoided, there remains a chance the accelerator could set off a chain reaction that would cause all protons in existence to decay.

Now, personally, I'd make the case that protons had it coming—after all, they do help to form the physical matter on which Celine Dion's music is recorded, and that's not something you're just going to get away with.

That said, I am reliably informed that certain things can't exist without protons, such as the universe or, more important, me. The question then is whether the eradication of the Celine Dion discography across all space and time is worth the permanent annihilation of all existence. I'm going to need some time to work this one through.

Asteroids: A few years back, a "skyscraper-sized asteroid" passed within 80,000 kilometres of Earth, which is pants-wettingly close in astronomical terms. A bigger rock is on target to come even closer around 2029. In fact, Canadian and American astronauts have long warned that our planet is a sitting duck for a massive asteroid—one of which may ultimately smash into Earth, dooming billions to death and prompting thousands to turn to their god and plaintively inquire: "Why? WHY?? *Why couldn't this have happened in 1983 when I still had four LPs left on my Columbia House commitment??*"

The most alarming warning comes from an organization once headed by Canadian astronaut Chris Hadfield. It's called the Association of Space Explorers, which surely ranks among the most badass and awesome-sounding of private clubs out there—although members do have to put up with Buzz Aldrin ending every argument with younger astronauts by hollering: "How did your moon walk go? Oh, right, you never walked on the moon like I walked on the moon! *[Pause.]* MOON!"

When it was released, the association's report about the asteroid menace got some coverage in the media. Permit me to direct you to a critical sentence from one of the news articles: "The United Nations is currently studying the report, which outlines plans to detect and deflect any objects that might threaten the planet."

Did you catch that? *The United Nations.* The UN's got our backs, people. They're totally on top of this. Even as you read these words, the Executive Secretary to the Director-General of the Under-Under-Secretariat is totally think-tanking the Proposed Action Item of facilitating the appointment of a Special Envoy for The Asteroid That Will Kill Us All. This will be followed by a decade of fruitless negotiations with the hurtling death rock.

> SPECIAL ENVOY: If you turn your agenda to page 4, you'll see it's time to discuss the unique heritage of your basaltic crust, after which I will talk reason with your nickel-iron core.
> *[ASTEROID methodically maintains speed and course to apocalyptic impact.]*
> SPECIAL ENVOY: Good idea. Muffin break.

I'm telling you: one toothless embargo and a series of empty, sternly worded resolutions later, the General Assembly will finally be ready to take decisive action against the imminent asteroid threat by passing a resolution condemning Israel for something.

(Not that the wholesale annihilation of our species would be all bad. For one thing, it would save me from confronting the backyard. I'm looking at it right now as I type this chapter and it's ... it's ... it's tragic out there. We had a bunch of people over last night and my "landscaping" consisted of taking a large flowerpot and placing it strategically over the gaping hole in our rotting deck. Sure, the lawn was still patchy and brown, part of the fence was falling down and there was a tire fire burning over in one corner—but that splintery limb trap was now somewhat less likely to claim a child's life. Look for me on the cover of next month's issue of *Lawsuit-Avoidance Gardening*.)

Anyway, where was I? Right, the threat of death by mega-rock. Hadfield and his colleagues say we urgently need to build on the efforts of Spaceguard, which sounds like an astronaut's deodorant but is actually an ongoing survey of the skies that scans for potential threats.

But why bother? If a big-time asteroid is coming our way, we're done for. In the movies, it's Bruce Willis and his gang of character actors to the rescue, saving humanity with the power of macho posturing and Aerosmith power ballads. But real life brings with it the grim fact of real governments. And how would they respond?

I think it's a safe bet that Russia would fire several nuclear warheads at the approaching asteroid. These missiles would destroy the Moon. Meanwhile, Sarah Palin and Rush Limbaugh would encourage Americans to run simultaneously in the same direction, thinking perhaps that this would speed up the Earth's rotation and let China take the worst of the impact. In Canada, Stephen Harper would dispatch an emergency mission to the asteroid, but only to put an Economic Action Plan sign on it.

Doubt my prediction? Consider this: the *New York Times* reported that more than a decade after the 9/11 attacks, and after billions of dollars spent, US officials still hadn't figured out how to allow firefighters and police officers from different jurisdictions to talk to each other over their radios at emergency sites. More than a decade! And these government guys are going to successfully deflect a 200-million-ton planetoid travelling at 30 kilometres per second? *Riiiight.*

It doesn't matter how much Spaceguard you apply—we might as well move straight to the widespread looting.

IF ALL THIS talk of your inevitable demise (and mine—but mostly yours) has got you down, here's a pick-me-up: there is a small but real possibility that you will never die. Unfortunately, that's because there's a chance that you don't actually exist.

A recent book by Brian Greene, a respected theoretical physicist, explores the theory that supercomputers will eventually become powerful enough to run simulations featuring "people" who believe they are real. Sounds fun, right? Who wouldn't want to re-create the past to be able to witness life in the fifteenth century or jump in and punch Bryan Adams in the balls at the exact moment he decides to learn to play guitar?

But wait. Hang on a minute. If such simulations will one day be possible, there's no guarantee that we aren't *already living inside a simulation*—"perhaps one created by future historians with a fascination for what life was like back on 21st-century Earth," Greene writes.

The downside: everything we have ever known, touched or loved never actually existed. The upside: same goes for Ashton Kutcher.

ACKNOWLEDGMENTS

Thanks to Cheryl Cohen, who edited this book with skill and diligence and whose browser history, as a result, is now that of a very troubled person, filled with queries like:

- Is Kesha's name still spelled with a dollar sign?
- In which year did Richard Gere reign as *People's* Sexiest Man Alive?
- What is the world record for number of fat jokes about Kirstie Alley because I think we're breaking it?

(Cheryl ultimately convinced me to change some of the Kirstie Alley fat jokes to fat jokes about other people, or to jokes that aren't about being fat at all, a genre that I was previously unaware of.)

I also owe a debt to Sarmishta Subramanian, who edits my column each week in *Maclean's* magazine. (Young people: a magazine is just like the internet, but with staples.) Sarmishta routinely makes my work either funnier or less unfunny, depending on your perspective.

And thanks to Silas White, Anna Comfort O'Keeffe and everyone at Douglas & McIntyre for publishing this book, which was super-nice of them.